All About
SOUTH AFRICA

ACKNOWLEDGEMENTS

The publishers wish to express their sincere gratitude to the following contributing consultants, organisations and individuals who offered their co-operation and advice in the compilation of this book throughout the different editions (1992—2013):

Africana Museum, Johannesburg; **Albany Museum**, Grahamstown; **Anglo-American Corporation of South Africa**; Anthony **Bannister**; Phillida **Brooke-Simons**; Dr Mike **Cluver**; South African Museum, Cape Town; John **Comrie-Greig**; Alex **Daneel**, Golden Gate Highlands National Park; Dr Patricia **Davidson**, South African Museum, Cape Town; **De Beers Consolidated Mines**; Jackie **de Klerk**, Department of Environmental Affairs and Tourism; Susan **de Villiers**, African National Congress; Aubrey **Elliot**; Magriet **Engelbrecht**, South African Communication Service; ESKOM; Kobus Fourie, South African Communication Service; Simon **Gear**, climatologist; **Gold Reef City**, Johannesburg; Anneke **Greyling**, Department of Political Studies, University of Stellenbosch; Dr Deirdre **Hansen**, Faculty of Music, University of Cape Town; Professor Martin **Hattingh**, Faculty of Agriculture, University of Stellenbosch; Don **Henning**, Armscor; Helmoed-Römer **Heitman**, defence journalist and author; **ISCOR**; Etta **Judson**, Voortrekker Monument; Gerald **Klinghardt**, South African Museum, Cape Town; **Koeberg Nuclear Power Station**; Astri **LeRoy**, chairman, Spider Club of Southern Africa; **Library of Parliament**, Cape Town; **Martin Spring Publications**; Reg **Morgan**, Clerk of Papers, Parliament, Cape Town; **National Sea Rescue Institute**, Cape Town Unit; Greg **Roberts**, South African Astronomical Observatory, Cape Town; Martin **Roos**, Agricultural Research Council; Pete **Roussos**, African National Congress; **SASOL**; Nerina **Skuy**, Apple Express; **SOEKOR**; **South African Astronomical Observatory**, Cape Town; **South African Chamber of Mines**; **South African Library**, Cape Town; **South African National Gallery**, Cape Town; **State Archives**, Cape Town; Fahiem **Stellenboom**, Baxter Theatre Complex, Cape Town; Professor HW **van der Merwe**, Centre for Intergroup Studies, University of Cape Town; **Volkskas Bank**

Struik Lifestyle
(an imprint of Random House Struik (Pty) Ltd)
Company Reg. No. 1966/003153/07
1st FloorWembley Square 2,Solan Road, Gardens, Cape Town 8001
PO Box 1144, Cape Town, 8000, South Africa

First published in 1992
Second edition published in 1995, reprinted in 1997
Third edition published in 2001, reprinted in 2002
Fourth edition published in 2004
Fifth edition published in 2005, reprinted in 2006, 2007, 2008
Sixth edition published by Struik Lifestyle in 2009, reprinted in 2010
Seventh edition published in 2013

ISBN: 978-1-43170-096-7

Publisher: Linda de Villiers
Managing editors: Wilsia Metz (1st ed), Sean Fraser (2nd ed), Cecilia Barfield (3rd-7th eds)
Editors: Susannah Coucher (2nd ed), Joy Clack (3rd ed), Samantha Fick (4th-5th eds), Glynne Newlands and Bronwen Leak (6th ed), Cecilia Barfield and Gill Gordon (7th ed)
Design manager: Beverley Dodd (7th ed)
Designer: Randall Watson (7th ed)
Image researcher: Colette Stott (7th ed)
Consultants: Jay Heale (general) (1st ed), John Comrie-Greig (natural history) (1st ed)
Text updated by: Brian Johnson Barker (2nd-5th eds), Rob Marsh (6th-7th eds)
Reproduction: Hirt & Carter
Printing and binding: Tien Wah Press (Pte) Limited, Singapore

FOREWORD

This edition of *All About South Africa* has been specially designed for young readers like you and is packed with plenty of facts, figures, colourful illustrations and photographs that will help you improve your general knowledge and make school projects and homework fun. It's full of information on our country, its people and their history and culture, our wildlife, technology and economy. So, if you want to know about the world around you and be a whizz in class, *All About South Africa* is just the book for you!

Contents

The Earth

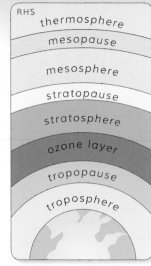

AIR ENVELOPE

The Earth's **atmosphere** is an envelope of gases about 800 km thick, held in place by the Earth's gravitational pull. The lower levels consist of 78% nitrogen, 21% oxygen, 0.9% argon and smaller quantities of other gases. The atmosphere becomes thinner and thinner until it finally reaches space. Oxygen allows us to breathe, and some of it changes to form a layer of ozone which filters the sun's harmful ultra-violet rays. Many scientists believe that a decrease in ozone and an increase in carbon dioxide has been caused by over-use of chemicals, engine exhausts and the burning of fossil fuels such as oil and coal. This has led to global warming, or the greenhouse effect, by trapping the sun's energy.

Scientists believe that the Earth probably began about 4600 million years ago as a cloud of gases and dust whirling around in space. As it spun, it shrank into a fiery hot, liquid globe to form the planet Earth. As the surface gradually cooled, a crust of solid rock developed which forms the mountains, soil and sand, that we live on today.

The Crust Cracks

Scientists believe that during the Earth's history its land areas were united into one enormous land mass, which they called Pangaea. About 300 million years ago, it began to crack into two parts – Laurasia to the north and Gondwana in the south. They were separated by a sea stretching from east to west, of which the Mediterranean may be a remainder. Later, these two landmasses also began to break up, Laurasia divided to form North America, Greenland, Europe and most of Asia north of the Himalayas. Gondwana split up into South America, Africa, India, Australia and Antarctica. The fragments of land that we know as continents today once fitted together, but over millions of years they drifted thousands of kilometres apart.

The Floating Crust

The cracked pieces of the Earth's crust are known as plates and are about 40 kilometres thick. They are able to float because their rocks are lighter than those of the molten mantle below. The plates collided and crumpled to form deep trenches in the oceans and to push up high mountains on the land. The **Himalayas** are the highest mountains on Earth, and are still being squeezed up as a result of a collision between India and Asia. The Great Rift Valley is a huge crack which runs from the Jordan Valley in Israel down the length of East Africa and into northern Mozambique. This crack is believed to have been caused when the Earth's crust collapsed between two plates that were moving apart.

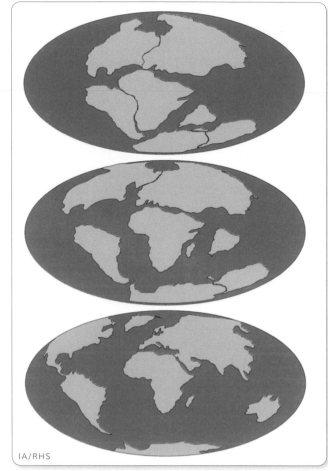

IA/RHS

Over the years, the single land-mass, called Pangaea, divided into two masses called Laurasia (in the north) and Gondwana (in the south). These later split to form the continents as we know them today

Our Changing Earth

The Earth is constantly changing. Not only are land-masses moving, but new crust is being made all the time. On the sea floor, molten rock bubbles up through the deep cracks between the plates to form ridges and islands. An example is the mountain range stretching below the Atlantic Ocean from north to south. Visible parts of this ridge are islands, such as Iceland and Tristan da Cunha, which have risen above the surface of the sea. A volcano erupting below the Atlantic Ocean south-west of Iceland created the new island of Surtsey between 1963 and 1967.

The theory that the continents were drifting slowly across the surface of the Earth, either separating or clashing together, was first put forward in 1912 by Alfred Wegener, a German meteorologist. Wegener's theory became known as the Continental Drift hypothesis. However, it was a South African geologist, Alexander L du Toit, who first suggested the existence of two primordial supercontinents, Laurasia and Gondwana, in his book *The Wandering Continents* (1937). Du Toit formed the world 'Laurasia' by combining the names of two cratons – Laurentia and Eurasia, and Gondwana means 'the land of the Gonds'. A craton is a stable, relatively immobile mass on the Earth's crust that is at the heart of a continent.

Great Rift Valley

The Changing Landscape

Wind erosion has carved fantastic shapes from the Cederberg rocks and rushing waters have gouged potholes out of the Blyde River bed at Bourke's Luck. Surf has scoured the Hole-in-the-Wall on the Wild Coast and sculpted the Bogenfels arch on Namibia's forbidden 'Sperrgebiet' or diamond coast.

FOUR LAYERS OF THE EARTH

Beneath the Earth's **crust** are three layers. The layer under the crust is the **mantle**, and is followed by the **outer core** and the **inner core**. In mountainous areas, the crust may be 50 kilometres deep, but under the oceans it measures only about 6 kilometres. The rocks of West Greenland are 3 800 million years old, and are probably the oldest rocks known on the Earth. The mantle (2 900 kilometres thick) consists of very slowly flowing currents of dense, semi-molten metals. Below it is the outer core – a 2 240 kilometre-thick layer of very hot, molten metals, mostly iron and nickel. The inner core at the centre of the Earth is probably solid. It consists mainly of metals and measures 2 440 kilometres across with a temperature of 3 700 °C at the centre.

LH/IOA

THE FAMILY OF PROTEACEAE

The botanical family Proteaceae provides a clue to the existence of the single, great land-mass of Gondwana: related members of the family, such as the **sugarbush** (*Protea repens*) are found growing in several southern lands although they are separated by thousands of kilometres of ocean.

inner core

outer core

mantle

crust

IA/RHS

CONTINENTAL DRIFT

The movement of the plates in the Earth's crust is known as **continental drift** and is still going on. North Africa was once covered with ice and was situated where the Antarctic is today. America is slowly moving away from Europe, and this has even caused telephone cables under the Atlantic Ocean to snap! In 50 million years' time Alaska may move right up to the Asian continent to form one land-mass.

WHY GONDWANA?

The Gonds were people who lived in prehistoric times in central India. When geologists surveyed the area they named the rock system found there 'Gondwana', meaning 'land of the Gonds'.

Early in the 20th century, naturalists discovered plant and animal fossils in South America, Africa and Australia similar to those found in what they had called Gondwana in India. They realized that this must mean that these continents had once been linked together.

BP/SPL

Rocks and fossils

JH/RHS

BANKET – A ROCK OR A TOFFEE?

'**Banket**' is the name of a traditional Dutch toffee with almonds in it. Because the rock in which gold is found looks like the sweet, it is also called banket. These rocks are conglomerates that have been pressed together. The spaces between them are filled with minerals, including gold.

GTY/GI

Early miners pan for gold on the Witwatersrand

Millions of years ago southern African mountains, valleys and plains were shaped by the forces of nature, such as volcanic eruptions, floods, wind, rain and the sun. Many early rock formations and fossils may be found in South Africa.

The Oldest of All

South Africa's oldest rock formations, found mostly in the Barberton area, consist mainly of rocks called granite, gneiss, lavas and chert. In some of the chert beds scientists have found tiny fossils of blue-green algae – the earliest forms of life. This proves that simple plants grew in South Africa at least 3 500 million years ago.

The youngest rock formations, such as the Kalahari group, are less than 65 million years old. They occur on the Namaqualand coast, parts of the Western and Eastern Cape and northern KwaZulu-Natal.

The Witwatersrand's Gold

During the one thousand million years after the simple plants appeared, the important rock formations of Gauteng came into being. The great Witswatersrand Basin was gradually filled with sediment carried in by rivers, and was eventually compressed to form sandstone and conglomerate. So much sediment was deposited that the basin sagged under the heavy load. Molten rock pushed up through the floor of the basin and formed the ridges and outcrops that we see in parts of Johannesburg today. The basin eventually dried out and the water left ripples on the sand, which were preserved and can still be seen today.

The Witwatersrand is the world's richest goldfield. Gold-bearing conglomerates are found in several layers. One, known as the Carbon Leader, contains millions of tiny plants which may have carpeted the Witwatersrand flood plain before it was filled.

Minerals of the Bushveld

Covering large parts of Limpopo and North West Provinces is a geological wonder known as the **Bushveld Igneous Complex**. Many of the minerals that bring wealth to South Africa are found in the Complex that was formed in two stages almost 200 million years ago. Molten lava (the word **igneous** means 'fiery') was forced into the Earth's crust and cooled to form a reddish granite. This is how Rooiberg in Limpopo Province got its name. Then there were even further intrusions of masses of hot, molten rock, and rock formations began to develop in colours that vary from red to dark grey.

The world's richest platinum and chrome deposits are found here. Tin, the rare vanadium and titanium, nickel, manganese and iron are some of the other minerals mined in this area.

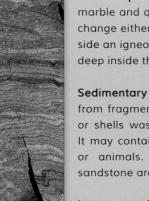

wind

IL/RHS

TABLE MOUNTAIN

The Cape System is a geological system found in various parts of South Africa, and even **Table Mountain** forms part of it. About 550 million years ago, massive movements of the Earth lifted layers of sandstone and rock deposited beneath the sea millions of years earlier. As the Earth rose, it crumpled to form the Cape Fold Mountains. Wind and rain eroded one section so that it eventually became the familiar flat-topped Table Mountain we know today.

Metamorphic rock   *Sedimentary rock*   *Igneous rock*

ROCKS

Metamorphic rock, such as slate, marble and quartzite, has undergone change either by being heated along-side an igneous intrusion or squeezed deep inside the Earth's crust.

Sedimentary rock is built up in layers from fragments of broken rock, sand or shells washed into a lake or sea. It may contain the remains of plants or animals. Limestone, chalk and sandstone are sedimentary rocks.

Igneous rock is molten rock from deep within the Earth. Once on or near the surface, it begins to cool down. Granite, basalt and obsidian are among the igneous rocks.

THE KAROO SYSTEM

The Karoo System stretches over more than 60% of South Africa. Scientists believe that these rocks were formed in four stages between 300 and 150 million years ago. The stages are identified by the different fossils they contain. The deepest layer is the **Dwyka Series**, which originated during an Ice Age. The overlaying **Ecca Series** contains a few scattered fossils, including a water reptile Mesosaurus. Plant fossils including coal are found in many parts of the Ecca Series. Above this is the **Beaufort Series**, rich in reptile and amphibian fossils. Fossils in the **Stormberg Series** closest to the surface include dinosaurs, fish and plants.

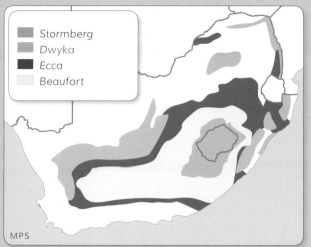

Stormberg
Dwyka
Ecca
Beaufort

MPS

FOSSILS

The remains of plants and animals preserved in rock are important in discovering the age of rock formations and how they were formed. Scientists study **fossils** to tell how the Earth has changed and learn about the plants and animals that once lived on it. For instance, fossilized shark teeth found in the Swartberg range near Oudtshoorn tell us that this area was once under water.

CMR

SURPRISING FOSSILS

Coal may seem like rock but it is really the remains of **ancient plants** preserved in the Earth and hardened over millions of years. The plants could be as small as algae or as large as trees that grew in swamps about 250 million years ago. Because of their origins, coal, oil and natural gas (such as the underwater gas 'field' off Mossel Bay) are known as 'fossil fuels'.

BP/AI

An erupting volcano and its lava flow

LOOKING FOR FOSSILS

Fossils are protected by the National Heritage Resources Act, and you need a permit to dig for or to remove them. If you find a fossil, don't remove it from the site, but report it to the nearest museum.

Fossils are often white and stand out clearly against the rocks. Scientists use special tools, like chisels and probes, in order to excavate specimens without damaging them; they often cover the fossil with protective plaster before trying to remove it.

The Great Assault

About 100 million years ago, powerful underground forces shook the great land mass of Gondwana, which split into the separate southern continents. In the south of newly formed Africa, massive amounts of lava flooded onto the surface to form the Drakensberg and Lesotho mountains. In other places, volcanic eruptions caused cracks, or 'pipes', to appear; some resulted in craters on the surface. The heat and pressure deep inside the Earth transformed carbon into diamonds, which then rose to the surface inside these volcanoes.

PLACES TO SEE

ℹ️ Iziko South African Museum, Cape Town

Life long ago

TRACKING DINOSAURS
When dinosaurs walked across soft mud flats, they sometimes left huge **footprints** behind. These tracks show how the giant animals walked and ran, as well as the size and shape of their feet. In Lesotho, there are huge fossilized footprints of a dinosaur that lived 200 million years ago!

ALL GREEK TO ME!
The names of many of the giant reptiles end with **-saur** or **-saurus**, which comes from a Greek word meaning 'lizard', **Gorgo** is Greek for 'frightening', which the nine metre-tall, flesh-eating Gorgosaurus certainly was. **Ichthyo** means 'fishy' and the Ichthyosaurus was part lizard and part fish. **Palaeo-** means 'ancient' so the Palaeozoic Era concerns the most ancient of animals. **Meso-** is Greek for 'middle' and **Caino** (usually written Ceno-) means 'recent'.

As the surface of the new Earth started to cool down, rain began to fall. It rained without stopping for centuries until water covered the whole globe, but for the first 1 000 million years, there was no life on Earth at all.

The Sea
About 3400 million years ago the first tiny, single-celled plants appeared. They were similar to seaweeds and produced the oxygen needed by all living things. The first animals were all single-celled but others followed, which were more complicated. Arthropods swam in the sea with sponges and jellyfish, and later snails, cuttlefish, shrimp-like creatures and sea-scorpions appeared.

The Plants
By about 400 million years ago, the seas started to dry up. Eventually plants appeared on the land. At first they had no leaves and no true roots. By about 280 million years ago, almost every important plant group known today was growing on the land, but there were still none with flowers or seeds. In what is today known as South Africa there were giant mosses and tree ferns that spread by means of tiny cells called spores. There were also many tall, cone-bearing trees.

Fish and Land Animals
Meanwhile, about 350 million years ago fish appeared. They were the first creatures to have a backbone in place of an external skeleton. For a long time there were no creatures on land, and there were no flying creatures. Later, some types of fish developed lungs. They dragged themselves up onto the land using their strong fins and became the first amphibians. Insects crawled from the swamps and began to eat the leaves of plants. Fossils found near Mooi River in KwaZulu-Natal show that some of these prehistoric insects had wings.

Coal and the Mammal-like Reptiles
After the end of the ice age 280 million years ago, most of South Africa was covered by a huge inland sea in which thick layers of sandstone were deposited. In the marshy hollows between the rocks, the wood and leaves of trees and plants fossilized to form coal, which is still being mined today.

Reptiles, which evolved from amphibians, were able to live on dry land away from the water. Although they had the

Mesosaurus fossil

scaly skin of true reptiles and laid eggs with leathery shells, many resembled mammals. Some of these early mammal-like reptiles were about one metre tall. Most of them ate plants, but some were flesh-eaters, which hunted the plant-eating reptiles.

Mesosaurus, one of the world's earliest reptiles, first appeared approximately 280 million years ago in what is now South Africa. It swam in fresh water and looked like a small crocodile.

The Coming of the Dinosaurs
The biggest and smallest dinosaurs lived between 195 and 65 million years ago. Although **dinosaur** means 'terrible lizard', some were no bigger than a cat and a great deal less fierce. However, *Stegosaurus*, which lived in North America and Europe, was nine metres long. It had two rows of bony plates down its back and horn-like spikes on its scaly tail. But this terrifying creature had no teeth in the front of its jaw, and its brain was about the size of a large acorn!

The biggest dinosaur in southern Africa was the plant-eating *Brontosaurus* or *Apatosaurus*. Its fossil bones have been found in the Eastern Cape. In life, it was about twelve metres long, smaller than the North American *Diplodocus* (the Earth's biggest animal) and it had a small head and a long, curved neck that enabled it to eat from tree tops.

Some dinosaurs were suited to swamps, some lived on land and others returned to the sea. A flying reptile, *Pterodactylus*, was probably not much bigger than a sparrow, and had fine needle-like teeth. *Pteranodon*, on the other hand, had a wingspan of twelve metres.

About 65 million years ago, the dinosaurs disappeared and no one is certain why. Floods or earthquakes may have killed them, or the Earth may have become too cold. But by this time, mammals and flowering plants had appeared.

A FISH WITH FOUR LEGS
In 1938, fishermen working off the coast of East London, caught a strange, purple-blue fish that had four fins, which looked like stumpy legs. When it was shown to Professor JLB Smith of Rhodes University, Grahamstown, he realized that it was a coelacanth – a fish that had first appeared about 300 million years ago and was thought to have become extinct. Coelacanths were among the first fish to have teeth and overlapping scales. The coelacanth caught in 1938 may still be seen at the East London Museum.

SOUTH AFRICAN DINOSAURS

The first dinosaur discovered in Africa was unearthed in the Eastern Cape in 1845. Since then, there have been many discoveries in the fossil-rich sandstone rocks of the Kirkwood Formation. In 1996, a new dinosaur was discovered and given the name *Nqwebasaurus thwazi*, which means 'fast-running lizard from Nqweba' (Nqweba is the Xhosa name for the Kirkwood region). This is the first dinosaur to have an isi-Xhosa name. *Nqwebasaurus* lived about 130 million years ago. It was about the size of a large hen and probably ate small mammals, reptiles and insects.

The fossilized remains of Nqwebasaurus thwazi, the 'lizard from Nqweba', also known as 'Kirky'

Fossilized bones of the right foot of Nqwebasaurus

Anusuya Chinsamy-Turan and Billy de Klerk, who discovered Nqwebasaurus, at the site of their discovery

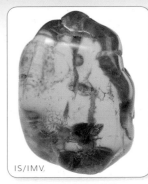

IS/IMV.

AMBER – A GEM OF A FOSSIL

For thousands of years man has treasured jewellery made from beautiful golden-brown **amber**. We know now that amber is not a gemstone but fossilized resin from trees that grew 40–60 million years ago. Extinct insects and plants have been found entombed within amber.

WK/IOA

A BOTANICAL WONDER

In the veld through which the dinosaurs roamed millions of years ago, there grew a fern-like plant, known as a cycad, with fruit resembling a pineapple. Cycads have survived almost unchanged for a very long time. They occur between the coast of Mozambique and Uniondale in the Western Cape. Some of the tallest cycads, up to 13 metres high, grow in a protected forest near Tzaneen in Mpumalanga.

PLACES TO SEE

- ℹ The East London Museum
- ℹ Iziko South African Museum, Cape Town
- ℹ The Dinosaur Park at Sudwala Caves near Nelspruit (Mbombela) in Mpumalanga
- ℹ West Coast Fossil Park, Langebaan, Western Cape

A skeletal reconstruction of Apatosaurus at the Geological Museum of the University of Wyoming at Laramie

11

Early humans

IL/RHS

TOOLS
One **stone** was used to chip flakes from another. These flakes were sharpened and carved on one side to form a cutting edge. If the stone was worked on both sides, an almond-shaped tool with two cutting edges was formed, and used to cut and dig. In time, sharp flakes were worked on to form arrow tips. Early man used animal **bone** as a hammer and made long, sharp blades from stone.

About 117 000 years ago, one of our first human ancestors walked across a beach at Langebaan, about 150 km north of Table Bay. Miraculously, her footprints remained intact, and slowly became fossilized as the sand hardened into sandstone. The prints are now kept in the Natural History Museum in Cape Town, and scientists agree that they are probably the oldest trace of a modern human being – *Homo sapiens* – in the world.

The Taung Child
A southern African child who died about three million years ago provides clues about human evolution. In 1924, near Taung village, 140 km north of Kimberley in the North West Province, a worker blasting limestone in a quarry discovered a small, fossilized skull embedded in the rock. His find was sent to Professor Dart, head of the Department of Anatomy at the University of the Witwatersrand, who realized at once that the skull was different from anything ever seen before. It was similar to the head of a small ape, but it had certain characteristics that were more like those of a human.

The teeth showed that the skull belonged to a child of about three or four years old. It had a brain no bigger than an ape's, but Professor Dart could tell that the child had walked on two legs like a human. He named the Taung child *Australopithecus africanus*, meaning the 'southern ape of Africa'. But he was still convinced that it was not an ape but a hominin, or member of the family of man.

Homo habilis
Homo habilis (capable or handy man) lived between two million and 1.5 million years ago. He is thought to have made and used tools of bone and stone, and may have been the first true ancestor of the modern human race (*Homo sapiens*). Although most fossils of *Homo habilis* have been found in East Africa, some scientists believe that fossil fragments found at Sterkfontein, a series of limestone caves in Gauteng, are also remains of this species. Sterkfontein, one of the richest sources of hominin (man-like) fossils in the world, has been proclaimed a World Heritage Site.

IL/RHS

Spearpoint and Willow leaf point

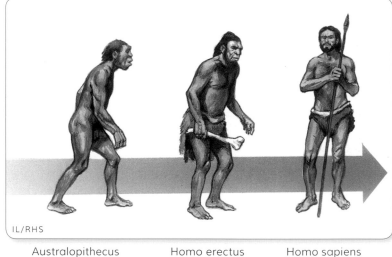

IL/RHS

Australopithecus africanus   Homo erectus   Homo sapiens

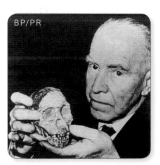

BP/PR

Professor Raymond Dart holds the Taung skull

MP

MRS PLES
Dr Robert Broom published a description of what he believed the Taung child would have looked like had it ever grown up. In 1947, while doing excavations at Sterkfontein, he unearthed a skull of an adult hominin. At first he thought it was a female of a species never seen before and named it *Plesianthropus transvaalensis* – nicknamed 'Mrs Ples'. On further examination 'Mrs Ples' proved to be almost identical to the Taung child and was therefore a specimen of *Australopithecus africanus*. Both were closely related to apes, but their human characteristics show that they were man's ancestors too. Recent studies indicate that 'Mrs Ples' may in fact be male!

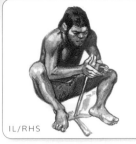

Homo erectus

The world of *Homo habilis* was a dangerous place in which to live. Much smaller and weaker than the big and ferocious animals around him, *Homo habilis*, who had neither claws nor fangs for defence and could not run as fast as these predators, was gradually replaced by *Homo erectus* approximately 700 000 years ago. *Homo erectus* (upright man) – whose remains were discovered in 1948 at Swartkrans, an archaeological site near Krugersdorp – had a sloping forehead, a ridge of bone across the brow, large teeth and a heavy jaw with a small chin. These hominins lived in caves and learnt to make fire, and may have developed some form of speech. Their large brain and nimble fingers enabled them to make tools and weapons, which they then used to hunt wild animals for food and skins.

Homo sapiens

In time *Homo erectus* was replaced by *Homo sapiens* (wise man) who is the direct ancestor of modern humans and lived all over the world. Although there were still some physical characteristics in common with *Homo erectus*, the brain was larger and more complex. Finally *Homo sapiens sapiens* (wise, wise man) which comprises all living people, emerged between 50 000 and 100 000 years ago. The ability to speak, write, calculate, invent, create and destroy was well developed. The heavy brow ridge disappeared, the forehead became higher, the teeth smaller and the jaw lighter with a pronounced chin. *Homo sapiens sapiens* now lives on every continent on Earth and, with the modern technology he has created, is even able to explore the moon and the planets.

FIRE!

The **first** fire seen by man was almost certainly a result of lightning striking dry vegetation. When man chipped at flints to make tools, sparks flew from them, but only after centuries did he learn to make his own fire by means of friction. *Homo erectus* lived during an Ice Age, so it would have been a comfort to warm himself beside his own hearth, where he learnt how to cook meat.

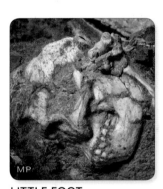

LITTLE FOOT

In 1997 Dr Ronald Clarke and his preparators, Stephen Motsumi and Nkwane Molefe, found the world's only complete hominin skeleton at Sterkfontein. Affectionately called **Little Foot** because it was found following the discovery of twelve of its foot bones, the skeleton is unique because it is the most complete *Australopithecus*, or ape man, ever found. It has revealed valuable information about how these creatures moved and behaved, and is one of the most important archaeo-logical finds ever made.

PLACES TO SEE

ℹ️ The Sterkfontein Caves near Krugersdorp (City of Mogale)

IL/RHS

The San and the Khoikhoi

The San, formerly called Bushmen, were nomadic hunter-gatherers who lived in harmony with the environment. In order to survive they had to know a lot about the animals and plants of the veld.

People of the Kalahari

Rock paintings and engravings show that the San people once lived all over southern Africa and were its main inhabitants. But when herders and farmers arrived, many San hunter-gatherers were either killed or driven into the harsh interior. Some intermarried with other groups and the only San that remained as hunter-gatherers were those in the Kalahari.

A San rock painting from the Cederberg

The Hunter-gatherers

All San groups lived as hunter-gatherers. The men became expert trackers. Big animals were hunted with poisoned arrows. Many kinds of poison were collected from different sources, including scorpion and spider venom and a liquid squeezed from beetle grubs. They also trapped birds and small creatures in snares or smoked animals like porcupines out of their burrows. Plant food formed the basis of their diet. Women gathered moisture-filled melons and dug up roots and bulbs. In times of drought, these plants were an important water source.

The San were skilled hunters

Living in Groups

Hunter-gatherers usually lived in family groups and, because they often moved about, they had few possessions. They usually had small families as a mother found it difficult to cope with more than two young children when she was travelling on foot.

Hunter-gatherers lived in caves, as well as temporary shelters made from branches and grass. Within their camps there would be a fireplace where people gathered to eat, share the meat after a kill and to make weapons and ornaments. They also played music and danced.

Some San families lived in huts covered with reeds and grass

A painting by Samuel Daniell of a Khoikhoi village

KHOIKHOI MUSIC
The Khoikhoi controlled cattle by playing **whistles** made from hollow bones. As they danced, they also played bell-like harmonies on **reed flutes**. From bows and arrows, they discovered that they could make music by attaching a **calabash** sound-box to the bow and then plucking the string. The **gorah** was a combination of a flute and a bow that produced a trumpet-like sound.

The Khoikhoi

The people living at the Cape when the first Europeans arrived in 1488, called themselves the Khoikhoi, meaning 'men of men' or 'the real men'. The European settlers traded with them, exchanging beads, copper, iron and tobacco for sheep and cattle, but could not understand their language. They noticed that whenever the Khoikhoi danced or sang they called out the word **Hautitou**. The Europeans thought that this was their name and called them **Hottentots**, but today the Khoikhoi are once again known by the name they had given themselves.

A Wandering Life

The Khoikhoi were nomadic herders who moved about in search of grazing and water. They were probably searching for new pastures when they first moved southwards to the Cape. They were also superb hunters and often hunted for food.

At first, the only animals the Khoikhoi kept were sheep. They ate the meat, and the women milked the ewes and made clothing from the skins.

Cattle later became a sign of wealth and were slaughtered only for special occasions and wedding feasts or funerals. The Khoikhoi used their oxen to transport goods.

The Khoikhoi packed up their huts when they moved on

Khoikhoi Houses

Khoikhoi huts had a framework of supple poles covered by reed mats, and some of these may still be seen in Namaqualand. Villages were made up of a circle of about 30 to 50 huts, with each low doorway facing the cattle enclosure in the centre. When the pastures were bare, or if a person died, the herders would pack up and move on to find another place to settle for a while.

The Strandlopers

Living along the shores of Table Bay and elsewhere along the coast were groups of people who ate mainly shellfish and wild roots. It is thought that they may have been Khoikhoi who had lost their livestock. The Dutch called them Strandlopers, meaning beachrangers, while the English called them Watermen. Fragments of their pottery and shell middens can still be found on some Cape beaches today.

The Khoikhoi are Dispossessed

After the Dutch settlers landed at the Cape, many of the Khoikhoi were attracted by the goods that the settlers offered in exchange for cattle and sheep. Soon there was fierce competition to trade with the Dutch, but some Khoikhoi lost their livestock. Others found that the Dutch would not let them graze their animals near the new settlement.

Robbed of their land, many of the Khoikhoi moved away from Table Bay. In raids on Khoikhoi camps, women and children were taken and made to serve the Dutch as slaves. War broke out, but the Khoikhoi could not compete with the guns and other weapons of the Dutch.

Smallpox and other diseases also killed many Khoikhoi, especially in the epidemic of 1713. There are few true Khoikhoi left today. Among the last survivors are those who live in the hot, dry Richtersveld National Park in northern Namaqualand. They are consulted on the park's management, but many of the adults are obliged to travel great distances to find work. Most families keep a few sheep and goats and struggle to raise basic crops in the harsh climate.

HOTTENTOTS HOLLAND MOUNTAINS
These mountains surround the Cape Flats and skirt the eastern side of False Bay. There is an interesting story to the name. In 1657, a group of free burghers encountered some Khoikhoi, the first people they met when they settled inland, tending their cattle in a beautiful valley beneath the mountains of the Cape Flats. The Khoikhoi explained that that was their home, just as Holland was home to the Dutch, and since then, both the mountains and the region have been known as Hottentots Holland.

PLACES TO SEE

Look out for Khoikhoi place names when you are travelling. Examples are Garies, Tsitsikamma, Keimoes, Outeniqua and Keiskamma

The Nguni-speakers

ENOUGH TO TURN HER HEAD
Married **Zulu women** took great pride in their headdress and rubbed their hair with red clay and styled it into various shapes. They wore beautiful bead necklaces and huge earrings in their stretched earlobes.

DRESSED TO KILL
The traditional battle dress of the **Zulu warrior** was a kilt of animal pelts and tails, an ox-hide shield and a short spear. Important men wore leopard skin and brave warriors wore a necklace of wooden beads. Today, a man may still wear a leopard skin when he gets married.

The Nguni-speaking people are thought to have originated in Central Africa, but later moved southwards and settled in what is now KwaZulu-Natal and parts of Mpumalanga. By 300 AD they were farming sorghum and millet and by 500 AD they had large herds of domestic cattle. Some of these people came down the coastal plain between the Drakensberg and the sea looking for an area to settle. By about 700 AD there were Iron Age farmers in the Eastern Cape. These early farmers were the direct ancestors of the present day Zulu, Xhosa, Swazi and Ndebele.

Lifestyle and Customs

In the old days, all the Nguni people lived in much the same way and spoke a similar language. The men were herders, hunters and warriors, and the women cultivated the land. Young girls worked in the fields and boys looked after the cattle. Large family groups lived together in scattered homesteads made up of circular huts grouped around a central cattle kraal. Marriages were arranged between families and cattle were exchanged as bride-wealth or *lobolo*. A man was allowed to have several wives, but the number depended on how much *lobolo* he could afford.

Chiefs were people of great importance and were much respected. Each family clan had its own chief and a group of clans was ruled by a paramount chief.

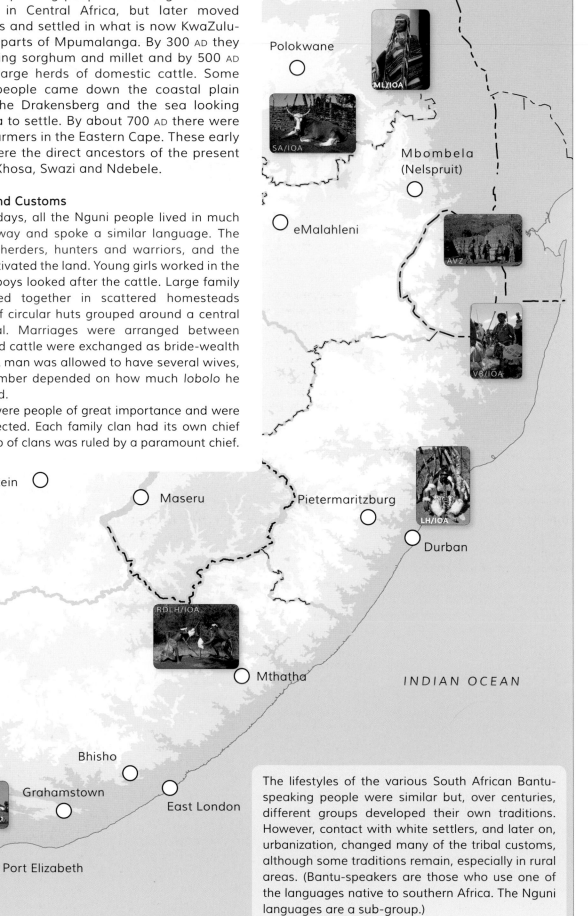

Polokwane

Mbombela (Nelspruit)

eMalahleni

Bloemfontein

Maseru

Pietermaritzburg

Durban

Mthatha

INDIAN OCEAN

Bhisho

Grahamstown

East London

Port Elizabeth

The lifestyles of the various South African Bantu-speaking people were similar but, over centuries, different groups developed their own traditions. However, contact with white settlers, and later on, urbanization, changed many of the tribal customs, although some traditions remain, especially in rural areas. (Bantu-speakers are those who use one of the languages native to southern Africa. The Nguni languages are a sub-group.)

The Zulu

One of the sons of Malandela and Nozinja who lived in the area formerly known as Zululand (now northern KwaZulu-Natal) was called Zulu, which means 'heaven' or 'sky'. When Zulu grew up, his brother Qwabe plotted to have him killed, so his mother took him to another part of the region, just south of the White Mfolozi River, where he established the Zulu clan. During the 18th century, powerful clans living north of the Tugela River overwhelmed the many smaller chiefdoms and eventually four separate groups – the Dlamini, Ndwandwe, Mthethwa and Qwabe – emerged.

The small Zulu chiefdom was part of the Mthethwa. Early in the 19th century, the great military commander, Shaka, seized the leadership of the Zulu chiefdom and, after conquering all the clans in Zululand, he united them to form the Zulu nation – one of the most powerful nations in Africa. The Zulu Kingdom still exists and exercises important political influence.

Today the Zulu, one of the largest Nguni-speaking groups in South Africa, are led by their King, Goodwill Zwelethini, a descendant of Senzangakhona, Shaka's father. Many Zulus live and work in towns and cities.

The former cultural organization, Inkatha Yesizwe, has become the Inkatha Freedom Party (IFP), which is a political party.

The Xhosa

The traditional home of the Xhosa is the coastal strip from the Mtamvuna River in KwaZulu-Natal to the Zuurveld of the Eastern Cape. Although they speak the same language with the characteristic click sounds derived from the Khoikhoi, they are divided up into a number of large, related groups, including the Mpondo, Thembu and Bomvana.

By the time that the white colonists began to move eastwards from the Cape, the Xhosa had become the most powerful people in the Eastern Cape. Between 1779 and 1878, nine bitter frontier wars were fought between the Xhosa and the Europeans who had settled in the area.

The Xhosa-speaking people traditionally lived in homesteads where all family members were related to the head of the group. As with the Zulu people, marriages were arranged between families and *lobolo* was payable. Both boys and girls went through a period of initiation rituals, which marked their passing from childhood into adulthood.

Many Xhosa-speaking people live in the Eastern Cape (formerly the Transkei and Ciskei). Transkei lay between the Mtamvuna and Great Kei rivers, whilst Ciskei lay between the Great Kei river in the east, and the Keiskamma and Tyume in the west. As a result of a disaster that occurred in the 1850s many Xhosa-speaking people moved to other parts of the country.

A young Xhosa girl, Nongqause, had a vision from her ancestors and told her people that they should destroy all their cattle and crops so that new cattle and crops could arise from the earth. When this was done, many thousands of Xhosa people died of hunger, while others moved away and became part of other communities.

Today many Xhosa-speaking people have become urbanized and live and work in cities and towns all over South Africa.

The Swazi

The Swazi are descended from the Dlamini clan. They are related to the Zulu and their language and culture also show certain similarities. They were led across the Lebombo Mountains to the area now known as Swaziland in the mid-18th century by Ngwane I and developed a political system where a Queen Mother counter-balanced the powers of the king. Later they took their name from their king, Mswati I, who built up a powerful army, reorganized along the lines of the Zulu age-group regiments. They waged many wars against neighbouring people but eventually came under the authority of the British. In 1968, Swaziland became an independent kingdom and is led today by King Mswati III.

The Swazi king is known as *Ngwenyama*, the Lion. His mother, *Ndlovukazi*, or the She-Elephant, has a powerful influence over him and the nation. Likewise, the mother of a headman also has an important position in a family group living together in a homestead and her hut, called *indlunkulu*, occupies a central place in the homestead. The king's wives and his children live in special royal villages.

The most important event in the year is the feast of the first fruits, or *incwala*, which is held after the last full moon in December. A party of men travels to the coast to collect sea water, which is believed to have special powers. Another group goes to the country's main rivers to collect fresh water.

When they return, the water is used in a ceremony during which the king is cleansed with certain medicines and a black bull is slaughtered. This sacred period in the lives of the Swazi lasts about three weeks. It symbolizes both a ritual strengthening of their king and the unity of their nation.

More than one third of the Swazi people live outside Swaziland, often staying close to its borders with Mpumalanga and with Mozambique. Because of their close historical links, the language and traditions of these people of KaNgwane are much like those of the people of the kingdom of Swaziland.

THE RED-BLANKET PEOPLE

Traditionally the **Xhosa** wore skin garments and later blankets dyed with a particular type of red earth. Women wore large turbans, beads, copper bracelets and braided skirts. A long pipe sometimes decorated with beadwork was the status symbol of a mature married woman.

THE SANGOMA

The **Sangoma** may be a man or a woman and is a trained spiritualist or diviner. Sangomas are believed to have a special relationship with powerful ancestral spirits and some people believe they can predict disaster and 'smell out' guilty people.

An *inyanga* is a traditional healer or herbalist and, like a *sangoma*, is trained in making herbal medicines.

PLACES TO SEE

- The KwaDukuza Museum, Stanger
- Shakaland near Eshowe in KwaZulu-Natal

17

People of the interior

THE RAIN QUEEN
According to legend, in the 16th century a daughter of a northern chief fled her country, taking with her the clan's rain-making secrets. She and her followers settled in the Molototsi River valley and formed the nucleus of the people known as the Lobedu. After subduing the local people, **Modjadji** emerged as their leader and rain queen. She believed that she was the closest link with the ancestors and became the most famous rain-maker in Africa. It is believed that the power passes from one generation to another. Currently, there is no ruling rain queen as the previous rain queen, Modjadji VI, died in June 2005 and her successor has not been named yet.

While some of the early Bantu-speaking people settled on the south-east coast of southern Africa, others moved from the north into the interior. After further migration, three groups could be identified – the Sotho, Venda and Tsonga – and each occupied a different area. They were all Bantu-speakers and although their languages are similar today, they are not identical.

The Sotho

Most Sotho-speaking people live north of the Orange River and west of the Drakensberg. Although they are divided into the northern and southern Sotho and the Tswana, the Sotho-speaking people share certain common customs. Villages consist of circular huts with an open-air enclosure called a **lapa**. Men are allowed to have many wives and the chief's most important wife is known as the 'light' of the clan.

The Northern Sotho

The largest group is the **Pedi**, who settled in the Steelpoort River valley. The Pedi were iron-workers who became wealthy through trading. Many live in Limpopo Province, between the northern Drakensberg and Soutpansberg ranges. A smaller but well-known group living near the Limpopo town of Duiwelskloof are known as the **Lobedu**, or Modjadji's people. They have strong cultural ties with the Venda.

The Southern Sotho

The **Basotho** have lived in what is now Lesotho and the surrounding area for centuries. Many Basotho also live on the Free State side of the Lesotho border, in the area known as QwaQwa.

In the early 19th century, a military leader named Moshoeshoe united a number of small chiefdoms to form the Basotho nation and in 1871 what was then Basutoland became part of the Cape Colony. Lesotho was recognized as an independent kingdom in 1966.

The Tswana

In the 16th century, the **Tswana**, the most important group of the western Sotho, settled in what is now the North West Province and divided into two main groups. The **Rolong** took their name from their chief, Morolong, meaning 'the metal worker' while the other group called themselves the **Bafokeng**, meaning 'people of the dew'.

Most Tswana people live in North West Province and the far Northern Cape, an area formerly covered by the 'homeland' state of Bophuthatswana, which had its principal city at Mmabatho (which means 'mother of the people') next to the historic town of Mafikeng. Mafikeng was besieged during the Anglo-Boer War.

The Venda

During the 18th century some of the Karanga-Rozwi people of Zimbabwe moved south to settle in Limpopo Province, along the Soutpansberg range.

Traditionally they cultivated land rather than farmed with cattle. They were also very good at metalwork and smelted iron, which they then used to make hoes and other instruments. In 1979 the area became the 'independent' state of **Venda**, but became part of the Northern Province (now Limpopo) in 1994.

The **Lemba**, a small group living among the Venda, are believed to have descended from Arabs, who, hundreds of years ago, travelled from the coast to trade with the people of the interior. The Lemba resemble Arabs in appearance, have Arab names and are also forbidden to eat pork. The women are expert potters and the men are fine metal workers. Today, the Lemba live widely dispersed in small groups.

GROWING UP
In every Bantu-speaking group there were special ceremonies to mark the beginning of adulthood. They entered initiation schools and were instructed in adult behaviour. For example, groups of circumcized Xhosa boys (amaKwetha) moved to an isolated hut marked with a white flag. To indicate that they were separate from the rest of the people, they painted their faces and bodies with white clay and at a later stage covered their heads with tall reed hats. They wore sheepskin cloaks and reed skirts. After the final stage their huts were burnt to symbolize the emergence of the boys into adulthood.

Huts or initiation shelters made of plastic sheets are still seen on the outskirts of cities.

The Shangaan-Tsonga

Five centuries ago, the Tsonga lived in Mozambique and became rich by trading with the Portuguese, exchanging copper and ivory for fine linen cloth. But in 1820, they were partly overpowered by Soshangane, leader of the Ndwandwe clan of Zululand, who was fleeing from Shaka. A part of the Shangaan group joined Soshangane's clan and, in the 1840s, settled with them in the Lowveld of Limpopo Province and Mpumalanga.

The Ndebele

The Ndebele, who are descended from Nguni-speakers, form three groups: the Ndebele of the Limpopo Province and those of Gauteng both moved from KwaZulu-Natal in about 1600. Two centuries later, the third group, which became known as the Matabele, moved north of the Limpopo River into Zimbabwe to escape Shaka.

The Ndebele mixed with the Sotho and today speak their language and have adopted many Sotho customs. The southern Ndebele still speak a language related to Zulu, and many live near Tshwane (Pretoria). Here they developed a bold visual culture – they are renowned for their strikingly decorated houses with walls painted in bright colours and many patterns. Traditional Ndebele homes used to be circular, of the type described as a 'cone on cylinder', but most are now built to a rectangular plan and have flat roofs.

AFRICAN ARTISTS

Many Ndebele women are gifted artists who create elaborate headwork. Some women wear heavy necklaces and anklets that are rarely removed.

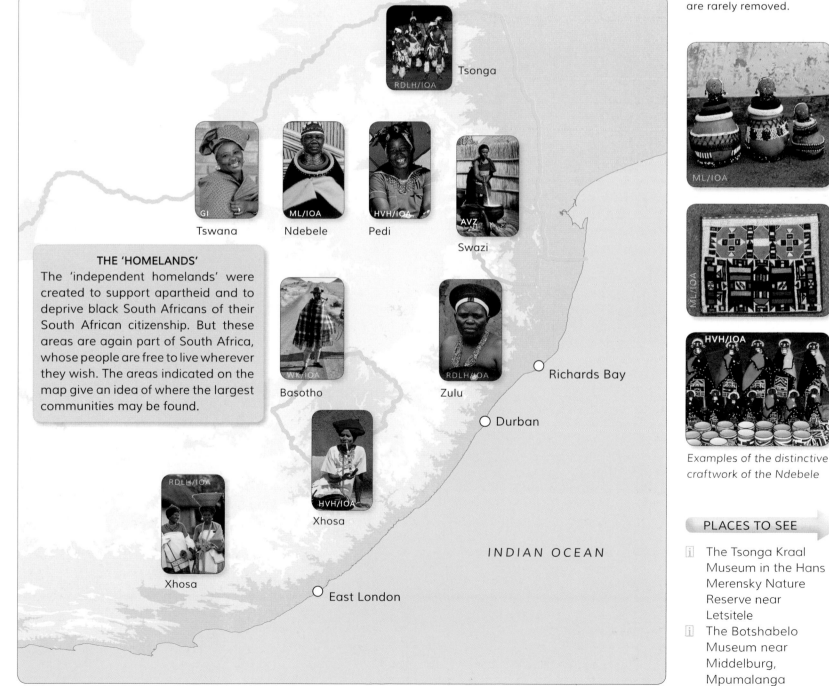

THE 'HOMELANDS'
The 'independent homelands' were created to support apartheid and to deprive black South Africans of their South African citizenship. But these areas are again part of South Africa, whose people are free to live wherever they wish. The areas indicated on the map give an idea of where the largest communities may be found.

Examples of the distinctive craftwork of the Ndebele

PLACES TO SEE

ⓘ The Tsonga Kraal Museum in the Hans Merensky Nature Reserve near Letsitele

ⓘ The Botshabelo Museum near Middelburg, Mpumalanga

Our earliest visitors

AE/GTY/GI

INSTRUMENTS TO SHOW THE WAY

Voyages of discovery took seamen far from landmarks and familiar star positions. To help them cross uncharted seas, instruments of navigation were improved. The magnetic compass, which had been used for over a thousand years, was improved by inserting a rotating iron pin in a waterproof brass box so that it always pointed approximately north. All 32 wind directions were painted on the base of the new compass.

The **astrolabe**, used to determine latitude since the time of the Roman Empire, was also improved. It consisted of a circular scale with a pointer fixed at the centre. Taking his sights at the sun or the stars along this pointer, the navigator would guess their angle above the horizontal and calculate the ship's latitude on astronomical tables.

THE POUNT

In March 1989, a remarkable vessel, the *Pount*, which means 'Land of the Gods', sailed into Cape Town harbour. It had sailed all the way from southern France. This vessel was a replica of Egyptian sea-going trading ships of around 1500 BC. It took the *Pount* two-and-a-half years to circumnavigate Africa.

From earliest times there has been trade between Europe and the Far East. Europeans paid high prices for the silks, spices and other exotic goods that could only be obtained in India and China. To satisfy this demand, merchants travelled between Europe and Asia. But by the early 15th century, wars in Asia Minor had made this overland journey impossible and traders had to find a new route to the Far East. Portugal in particular embarked on a number of 'voyages of discovery' to establish a sea route to the spice-rich lands of India and China.

Finding a Sea Route to India

In 1488, **Bartolomeu Dias** sailed along the west coast of Africa in the hope of rounding the southern tip of Africa and then sailing on to India and the Far East. Dias' ships, the São Cristovão and São Pantaleão, had sailed along the African coast, but strong winds blew them out to sea. When Dias next saw land, he realized from the position of the sun that he was heading northwards and that his ships had rounded Africa's southernmost point.

He sailed on until his exhausted men forced him to turn back. Dias called at several places on his way home. Although he did not enter Table Bay, he named the headland that guarded the southern seas 'Cabo de Boa Eperança' – the Cape of Good Hope. He had not reached India, but discovered that a sea route to the East was possible.

In 1497, **Vasco da Gama** led a second expedition to the East. Four ships left Lisbon and, after four months at sea, they anchored off the Cape in a bay Da Gama named after **St Helena**. Da Gama sailed on and when he passed the lush east coast on Christmas Day, when

Christians celebrate the birth of Christ, he named it **Natal**, meaning 'birth'. Early in 1498, the Portuguese ships reached Malindi, in today's Kenya, and an Arab pilot guided them across the Indian Ocean. At last a sea route to India had been discovered and soon other nations, most notably the British and the Dutch, began sending their ships around the Cape.

CHINESE MAP-MAKING

China has a long and illustrious history of map-making, dating back almost 2 500 years. Aided by the early discovery of the compass, an advanced knowledge of astronomy and the development of a grid mapping system, geographic maps had been used since the Chin Dynasty (265–289 BC).

Map-making developed further during later dynasties, but the real impetus for the drawing of world maps would come during the Mongol Yuan Dynasty (1260–1368).

As a result of the conquests conducted during this period, China was able to extend its sphere of influence as far as the boundaries of Europe. This, in turn, led to an increase in intellectual and commercial contacts, especially with Persia and Arabia, allowing Chinese cartographers to draw on knowledge from other countries and integrate it with their own.

As far as it is possible to establish, the first map to depict the south-pointing peninsular shape of the African continent was drawn by Zu Siben (1273–1337), almost two centuries before Africa was circumnavigated by the Portuguese.

It is noteworthy that maps accurately displaying Africa – in terms of shape and proportion – only appeared in Europe in the 16th century.

CTAR

Bartolomeu Dias

CTAR

A caravel with triangular sails

The first contact between the Khoikhoi and European seafarers took place when the Portuguese captain, Antonio de Saldanha, landed in Table Bay in 1503.

Before the Portuguese

There is a suggestion that an Egyptian Pharaoh, Necho, sponsored a Phoenician expedition that successfully sailed around Africa at the end of the 6th century BC, almost 2 000 years before Vasco Da Gama. There is also evidence that at least three of the seven 'Treasure Fleets of the Dragon Throne' that left China to explore the Indian Ocean from 1403 to 1435 visited East Africa.

But why do we know so much about the Portuguese 'voyages of discovery' and so little about the other early visitors to our shores? Firstly, evidence to prove that the Phoenician expedition occurred remains sketchy, although compelling. Secondly, China underwent a dramatic political change in about 1435 when a new Emperor came to the throne. Indian Ocean voyages that had been taking place for over 30 years were abandoned and priority was given to defending China's vast land frontiers. Following this decision, China withdrew into itself.

At the same time, Europe was suddenly awakening from a 1 000-year slumber. The Renaissance, which began in Italy in the 1400s and quickly spread to the rest of Europe, was an intellectual re-birth that provided new impetus for learning and discovery.

Thus, by the middle of the 15th century, quite separate events on opposite sides of the world had set the scene for Europe's influence to increase and for China's influence to decline.

AT THE RATE OF KNOTS
An old method of calculating distance at sea was known as **dead reckoning**. A cord was tied to a log and tossed into the sea from the ship's bow. The person holding the cord would count the seconds it took to move towards the stern. As they knew the ship's length, they could calculate its speed. After several hours, sailors would have a rough idea of the distance travelled. Another method involved the paying out of a line in which a series of knots were tied. From this we get the term 'knots', which is still used at sea or in the air today. (One knot equals about 1.85 kilometres per hour.)

A Chinese junk, circa 1300 AD

One of the ships in Vasco da Gama's fleet

THE PHOENICIANS: ANCIENT SEAFARERS

According to the Greek historian Herodotus, Pharaoh Necho of Egypt supported an expedition to circumnavigate Libya (Africa) at the end of the 6th century BC. In his book *History*, Herodotus says, '... And so the Phoenicians set out from the Red Sea and sailed the southern seas ... they sailed on so that after two years ... they rounded the pillars of Heracles (the Straits of Gibraltar) and came to Egypt. There they said (what some believe but I do not) that in sailing around Libya they had the sun on their right hand.'

The story told by Herodotus is astounding – not only because it implies that at the time of writing it was common knowledge that Africa was surrounded on three sides by water, but also because of the claim made by the mariners that they had sailed with 'the sun on their right hand'. No one would have known at that time that below the equator, the sun is not in the south but in the north, unless he had sailed westwards in the southern hemisphere!

PLACES TO SEE

ⓘ Bartholomeu Dias Museum Complex in Mossel Bay

Early days at the Cape

The Drommedaris

The *Drommedaris*, the *Reijger* and *De Goede Hoop* sailed into Table Bay on 6 April 1652. The Dutch East India Company in Amsterdam had instructed Commander Jan van Riebeeck to start a refreshment station for ships travelling to and from the East. Fresh vegetables and meat that could be bought from the Khoikhoi, would prevent scurvy, a disease from which many sailors died.

WC/CBD

Jan van Riebeeck and his party of Dutch settlers land at the Cape

A LUCKY ACCIDENT

On 22 December 1846 the Dutch East India vessel *Nieuwe Haerlem* sailed out of Batavia in the East Indies with a cargo of spices, gold cloth and Chinese porcelain. It dropped anchor in Cape Town on 22 March 1647. Three days later it was driven ashore near present-day Milnerton during a storm and wrecked. Most of the crew reached safety, but there was no ship to take them back to Holland. For over a year the captain and crew remained at the Cape where they were able to raise crops and traded copper and tobacco for cattle and sheep from the local people. They obtained salt from the salt marshes along the Diep River and lived off penguins, penguin eggs and cormorants.
In March 1648 a fleet of twelve ships stopped at the Cape on route to Holland. On one of these ships was Jan van Riebeeck. When van Riebeeck returned to Holland he convinced the Dutch East India Company to establish a '**refreshment station**' at the Cape. He returned to the Cape as head of this expedition in April 1652.

The People at the Cape

The ships brought **Jan van Riebeeck**, his wife, Maria de la Quellerie, and their baby son, and about 90 men, women and children to the Cape. Van Riebeeck made contact with the Strandlopers along the shores of Table Bay, while the Khoikhoi brought cattle and sheep to graze near the Cape Peninsula. Trading began, but trouble arose as neither group understood the other's concepts of owning land or livestock.

There was so much work to be done in the new and expanding settlement that men from passing vessels often stayed behind to help. The growing community soon included builders, blacksmiths, carpenters, fishermen and farmers.

CTAR

CTAR

Jan van Riebeeck (top) and Maria de la Quellerie (above)

SA/IOA

THE CASTLE OF GOOD HOPE

In January 1666, Commander Zacharias Wagenaer laid the foundations of a stronger fort than Van Riebeeck's original **Fort de Goede Hoop** to defend the settlement from the English. The fort was built by about 300 soldiers and many slaves. Timber came from Hout Bay, stones from Table Mountain and the mortar was made from Robben Island seashells. In addition, wood, bricks and tiles were imported from the Netherlands. Work was slow, but in April 1679 the Castle of Good Hope was officially completed. The following year, Simon van der Stel moved into the commander's quarters. All the old plans refer to the Castle as a citadel – a refuge within a city. The star-shaped Castle has five pointed bastions, named **Buren**, **Katzenellenbogen**, **Nassau**, **Oranje** and **Leerdam** after the titles of the Prince of Orange. These housed the armoury, kitchen, food store, soldiers' barracks and prison. The Castle's first entrance was so close to the sea that waves often swamped it. In 1695 a wall (the 'Kat') with a beautiful balcony was built across the courtyard for extra defence. For over a century all important decisions were made at the Castle of Good Hope, but never, in its over 300-year-old history, has a shot been fired against the enemy.

The Expanding Settlement

Crops that were planted in Green Point were flattened by the wind, so fields were planted along the Liesbeeck River valley and the Company erected a large barn ('De Schuur') on the slopes above it.

It was from this valley that the Khoikhoi were permanently expelled in 1657. Because the company could not provide enough produce, nine farmers or **free burghers** – were given permission by the Company to trade, grow crops and keep cattle and sheep. Small forts had to be built to protect them from the Khoikhoi whose land they now occupied.

Jan van Riebeeck Leaves the Cape

When Jan van Riebeeck left the Cape, just ten years after his arrival, the permanent population had grown to 953, including 191 slaves. The new settlement was quickly developing into a village and thatched cottages stretched down the single street from the Company's Garden to the busy jetty.

Simon van der Stel leaves his mark

In 1679, Simon van der Stel was appointed as the first Governor of the Cape. He soon set about the planting of vines for wine-making (in those days, wine was often safer to drink than water!). He built the beautiful Groot Constantia homestead (below) on land granted to him in 1685, and established the town of Stellenbosch.

THE GARDENS

The Cape's first gardener, Hendrik Boom, uprooted the natural fynbos, laid out the Company's Garden in Table Valley, and sowed vegetable seeds. Fruit trees were imported from Europe and the East and the first vines were planted. Soon wheat was growing at Green Point.

TRAGIC EVA

A young Khoikhoi woman, named Krotoa (known as Eva) was educated by the Van Riebeeck family. She acted as interpreter for the Dutch and in 1664 married the surgeon Pieter van Meerhoff. After his death in 1667 she was rejected by both the Khoikhoi and the white communities, although she had played a vital part in relations between them. She was sent to Robben Island several times and died in 1674, aged only about 30, and was buried in the chapel inside the still uncompleted Castle.

PLACES TO SEE

- The Castle of Good Hope in Cape Town
- Explore a replica of the *Drommedaris* at Santarama Miniland in Johannesburg, although it is in a state of neglect
- The Company's Garden in Cape Town
- Groot Constantia homestead in Constantia, Cape Town

Slaves at the Cape

SHOES FOR THE FREE

Because slaves were not paid, they could not afford to buy or even make clothes, and the rags they wore were given to them by their masters. They never wore shoes so bare feet came to mean that you were a slave. Only 'free blacks' could afford to buy shoes.

FREE BLACKS

Some slaves, especially those who had been baptized into the Christian religion as children, were manumitted (set free) in adulthood. Most freed slaves came from the towns, and were called **free blacks**. Although free blacks had some rights, they were forced to carry passes when travelling and women were told how to dress. Some free blacks became craftsmen or fishermen and were very successful. Many women took in laundry and some free blacks bought farms.

Jan van Riebeeck did not have enough workers to help him complete the enormous tasks that he had been given. Only two months after his arrival he asked the Company to send him slaves from the East. The Khoikhoi, who still had their lands and their livestock, refused to work for the Dutch and hoped that they would soon go away.

The First Slaves Arrive

On 28 March 1658, the Amersfoort, carrying nearly 200 young Angolan slaves, dropped anchor in Table Bay. Many older and weaker slaves had died at sea, and those that remained were mostly young boys and girls. Some worked in the fields and gardens and the rest were given to Company officials. Two months later, 150 more slaves arrived and, from then on, slaves were regularly shipped in from East Africa, Madagascar, Mozambique and the East. Conditions on the ships were dreadful and many slaves died from disease, while some lost their lives trying to swim ashore.

Working for the Company

The Company's slaves cut timber, worked in the harbour, on buildings and in the gardens. They were given very little food and worked long hours, resting only on Sundays. The Company's slaves lived in the damp and overcrowded Slave Lodge, which was badly ventilated and unhealthy. After 1811, the building was rebuilt as government offices. Since 2000 it has been converted into the Iziko Old Slave Lodge Museum, which tells the story of slavery at the Cape.

Sold by Auction

When a shipment of slaves arrived at the Cape, those not needed by the Company were auctioned. Most people wanted young, strong men, but some wanted women too. Buyers inspected slaves as they would cattle. Husbands and wives could be sold separately, and some children were parted from their parents for life. The site of the tree under which many auctions took place, is marked by a plaque in Spin Street, Cape Town.

An African slave market

Etching depicting native Africans sold into slavery, circa 1875

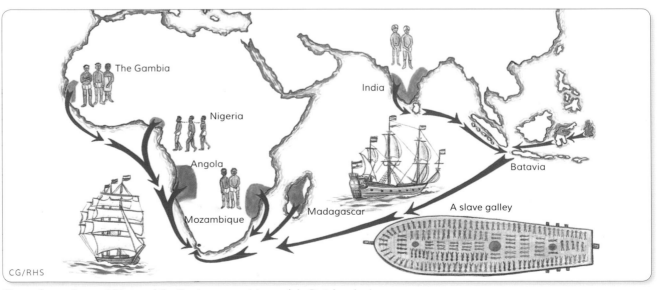

Slaves from all over Africa and the East were sent to work in Dutch colonies

On the Farms

Many slaves worked in the vineyards and pressed the grapes for wine. After washing their feet they would climb into a wooden cask of grapes and trample the fruit until the juice ran out. Slaves on the wheat farms harvested and threshed the grain. They also loaded wagons, ploughed the fields and tended the livestock.

On small farms, slaves slept in the kitchen or barn, and on large farms they had slave quarters. Some farmers allowed their slaves to grow their own crops and vegetables on their land.

The Town Slave

Rich people had many slaves. They worked as house servants, fetched water from the public pump and collected firewood. Some slave women were expert laundresses and needlewomen. Many slaves from the East were craftsmen, while others learnt trades at the Cape. They included plasterers, coopers (who make wine-barrels), tailors and metal-workers.

The End of the Slave Trade

In 1806 the British occupied the Cape for the second time and abolished the slave trade the following year. This did not end slavery, but meant that slaves could not be brought from other countries. Slaves taken from foreign ships at sea by the British Navy were hired out as 'apprentices' at the Cape. The trading of slaves within the colony continued and prices rose.

Free at Last

By the 1820s, people began to realize that slavery was cruel. Others thought it cheaper to pay free labourers than to support slave families.

In May 1833 the British parliament freed all slaves in the colonies, but they continued to work for their owners for five years until they were eventually released on 1 December 1838. Some slaves were quite sorry to leave their owners, but most were overjoyed.

The British government had promised to pay slave owners part of the value of their slaves, but as they had to fetch their money in London, many never received payment. But owners still had some control as they were allowed to punish servants who tried to leave before their contracts expired.

THE SLAVE BELLS

Special **slave bells** were rung to summon slaves to work and to declare the end of their working day. These big bells, mounted between two tall pillars, were quite common on large farms, but few remain today.

RUNAWAY SLAVES

Many slaves were lonely, hungry and afraid when they arrived at the Cape. They were in a strange land and could not understand the language. Sometimes they were cruelly treated and many tried to escape, then facing danger from unfriendly Khoikhoi and prowling wild animals. For over 100 years, runaway slaves lived at Hangklip on False Bay. They ate fish or took food from passing wagons.

HUMAN TRAFFICKING

Slavery remains alive and well, nowadays referred to as 'human trafficking'. People are bought, sold and transported all over the world. There are no official records, but some estimates suggest as many as 27 million people are enslaved worldwide. It is thought that about one third of all the people trafficked are under 18.

An enslaved man

Sale of Prize Slaves.
This Day the 3d of October,
Will be Sold by Public Vendue,
At the Garden of F. Kannemeyer,
SEVENTY prime male and female Slaves, captured in the French vessels, La Raisonable and Le Glaucus, and condemned as prize in the Court of Vice Admiralty.
Cape Town, 28th Sept. 1801.

A poster advertising a slave sale

AN EASTERN FAITH AT THE CAPE

The **Islamic community** (formerly known as the Cape Malays) is descended from slaves from the East and its members still follow the **Muslim** faith. Many try to make the journey to the Holy City of **Mecca** at least once, but otherwise visit the five **kramats**, or tombs of holy men, in Cape Town. The most important is the shrine of Sheik Yusuf (or Joseph), who was exiled to the Cape in 1693 after leading a revolt against the Dutch in Java.

All Muslims keep the fast of **Ramadan** in commemoration of the revelation of the holy book, *The Koran*, to the prophet **Muhammad**. On the 27th night, sins are forgiven and miracles are said to occur. During the month-long fasting period, houses are spotless, candles are lit and new linen is laid on the beds. The fast ends with the sighting of the new moon.

PLACES TO SEE

- Iziko Old Slave Lodge Museum, Cape Town
- Slave bells at Stellenbosch and (replica) in Gardens, Cape Town

Change at the Cape

By the mid-1790s, Britain had become the richest trading nation in Europe and the Dutch East India Company had lost much of its wealth and power. The Netherlands had been invaded by the French and Prince William V of Orange had fled to England. Many officials at the Cape were considered to be extravagant and dishonest, and there was serious unrest in the interior.

VAN RIEBEECK STAD
In its early days, Cape Town had no name and was known only as **De Kaapsche Vlek** ('the Cape village'). The name 'Kaapstad' followed naturally. In July 1804, when Cape Town was granted its new coat of arms, which included the Van Riebeeck family emblem, Commissioner de Mist suggested that the town's name be changed to 'Van Riebeeck Stad'. However, nothing came of the proposal.

'A WEAK OLD SOUL'
Although he opened the first theatre in the Cape and established a printing press, British governor Sir George Yonge, was inexperienced. Lady Anne Barnard described him as 'a very, very weak old soul'. He quarrelled with important people, and was accused of extravagance, bribery and fraud.

THE FRENCH LINES
For years prior to the British Occupation, the Dutch at the Cape expected a British attack, and their French allies sent soldiers to help protect the Cape. They built a line of forts stretching from Fort Knokke, where Woodstock railway station is today, through Zonnebloem farm, to the foot of Devil's Peak. When General Craig became the military commander he extended the French Lines up the mountainside. Several new forts were built and the ruins of the Queen's tower and King's blockhouse (above) can still be seen today. The latter, on Devil's Peak, is visible from the Castle and from False Bay, and was used for sending signals. It is still a fine viewing site.

A British Invasion
On 11 June 1795, a British fleet, commanded by Rear-Admiral George Elphinstone and General James Craig, sailed into Simon's Bay with orders to occupy the Cape peacefully. This would prevent France from taking over the important halfway-house to the East Indies. But the Commander at the Castle, Abraham Josias Sluysken, refused to surrender the colony and assembled his troops at Muizenberg.

Battles at Muizenberg and Wynberg
The Dutch troops were outnumbered, badly trained and short of guns, and General Craig's British troops easily managed to drive them back as far as Wynberg, where the Dutch were again defeated. Two days later, a peace treaty was signed and the Cape came under British rule. General Craig became military commander of the Cape and, determined that the colonists accept British rule peacefully, he tried hard to get rid of corruption among government officials.

Troubles Inland
Even before the British arrived, colonists in Graaff-Reinet and Swellendam rebelled against the Dutch East India Company. They would not agree to British rule so General Craig cut off their supplies and sent soldiers to the area. The districts grudgingly accepted British protection. **Earl Macartney** became governor after Craig left the Cape in 1797. He improved government salaries so that officials were no longer tempted to accept bribes, and abolished torture as a means of punishment and interrogation. Trade was freer and colonists became wealthier.

The Battle of Muizenberg

CTAR

Under the Batavian Republic

In 1802, the Treaty of Amiens ended the nine-year-old war between Britain and France. On 21 February 1803, Britain officially returned the Cape to The Netherlands, which by then had become the Batavian Republic.

Commissioner Jacob de Mist (right), and Governor Jan Janssens, began to reorganize the administration of the Cape. Ministers of religion had less control over the lives of the people in their communities. Marriages could now take place in a magistrate's court. Agricultural methods were improved and trading regulations were reduced.

CTAR

The Second British Occupation (1806)

But Britain and France were soon at war again and in January 1806 a British fleet of 63 ships sailed into Table Bay. Over 6 000 troops landed at Blaauwberg, and attacked General Janssens' 2 000-strong force of foreign mercenaries, untrained burghers, Khoikhoi and slaves. Most of the mercenaries fled, leaving the burghers and the Khoikhoi, aided by some French marines, to face the attackers. After one day of fierce battle, General Janssens ordered his men to retreat. With his remaining troops, Janssens then fled from the Battle of Blaauwberg and took refuge in the Hottentots Holland Mountains.

General David Baird marched to Cape Town and on 10 January 1806 signed the peace terms at Papendorp (today's Woodstock). From the time of the second British occupation, the Cape remained a British colony until it was incorporated into the Union of South Africa in 1910. The Union became the Republic in 1961.

THE DE MISTS

Julie Philippe Augusta de Mist was the youngest child of Commissioner de Mist. She accompanied her father to the Cape where, aged 19, she acted as his hostess at Stellenberg, their home in Kenilworth. Commissioner de Mist founded the first girls' school in the Cape. At a time when schools only for girls were almost unheard of in Europe, he opened his 'superior seminary' for young ladies in 1804. It was situated in the Keisersgracht (today's Darling Street). At first the school was a success, but falling numbers eventually forced it to close in 1809. It was many years before another girls' school was established.

MA

British forces clash with General Janssens' Dutch troops at Blaauwberg

LADY ANNE BARNARD

Earl Macartney's wife could not accompany him to the Cape, so Lady Anne Barnard, wife of his secretary, acted as his hostess. Her letters, sketches and journals describing life at the Cape in the 18th century are some of the most fascinating historical accounts on record. Apart from paintings of people she met and places she visited, Lady Anne also painted a view of Cape Town from the roof of the Castle. It shows a town of white, flat-roofed houses and straight, tree-lined streets stretching from the harbour to the Company's Garden.

NLSA

The Castle grounds, as painted by Lady Anne Barnard

A STEPPING STONE TO ASIA

The British invaded the Cape in 1795 and again in 1806 to stop it from falling into French hands. The Cape was seen as a valuable stepping-stone to the **Far East**, where the British East India Company was conducting a highly profitable trade. At first, the British had no interest in the territory inland from the coast.

PLACES TO SEE

ℹ The King's blockhouse on Devil's Peak in Cape Town

On the move

Many travellers, explorers and trekboers made discoveries in southern Africa quite by accident. Some were searching for precious minerals. Others were escaping from harsh laws. Missionaries were seeking converts. Naturalists were studying plant and animal life. Hunters were shooting animals for skins and ivory. Often by chance, these people came across unexplored places, unknown races and undiscovered things. Some recorded their adventures in writing and made South Africa known to the wider world.

Terra Incognita
When Bartolomeu Dias reached the Cape of Good Hope in 1488, Europe knew almost nothing about Africa south of the Sahara Desert. On maps of the time, the interior was often labelled *Terra incognita* – the unknown land. It was an area supposedly filled with strange peoples and terrible monsters. Sometimes European map-makers labelled the region 'Here be Dragons'.

The Castaways
In the 15th and 16th centuries many Portuguese ships were wrecked along our coastline. Hundreds of people drowned but some survived to write the earliest records of exploration in southern Africa. In 1552, the São João was wrecked at the mouth of the Mzimvubu River. The 500 survivors set off towards Mozambique, struggling over rugged mountains and desolate country. Some died from exhaustion or thirst, others were killed by wild animals. In May 1553 a handful of survivors reached their destination. Port St Johns is named after their ship.

A Mountain of Diamonds and Pearls
Early explorers at the Cape always hoped to find precious minerals. On an October morning in 1657, Abraham Gabbema and Pieter Potter discovered a mountain crowned by huge rocks that glistened like jewels. They called it **den Diamandt en de Peerlbergh**, the Diamond and Pearl Mountain. When a town was established under the mountain it took its name, 'Paarl', from the shiny granite rocks.

The Call of the Wild
By the late 17th century, many colonists wanted to escape from the restrictions at the Cape. They needed grazing for cattle and wanted to hunt game. In 1703, Governor Wilhem Adriaen van der Stel gave permits to people to farm in the interior. Many burghers began to move away and were soon known as **trekboers**.

THE LURE OF MONOMOTAPA
In 1659 Jan van Riebeeck sent seven free burghers to look for the legendary, rich kingdom of Monomotapa in Central Africa, but they turned back before they reached the Great Berg River. Jan Danckaert and Pieter Cruythoff also searched for the kingdom, but got no further than Clanwilliam.

ROBERT JACOB GORDON
Born in The Netherlands in 1743, **Robert Jacob Gordon** became a professional soldier and commander of the Cape garrison in 1782. His journeys took him further than any settler had been before, and he discovered fragments of Dias' padrão at the mouth of the Bushman's River. After he explored the False Bay coast, Gordon's Bay was named after him.

ANDERS SPARRMAN'S ADVENTURES
When the Swedish doctor **Anders Sparrman** arrived at the Cape in 1772 he had already been to China. After teaching for a while in Simon's Town, he joined Captain Cook and sailed around the world, visiting New Zealand, Tahiti, Easter Island and Antarctica. Sparrman returned to the Cape in March 1775, but set off into the interior. He later wrote his famous book, *A Voyage to the Cape of Good Hope.*

A museum reconstruction of a trekboer

When a trekboer was tired of his new farm, he left it and moved further from Cape Town. Trekboers no longer bothered about permits or kept within boundaries. If the land was fertile, the sons would remain with their father and build separate homesteads. In dry regions, the son would move a little further and then claim the area beyond that point as his own. Sometimes he would not even build a house, but would live with his family in his ox-wagon, moving on whenever he wished.

The Great River
In July 1760 a farmer, Jacobus Coetsé, discovered a wide river while hunting elephant in northern Namaqualand. Its Khoikhoi name was Gariep, but he called it the Great River. In 1777, Captain Gordon named it the Orange, in honour of the Dutch royal family. While in Namaqualand, Gordon met Hendrik Wikar, a deserter from the Dutch East India Company, who provided the first written record of the Augrabies Falls.

The Augrabies Falls

The Griquas
The Griquas were nomads who lived by hunting south of the Orange River. One clan followed **Adam Kok**, a freed slave from Piketberg, and another clan was led by Barend Barends. Missionaries persuaded both clans to settle near Klaarwater in the Northern Cape, but they quarrelled about who should be leader. Eventually, the missionaries took control, so Barends's followers moved away and Adam Kok's grandson, Adam Kok II, became leader. They were known as the Griquas and Klaarwater became Griquatown.

A TRADING NETWORK

Mapungubwe has been described as South Africa's first city. It was located at the confluence of the Shashe and Limpopo rivers, and was powerful around 1100 AD. **Thulamela**, which is near Pafuri in what is now the Kruger National Park, was at the height of its power between 1400 and 1600 AD. Both these sites were part of an important trading network in the region. They had highly organized societies and were home to skilled metalsmiths who produced gold and golden objects, which they traded with Islamic traders from the East Coast of Africa for goods from as far away as India and China. Mapungubwe was declared a Unesco World Heritage Site in 2003.

GRIQUATOWN

Griquatown, the first town to be established north of the Orange River, was founded in 1803 around a church serving the Griquas. Sometimes, adventurers, hunters, liquor traders and cattle thieves were hanged from a tree that still grows today. Travellers, explorers and missionaries who called there on their way north, included **David Livingstone** whose wife, Mary Moffat, was born at the mission.

Adam Kok III

The Griquas of Kokstad

After further quarrels, Adam Kok II gave up his leadership and settled at the Philippolis mission station. In 1861, Adam Kok III gathered his followers and trekked across the Drakensberg to the border area between KwaZulu-Natal and the Eastern Cape. The region was known as No Man's Land, but after the Griquas' arrival it was called **East Griqualand**. Kokstad was named after their leader, and the descendants of Adam Kok and his followers still live there.

The Dorstland Trekkers

In 1874, a group of trekkers left Rustenburg in the North West Province and headed for the dry Kalahari where they hoped to find a new home. They became known as 'thirstland trekkers'. Three groups trekked across what

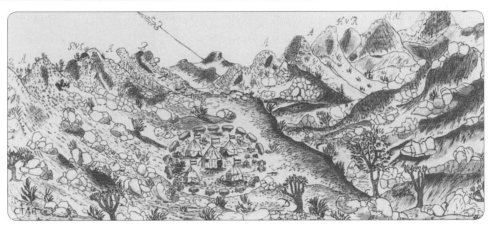

Van der Stel's camp in Namaqualand's copper mountains

are today Botswana and Namibia, and separated into smaller groups. Water was scarce, their livestock died and malaria struck. In desperation, people ate wild plants and were poisoned, or died from sunstroke, thirst, fever and starvation. In 1879, the survivors settled near the Etosha Pan but, when the Cape government took control of the area, the trekkers packed their wagons and headed towards the Kunene River and into Angola.

A typical trekker camp of the later 19th century

THE SEARCH FOR COPPER

In 1681 Nama people brought ore from Namaqualand to the Cape. Oloff Bergh and Isaq Schrijver went in search of the **copper mountains**, and in 1685, Simon van der Stel organized his own expedition. In two months he reached the fabled copper mountains, but there simply was not enough copper to mine.

PLACES TO SEE

- The Mary Moffat Museum, Griqutown, Northern Cape.
- Museum Transgariep, Philippolis, Free State.

The 1820 settlers

THE GRAHAM'S TOWN JOURNAL

The Graham's Town Journal, edited by Robert Godlonton, appeared in 1831, and was the first South African newspaper published outside Cape Town. Through the journal, people and the colonial government learnt about the settlers' hardships, needs, rights and opinions. In 1920 it merged with *Grocott's Mail*, which is still published today.

THOMAS PRINGLE

Pringle, a Scottish journalist, became South Africa's first poet of distinction. He strongly supported freedom of the Press and the emancipation of slaves.

Two settlers tried to bring a printing press with them to the Cape, but it was confiscated by the authorities when their ship docked in Cape Town, on its way to Algoa Bay

When the British government announced in July 1819 that it would settle British families in the Cape Colony, many people were eager to escape the poverty, high taxes and unemployment in Britain. About 4000 people came to the Cape, including ministers of religion, teachers, soldiers, and tradesmen. Many of the emigrants were poor.

Immigration Plans

The Cape governor, Lord Charles Somerset, wanted more white farmers in the Eastern Cape so they could act as a 'buffer' protecting the Colony from the Xhosa beyond the Great Fish River. There would then also be

more English-speakers in the area, known by the local Boer farmers as the Zuurveld. Although the land between the Bushmans and Great Fish Rivers appeared fertile, the soil was sour and barren and the rainfall uncertain.

Lord Charles Somerset

The Settlers Arrive

The *Chapman*, the first of twenty-one emigrant ships to reach Algoa Bay (now Port Elizabeth), arrived on 9 April 1820. Tents, stores and wagons were provided and Colonel Jacob Cuyler, the landdrost of Uitenhage, accompanied the settlers to their land near the mouth of the Great Fish River. 'When you plough the fields,' he told them, 'never leave your guns at home.' It was the settlers' first indication of the resistance they would encounter.

The acting governor, Sir Rufane Donkin, decided that the settlers should have a capital. The town of Bathurst was established about 60 kilometres south-east of Grahamstown, and a magistrate was appointed to control their affairs.

An 1820 Settler family

The Hardships of Pioneering

Life was difficult in the new settlement. Governor Donkin wouldn't allow the settlers to travel without special passes and, with winter approaching, they still lived in tents while building their simple mud houses. Few settlers knew how to farm but they persisted. Drought, floods and pests destroyed the wheat, and many sheep and cattle were eaten by wild animals. Some settlers died of disease and a few were killed in quarrels with the Xhosa, on whose land they had settled.

Groups of 1820 Settlers arriving in Algoa Bay

Settler Enterprise

As a result of these hardships many settlers were penniless and gave up farming. Some moved to the towns to find work as artisans, butchers, carpenters, shoemakers and coach makers. Others traded as pedlars, while those who could afford it, bought ox-wagons and bartered with the Xhosa for ivory and animal hides. Grahamstown was their base and, as trade increased, its citizens prospered, especially when the trade restrictions were lifted. Those who remained on the farms imported Merino rams and ewes. These animals adapted to their new environment. The land was unsuitable for crops, but was ideal for sheep.

War Breaks Out

In December 1834, war broke out again. Xhosa invaded Albany to retake their lands. Homesteads were burnt down and the settlers lost thousands of cattle and sheep. About 9000 settlers, Boers and Khoikhoi fled to Grahamstown and many never returned to their farms. When the war came to an end, 15 years had passed since the 1820 settlers had arrived. Many had been hard-working and brave and their sufferings, together with the disaster of war, had bound them together.

DISPUTED TERRITORY

The Zuurveld had been a **disputed territory** for many years before the 1820 Settlers arrived. It had originally been occupied by the Xhosa, who were driven eastwards beyond the Fish River by the British in 1811 and 1812. Then, in 1819, the Xhosa invaded the region and attacked the new garrison town of Grahamstown. Following this attack, the Xhosa were driven eastwards once more. Hoping to keep the settlers and the Xhosa apart, the British government then declared the land between the Fish and the Keiskamma rivers to be a 'neutral belt'. This measure failed because there was pressure from both sides to occupy the land. European settlers were arriving in the region all the time and thousands of African refugees were flooding southwards from Natal, having been driven from their homes by Shaka's Zulu army.

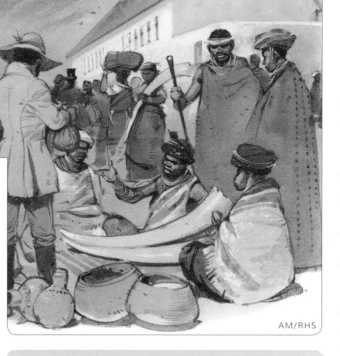

NO WAR AT THE VILLAGE OF PEACE

The settler village of Salem (which means 'peace') was built by Quakers, a religious group that believes in pacifism. During the war of 1834–35 the village was in danger of an attack by Xhosa, who had gone to war in an attempt to recover their lands. A Salem tradesman, Richard Gush, decided to try to settle differences by talking rather than fighting. Unarmed and accompanied by an interpreter, Gush spoke to the leader of the Xhosa. In response to the Xhosa saying that they were hungry, Gush collected bread and gave it to them, an act that suggested that the land could be shared peacefully. The Xhosa passed by without attacking Salem and, although this incident did not end the war, it did show that goodwill could help to solve difficult problems.

TALES OF SETTLER CHILDREN

In the Albany Museum in Grahamstown there is a china doll whose dress and feet are charred. Young **Hannah Dell** was clutching it when her family's wagon was set alight by Xhosa. Fortunately, Colonel Harry Smith (later Governor) rescued the family and took them to Grahamstown.

When little **Maria Marshall** was lost in Beggar's Bush near Grahamstown, family and friends searched for three days before they found her, exhausted but unharmed. Maria told how she had tried to separate two fighting snakes, and later how a big black 'cat' had shaken its long hair at her and roared. Her father trembled when he realized that the 'cat' was probably a lion!

Sophia Pigot was 15 years old when she arrived at Algoa Bay in May 1820. The journal that she kept until the end of 1821 describes the settlers' experiences on the long voyage to the Cape and after their arrival at their new home.

PLACES TO SEE

The Historical Section, Albany Museum, Grahamstown

The great trek

THE VOORTREKKERS
The 80-metre high
Voortrekker Monument
in Pretoria was designed
by Gerard Moerdijk. It is
surrounded by a symbolic
laager of 64 stone ox-
wagons depicted on its
perimeter wall. A symbol
of Afrikaner unity, it took
eleven years to build and
contains a Hall of Heroes
depicting scenes from
the Great Trek carved in
marble. The monument was
unveiled in 1949.

VOORTREKKER GUNS
Every Voortrekker had
rifles and pistols, and
Gert Maritz even had two
primitive cannons. The rifles
were muzzle-loaders or
voorlaaiers and, although
loading them required great
skill, some Voortrekkers
could do so on horseback.
They used a heavy
elephant-gun for hunting
big animals. Women would
help by casting round lead
bullets in home-made
moulds and loading the
guns in battle. They became
quite skilled in handling and
cleaning firearms.

During 1836 and 1837, hundreds of families of Dutch origin left the Cape in their ox-wagons to seek a new life in the interior. For the next two or three years, the swaying, jolting wagon was to be their only home. It became a symbol of the trekkers' security in an unknown wilderness.

Why They Left
The Graham's Town Journal of 2 February 1837 published **Piet Retief's Manifesto**, which gave ten reasons why the Voortrekkers had decided to move on. These included the unsettled border, Xhosa raids on farmers' houses and cattle, and the losses suffered when their slaves were freed in 1834.

The trekkers wanted to 'live a peaceful and ordered life, where they, under God's protection, would treat the surrounding clans with justice.' Retief believed the British needed nothing from Boer farmers and would not interfere with their plans.

Home on the Wagon
Before they left their farms and said farewell to relations, the Voortrekkers carefully prepared for the journey. In the veld, there were no towns where they could buy supplies. They loaded their wagons with rusks, biltong, cooking utensils and clothes and, because they could not take heavy furniture, packed only beds, stools and wooden chests. They also carried ammunition and guns for hunting and protection.

Life on Trek
The wagons travelled two or three abreast and each was drawn by a team of eight to 16 oxen, yoked together in pairs. They were led by a young boy called a **voorloper** carrying a whip called a **sjambok**. The driver sat in front on a chest or **wakis**.

Most families had one or two wagons, but an important trek-leader, like Gert Maritz, might have as many as seven. Each wagon was covered by a canvas tent stretched over a framework of quince hoops, and pots, pans and chicken pens hung under the wagon.

Because large herds of sheep, goats and cattle travelled alongside the wagons, the trekkers moved slowly, probably covering no more than 10 kilometres a day. When they had to hack rough paths through the bush or cross rivers and mountains, the pace would become even slower. Some wagons even tumbled down the steep cliffs.

Household goods used by Voortrekkers

The ox-wagons were packed with all the Voortrekkers would need on the long journey north

Voortrekkers lived much like 18th-century trekboers

Life in the Veld

In the evening the trek would outspan and form a laager for the trekkers' protection. The animals were kept in a kraal ringed by thorn-tree branches. The women prepared meals of meat and **roosterkoek** (griddle-baked bread) over an open fire. Coffee was made from dried figs or ground roots.

After the morning prayers and Bible-reading, there would be breakfast and lessons for the children, who were taught to read and write from the Bible. If the trek was resting for the day, the boys would herd animals in the veld while the girls helped their mothers.

A Woman's Work

In addition to cooking and washing, there was sewing. Linen was beautifully quilted and buckskin was made into jackets and trousers. Women nursed the sick with 'veld remedies' from a small medicine-chest or **huisapteek**. Plants, such as buchu, were believed to cure certain illnesses. Cobwebs were packed onto a wound to stop bleeding and septic sores were treated with mouldy bread.

THE TREKKER OX-WAGON

The trekker wagon had three separate parts: the chassis (**onderstel**), the bottom boards (**buikplanke**) and the body, which consisted of the wagon-sides and the hooped tent-cover. Because it was shaped rather like the jawbone of a horse or ox, the wagon was known as a **kakebeenwa** (jawbone-wagon).

A wooden yoke (**juk**), linked by a pin (**jukskei**), was attached to the necks of each pair of oxen. When the wagon was outspanned, the *jukskei* would be removed and used in a game.

SOME VOORTREKKER LEADERS

Louis Trichardt (1783–1838) trekked north from the Eastern Cape to the Soutpansberg, and then to Delagoa Bay (Maputo) where he and many other trekkers died of malaria.

Hendrik Potgieter's (1792–1852) group set off from Tarka, near Cradock, to north of the Limpopo River exploring the western Transvaal and Natal. He founded Potchefstroom in 1838.

Gert Maritz (1797–1838) led his party from Graaff-Reinet across the Drakensberg into Natal. After Piet Retief's violent death, Maritz became an important leader. The town of Pietermaritzburg was named after Retief and Maritz.

Piet Retief (1780–1838) left Grahamstown with 100 wagons and 100 men. He crossed the Drakensburg into the Zulu Kingdom where he and his men were killed by Dingane, the Zulu chief, in 1838.

Andries Pretorius (1798–1853) set out from Graaff-Reinet and travelled to Natal where he led a military expedition of Voortrekkers. The Zulus were defeated at Blood River on 16 December 1838. Pretorius later settled north of the Vaal. Pretoria is named after him.

Going Hunting

Voortrekkers seldom slaughtered their livestock, but generally hunted for their meat on horseback. Boys were taught how to hunt with guns and learnt where game was to be found. The Voortrekkers became skilled marksmen and experts on wild birds and animals.

No part of an animal was wasted. A boy would help his father cut the hide into long narrow strips called **riems**, which were used for ropes, animal-tethers, whips or the seats of stools. Hollowed horns were used to stored gunpowder, while candles were made from animal fat. A mixture of tallow and wild ganna plant were boiled and used to make soap.

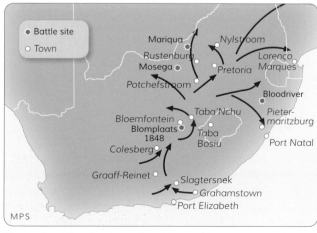
The routes taken by the various Voortrekker groups moving northwards from the Cape

Battle site
Town

Mariqua · Nylstroom · Rustenburg · Mosega · Pretoria · Lorenço Marques · Potchefstroom · Bloodriver · Taba'Nchu · Pieter-maritzburg · Bloemfontein · Blomplaats 1848 · Taba Bosiu · Port Natal · Colesberg · Graaff-Reinet · Slagtersnek · Grahamstown · Port Elizabeth

A Voortrekker cannon

BRAVE CHILDREN

Many children, both on the side of the Voortrekkers and of the clans against whom they fought, were caught up in the horrors of war. The names of only a few have been recorded. Among these is **Dirkie Uys**, who refused to leave his wounded father during a battle against the Zulu near Italeni in KwaZulu-Natal in 1838, and so was killed with him.

PLACES TO SEE

- The Voortrekker Monument and Museum in Pretoria.
- The Voortrekker Museum in Pietermaritzburg

The warrior king

THE HUNGRY PEOPLE

During the Mfecane, a peace-loving clan fled south of the Mzimvubu River and about 20 000 exhausted survivors reached what is now the Butterworth district. When the Xhosa asked them who they were, they answered **'Siyamfenguza'**, meaning 'We are hungry people'. Today they are known as Mfengu or Fingos.

Towards the end of the 18th century, there were three main Nguni clans living north of the Tugela River in KwaZulu-Natal. The Ndwandwe were led by their chief, Zwide. The Gwane were under Sobhuza, and Dingiswayo led the Mthethwa who lived between the Mfolozi and Mhlatuze rivers. When Dingiswayo became paramount chief of the Mthethwa, he reorganized the army. It became so powerful that the Mthethwa conquered most of the neighbouring clans.

Shaka's Rise to Power

Shaka was the son of Senzangakhona, head of the small Zulu chiefdom, but both Shaka and his mother, Nandi, were cruelly treated by the clan and were forced to leave. Eventually, they reached the territory of the Mthethwa. Shaka joined Dingiswayo's army and became a mighty warrior. In 1815 Shaka's father died and Dingiswayo helped Shaka take the chiefdom from his half-brother. Shaka gave his mother the name Great She-Elephant and sentenced to death those who had tormented him as a child. Like Dingiswayo, he built up the Zulu army. When Dingiswayo was killed by Zwide in 1818, Shaka became chief of the Mthethwa as well.

The Mfecane

Mfecane means 'crushing', and is used to describe Shaka's destruction of the neighbouring clans and the scattering of many others. Sometimes it is called the **Difaqane**, or forced migration.

By 1824 the huge Zulu nation had conquered or scattered many tribes. Grazing land had been ruined and cattle and grain stores plundered. Soshangane, one of Zwide's Ndwandwe chieftains, fled to Mozambique and created the Gaza kingdom between Delagoa Bay and the Zambezi River. Another group of Ndwandwe refugees was driven north of the Zambezi, while others went south, joining the Nguni in the Eastern Cape. Some fled to the fringes of the Kalahari and lived among Adam Kok's Griquas. Thousands escaped across the Vaal River, but fought among themselves, causing chaos among the Tswana.

LC/RHS

Shaka, king of the Zulus

LC/RHS

Dingiswayo

The Reign of Terror

Shaka was now a powerful king with the strongest army in southern Africa. His organized warrior regiments defeated all his rivals, including the Ndwandwe. Some clans became part of the Zulu nation and their young men were drafted into his army. Other clans were destroyed or fled. By 1824, the powerful Zulu kingdom stretched across much of KwaZulu-Natal.

Shaka was curious about the culture of white people and respected their knowledge and guns. The traders were horrified at the way Shaka punished his subjects for minor offences. As his kingdom expanded, Shaka wanted even more power and sent his Zulu armies to war against tribes far away. But his warriors wanted to stay at home and start families, so his half-brothers, Mhlangane and Dingane, plotted against Shaka and, in 1828, they stabbed him to death.

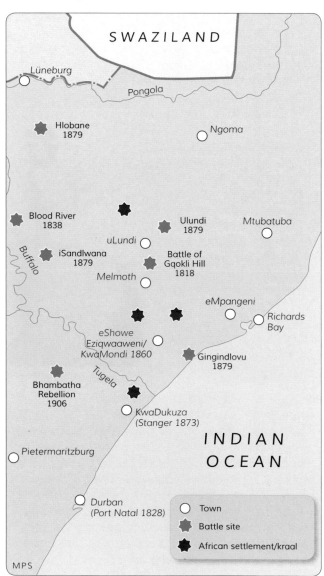

Mzilikazi and the Ndebele

Mzilikazi was one of Shaka's most successful officers until he rebelled in about 1821. He fled north-west with 500 followers and settled in the Magaliesberg where he founded the kingdom of the Ndebele.

During the 1830s, Mzilikazi's kingdom was attacked by both the Zulu and the Griquas. Mzilikazi then moved to the Marico River valley where he clashed with the Voortrekkers before fleeing yet again. Some Ndebele moved to Zimbabwe and into an area called Matabeleland. The rest followed their chief through today's Botswana. In 1839, Mzilikazi reunited his Ndebele people at the new capital he founded at Bulawayo.

LC/RHS

SHAKA'S ARMY

Shaka's army included all Zulu men under the age of 40. They lived in barracks, or **amakhanda**, and each regiment, or impi, had its own headdress and shield. Shaka carefully watched the youngest warriors and their barracks were near his headquarters not far from present-day Eshowe. Shaka replaced the long, traditional throwing assegai with a short, stabbing spear. Once the enemy had thrown their assegais, the Zulu warriors, carrying huge ox-hide shields, which covered the entire body, closed in on them in deadly hand-to-hand combat. Instead of a straight line, Shaka's impis approached the enemy in a head-and-horns formation. While the regiment at the centre (the head) led the attack, those on the sides (the horns) surrounded the enemy, forcing them to turn away from the main 'head' attack. Shaka's warriors were never allowed to rest and once one battle was over, they would fight another. They could not wear footwear and Shaka made them run long distances to toughen their feet. Because he wanted his men to concentrate on war, only soldiers over the age of 40 could marry.

THE BATTLE OF VEGKOP

In August 1836 the Ndebele attacked those Voortrekkers who had crossed the Vaal River. When the trekker leader, Andries Pretorius, returned from a scouting expedition, he formed a laager with about 50 wagons near Vegkop in todays district of Heilbron. Followed by 40 men, Sarel Cilliers rode out to meet the thousands of approaching Ndebele warriors and asked what harm the white men had done. But their leader only shouted 'Mzilikazi!' and the warriors charged. The trekkers fled to their laager, firing shots and killing 430 Ndebele. Only two Voortrekkers were killed at Vegkop.

A painting of Moshoeshoe's mountain fortress, Thaba Bosiu, which means 'mountain of light'

Moshoeshoe's Mountain Kingdom

The Basotho chieftain Moshoeshoe lived in the mountain fortress of Thaba Bosiu, not far from the Caledon River. Determined to end the lawlessness of the refugee clans in his territory, he gave their chiefs cattle and allowed their people to live in their own villages and keep their own traditions. Recognizing some advantages in Western education, he invited three French missionaries to stay. Though frequently attacked, his Thaba Bosiu was never defeated, and Moshoeshoe accepted the conquered people into his kingdom. By 1840 his subjects numbered over 40000, but Moshoeshoe realized that his army was powerless against the guns of the approaching Voortrekkers and British. When he asked the British for help in 1868, they took over Basutoland (now Lesotho). Moshoeshoe died two years later aged 84.

MOSHOESHOE

Moshoeshoe, who was first called Lepoqo, belonged to a small Basotho clan. He became known as Moshoeshoe when he stole cattle from a neighbouring clan. The word sounds like a sharp blade shaving a stubbly beard and means 'the man who shaved the beard of the enemy'.

BIRTH OF THE SWAZIS

The Swazis existed even before Shaka rose to power. Between 1815 and 1836, Sobhuza's Ngwane people were driven from the Phongolo River area by Zwide's Ndwandwe and moved north where Sobhuza built a new state in the mountains. It was later called Swaziland, named after Mswati, Sobhuza's successor.

PLACES TO SEE

[i] Shakaland near Eshowe in KwaZulu-Natal

Wars in the Eastern Cape

THE MISSIONARIES
In the early 19th century, the Cape government treated black people very harshly, but missionaries, such as **Robert Moffat**, who had come to the Cape to teach and preach the Gospel, believed that all people should have the right to work where they pleased, learn trades and own houses.

DR VAN DER KEMP
Dr Johannes Theodorus van der Kemp arrived at the Cape in 1799 and spent a year among the Ngqika near today's King William's Town. He founded a settlement for homeless and ill-treated Khoikhoi labourers at Bethelsdorp north of Algoa Bay, but local farmers accused him of sheltering criminals.

When the trekkers reached the Zuurveld between the Bushmans and the Great Fish rivers, in the late 18th century, the area was already occupied by the Xhosa. The Xhosa believed that the land belonged to the entire community, but the trekboers felt that a farmer had the right to own land that he could claim for his own use and on which no one else could farm or graze cattle.

The Fish River Boundary
In 1778 Governor Joachim van Plettenberg made the Great Fish River the boundary between the Xhosa on the east and the trekboers on the west. But it was a lawless area and both sides frequently crossed the Great Fish River to steal one another's cattle. These clashes led to nine outbreaks of bitter fighting in this eastern region between 1779 and 1878. They ended only after the entire region had become part of the Cape Colony.

The Wars of Dispossession
THE FIRST WAR (1779–1781) When Xhosa people began to settle west of the Great Fish River, Commandant Adriaan van Jaarsveld was instructed to remove them peacefully. His methods were brutal, and many Xhosa died and numbers of cattle were captured.

THE SECOND WAR (1789–1793) In 1789, two warring Xhosa clans crossed the Fish River into the Zuurveld. Some farmers helped Ndlambe, a Xhosa chief, to attack the Gqunukhwebe clan. But the farmers' commandos broke up because they had no confidence in their leader, Honoratus Maynier, and the Xhosa remained in the Zuurveld.

THE THIRD WAR (1799–1803) During the four years of the Third War, discontented Khoikhoi and Xhosa moved across the Zuurveld to the Graaff-Reinet district. The British forces tried to calm these troubled areas. When the Dutch took over the Cape in 1803 they made peace with the Khoikhoi, but the Xhosa refused to move beyond the Fish River.

THE FOURTH WAR (1811–1812) When the British returned to the Cape in 1806, the Zuurveld was unsettled. In 1812 soldiers and burghers led by Lieutenant-Colonel John Graham forced 20 000 Xhosa back across the Fish River. To protect the new settlements, 27 forts were built and troops were posted to the new towns of Grahamstown and Cradock.

THE FIFTH WAR (1818–1819) In 1818, Governor Somerset promised to reward Chief Ngqika if he could end cattle-thieving in the Zuurveld. As a result, Ngqika's uncle and rival, Ndlambe, raided and defeated Ngqika. British troops then attacked Ndlambe and seized 23 000 cattle. In April 1819, Ndlambe's war doctor, Makanna, attacked Grahamstown with 6 000 warriors. Many Xhosa were killed, but the British, fighting from behind barricades, lost only two men.

THE SIXTH WAR (1834–1835) In 1829, the Cape government settled 4 000 Khoikhoi and Griqua in the fertile Kat River valley, the home of the Ngqika. Chief Maqoma was enraged. In December 1834, Xhosa invaded the Cape Colony, burnt farms and killed many settlers. The Gcaleka chief, Hintsa, who had given himself up to Colonel Harry Smith, was shot and killed by a settler. Although peace was made in 1835, the Xhosa never actually surrendered.

A camp along the banks of the Great Fish River

THE SEVENTH WAR (1846–1847) Trouble in the Zuurveld intensified when a man named Tsili stole an axe from a Fort Beaufort store. This led to the bitter War of the Axe. Both the Xhosa and the colonial forces suffered heavy losses. The Xhosa burnt the veld and thousands of people starved. It was the British troops that finally won in October 1847.

Ngqika's men prepare to attack in the Boomah Pass

THE EIGHTH WAR (1850–1853) On Christmas Eve 1850, the Ngqika chief, Sandile, attacked a colonial patrol in the Boomah Pass through the Amatole mountains and the next day, destroyed three white settler villages. Sandile was joined by other Xhosa clans; Khoikhoi from the Kat River Settlement and Khoikhoi soldiers who had deserted the British, and taken their guns with them. It was two years before the British drove the Xhosa from the Amatole, but the war did not end until 1853.

The British and Xhosa fight the War of the Axe

THE NINTH WAR (1877–1878) This war started at a wedding party in 1877 when a quarrel flared up between a Mfengu guest and a Xhosa chieftain. Cape Frontier Police were sent to protect the Mfengu who had fought for the British in the Eighth War. By the time the war ended in 1878, the Xhosa endured heavy losses: 4000 men died and 45000 head of cattle were taken. The power of the Xhosa was finally broken.

XHOSA PARAMOUNT CHIEFS

Many Xhosa chiefs were descended from the Rharhabe paramount chief, Phalo. Much-feared by his people, **Gcaleka** became paramount chief of the Gcaleka Xhosa after a quarrel with his brother Rharhabe. His grandson, **Hintsa**, was killed while trying to escape from Colonel Harry Smith during the Sixth War of Dispossession. **Sarhili** was Hintsa's son and became paramount chief of the Xhosa in 1835. He made peace with the British in 1835 and 1844, but turned against them in the Seventh and Eighth Wars. His clan's quarrel with the Mfengu led to the Ninth War.

When Rharhabe died, his son, **Ndlambe**, acted as regent as his nephew, **Ngqika**, was too young to rule. When Ngqika finally became chief, he agreed with Lord Charles Somerset's plan to create a neutral zone between the Fish and Keiskamma rivers. But Ndlambe hated the British and fought Ngqika during the Fourth War. He was defeated in Grahamstown in 1819 and Ngqika was officially recognized as chief.

Ngqika's son, **Maqoma**, strongly opposed the creation of a neutral zone between the Fish and Keiskamma rivers, and invaded the area south of the Winterberg, resulting in the Sixth War. He remained neutral during the War of the Axe, but was captured while fighting the Eighth War and banished to Robben Island.

Sandile, Ngqika's other son and the last paramount chief was involved in the Seventh War. He refused to meet the governor in 1850 and was deposed as chief. His attack on British soldiers in the Boomah Pass in 1850 led to the Eighth War. Sandile was killed during the Ninth War.

Sandile was the last paramount chief of his clan

DR PHILIP
Because **Dr John Philip** of the London Missionary Society criticized the treatment of the Khoikhoi he was unpopular with the Cape government and white colonists. But it was largely due to his efforts that the so-called 'Hottentot Charter', or 50th Ordinance, was passed in 1828, giving the Khoikhoi the same rights as whites.

ON COMMANDO
Commandos were groups of ordinary citizens (burghers) who helped troops perform military duties. During the frontier wars they often came to the assistance of the army.

Colonel Harry Smith

PLACES TO SEE

ℹ Fort Selwyn, Grahamstown

Conflict in the East

DRESSING FOR WAR

During the summer of 1879, while waging war against the Zulus, Lord Chelmsford's soldiers wore uncomfortable, unsuitable uniforms, consisting of long-sleeved woollen jackets with large brass buttons and stiff, uncomfortable collars. Ammunition was carried in a leather pouch attached to a broad belt. The **infantry** wore red jackets (hence the term 'redcoats'), and the **artillery** wore blue. Their dark blue woollen trousers with red stripes were tucked into black leather leggings, and they wore white tropical helmets.

THE TRAGIC PRINCE

Napoleon III's son, Louis Eugène Jean Joseph Napoleon, volunteered to fight in the Zulu War. On 1 June 1879, he and Lieutenant JB Carey's scouts set out to choose a camp site for the army marching to Ulundi. When they were surprised by a Zulu impi, Lt Carey and his men fled, deserting the Prince Imperial. He died facing the enemy, his body stabbed by 18 assegais.

By the time Dingane succeeded Shaka in 1828, the Zulu army had become the mightiest in Africa. Since 1824, English traders and ivory-hunters had been living at Port Natal (today's Durban) on land that Shaka had granted them.

The Tragedy of Piet Retief

Piet Retief hoped that Dingane would allow his party to settle in Zululand. On his way to the royal kraal of Mgungundlovu to discuss the matter, he camped on the edge of the Drakensberg, but on 6 February 1838 he and his companions were killed by Dingane. This was the Voortrekkers' first clash with the people of KwaZulu-Natal. Dingane was determined to fight against the Voortrekkers who had invaded his land, and his Zulu impis attacked many Boer camps.

AVZ/GTY/GI

Piet Retief's grave, Mgungundlovu

The Battle of Blood River

Led by Andries Pretorius (pictured), a commando of 470 Voortrekker men set out to draw the Zulus into battle. They formed a laager of 64 wagons between a donga and the banks of the Ncome River. On 16 December 1838 the Zulu attacked, but were driven off – with heavy losses due to the Voortrekkers' muskets and cannons, before they could get close enough to fight with their spears and clubs. By evening, 3000 Zulu lay dead and the Ncome River turned red with their blood. In honour of a vow they had made, the Voortrekkers built a church in Pietermaritzburg. Today, their church is a museum.

CTAR

MC

Boers use a cannon called 'Ou Grietjie' during the Battle of Blood River

WK

THE BLOOD RIVER LAAGER

When the laager was formed, some of the wagons were positioned in a straight line, parallel to a donga, while the remaining wagons formed a crescent from one end of the line to the other. All the wagons were linked together with trek-chains and the gaps closed with **veghekke** or 'fighting gates'. Small cannons were mounted at the corners and the livestock was herded into the middle of the laager.

The Republic of Natalia

While Dingane was in power, the Voortrekkers couldn't establish their own republic in KwaZulu-Natal. Dingane's brother, Mpande, wanted to seize the throne, so in 1840 he helped the Voortrekkers to invade the Zulu Kingdom. Dingane fled to Swaziland where he was murdered and Mpande became King. The trekkers founded the Republic of Natalia with Pietermaritzburg as its capital.

The British Take Over

Britain still regarded the Voortrekkers as her subjects and in May 1842, troops arrived at Port Natal to take over the Republic of Natalia. The Boers refused to give up their republic and, led by Andries Pretorius, they marched towards Port Natal and camped at Congella. The British attacked, but Pretorius fought back for a month. Dick King and his servant Ndongeni, set off on horseback to fetch reinforcements for the British from Grahamstown. King covered 960 km in 10 days on his horse, Somerset. The British sent more troops and the Boers were driven off. The following year Britain took possession of the Colony of Natal, and the Republic of Natalia ceased to exist.

The British Make Demands

Britain, then the most powerful nation in the western world, was determined to stop the mighty Zulu nation that Cetshwayo had inherited from his father, Mpande, in 1873. The British sent Cetshwayo a demand which, among other things, stated that the Zulu king should disband his army within 20 days. When Cetshwayo did not react to this ultimatum, Britain finally invaded Zululand on 11 January 1879.

The Battle of Isandhlwana

On 22 January, about 20000 Zulu warriors attacked. Using the traditional bull-and-horns shape, they encircled Lord Chelmsford's troops camped along the slopes of Isandhlwana hill in western Zululand. The British were taken by surprise and their ammunition soon ran out. A bloody battle followed. Almost 1300 British soldiers and over 1000 Zulu were killed in two hours of battle, which was won by Cetshwayo's army.

The site of the Battle of Isandhlwana

THE OLD ZULU ORDER

The age-grouped regiments, or impis, carrying short-handled assegais and tall ox-hide shields (which Dingiswayo introduced and Shaka perfected) were used by Mpande and Cetshwayo. So was the deadly bull-and-horns fighting formation. Because warriors had no heavy uniforms, and feet as tough as boot-leather, they moved about swiftly and silently. Before a battle, they stood in a semicircle, stamping their feet and rattling their assegais against their shields. When the command was given, they fearlessly charged the enemy. Even their enemies respected the Zulus for their courage. There is a plaque where the Battle of Ulundi was fought. Its inscription reads: 'In Memory of the Brave Warriors who fell here in 1879 in Defence of the Old Zulu Order.'

The Battle of Rorke's Drift

Rorke's Drift

Two exhausted officers fleeing the battle at Isandhlwana arrived at the British hospital at Rorke's Drift in the Colony of Natal. They told of the horror that had happened only ten kilometres away and warned that about 4000 Zulu were approaching.

The two lieutenants in charge hurriedly erected barricades of mealie bags and biscuit boxes, before thousands of Zulu advanced across the veld and attacked. The thatched roof was set alight but the defenders fought on, losing only 17 men. After losing about 350 warriors, the Zulu impi withdrew.

The Final Battle

The war between British and Zulu forces continued for five more months, and the last battle was fought on 4 July 1879 at Ulundi, barely three kilometres away from Cetshwayo's royal kraal. Lord Chelmsford's 5000 troops crossed the White Mfolozi River at dawn and faced the entire Zulu army. Cetshwayo lost over 1000 of his 20000 warriors in an hour, while the British lost only ten men. The Zulu army had been defeated.

CETSHWAYO

After the Zulu War, the reluctant **Cetshwayo** was exiled to Cape Town. Supported by Bishop Colenso of Natal he wrote to Queen Victoria, begging to be allowed to return to his kingdom. Despite opposition, he met the Queen, in England, in 1882 and she agreed to restore him as king. But he was soon attacked by a rival chief and again driven from Ulundi. He fled to Eshowe where he died the following year. The Zulus still respectfully guard his grave in the Nkandla forest.

BRITAIN'S HEROES

The Victoria Cross, established by Queen Victoria in 1856, is awarded for outstanding bravery. It is a bronze cross with the words 'For Valour' engraved on it. During the Battle of Rorke's Drift, the Victoria Cross was awarded to eleven British soldiers, the largest number of heroes to be honoured in this way in a single battle.

PLACES TO SEE

- The Voortrekker/ Msunduzi Museum in Pietermaritzburg
- Rorke's Drift Mission and Museum, Rorke's Drift

Boer versus Briton

EMILY HOBHOUSE (1860–1926)

Emily Hobhouse, an Englishwoman, came to South Africa and visited British concentration camps where, during the second Anglo-Boer War, Boer women and children were being held. Horrified at their shocking living conditions, she started schools and helped those who had suffered. Her ashes are buried at the Women's Monument in Bloemfontein.

CHURCHILL AS A PRISONER

As a war correspondent, **Winston Churchill** was captured by Boers in an ambush on an armoured train. The young man who was to become Britain's Prime Minister during the Second World War and again between 1951 and 1955, was imprisoned in a school in Pretoria. He made a daring escape a month later and jumped a train to Lourenço Marques (today's Maputo).

In 1877, Britain took over the Zuid-Afrikaansche Republiek (ZAR) founded by the Transvaal Voortrekkers 25 years earlier. The Boers were outraged and, at a meeting at Paardekraal on 16 December 1880, they declared their country's independence.

The First Anglo-Boer War (1880–1881)

On 20 December 1880, British troops at Bronkhorstspruit were attacked by Boers. While the Boers lost only two men, 150 British soldiers were killed or wounded in ten minutes. British forces from Natal were again defeated at Laing's Nek on the Transvaal border, and ambushed by Boers at Schuinshoogte.

The Battle of Majuba

On 27 February, British soldiers gathered on Amajuba Mountain, then called Majuba Hill, to drive the Boers from Laing's Nek below. When the Boers saw the redcoats, they climbed the mountain and surprised the British. The British general, Sir George Colley, was killed and the British losses were so great that they surrendered. On 23 March 1881 a peace treaty was signed to end the war and the Transvaal was returned to the Boers.

The British unsuccessfully fought off the Boers at Majuba

The Jameson Raid

Gold was discovered on the Witwatersrand in 1886 and fortune-hunters from many countries flocked to the tent-town of Johannesburg. But the **Uitlanders** (foreigners) complained because, although they paid taxes, they could not vote. The Cape Prime Minister, Cecil Rhodes, sympathized with the Uitlanders. He hoped to overthrow Kruger's government so that Britain could take over the Transvaal with all its gold. At the end of 1895, **Dr Leander Starr Jameson** and 500 mounted men invaded the Transvaal from Bechuanaland (Botswana), but were overwhelmed by the Boers. Because Rhodes supported the Raid, he had to resign.

Dr Leander Starr Jameson

The Second Anglo-Boer War (1899–1902)

The Jameson Raid resulted in increasing bitterness between the Boers and the British. On 9 October 1899, the Transvaal demanded that the British withdraw from its borders and that troops on their way from Britain be turned back. The British ignored the demands and, on 11 October 1899, the Boers declared war. They blew up an armoured train and completely surrounded the town of Mafeking (now Mafikeng).

During the first battles in Natal the Boers were soundly defeated outside Dundee. However, they regrouped and on 2 November attacked and besieged Ladysmith. The British troops made three unsuccessful attempts to relieve the town at the battles of Colenso (15 December 1899), Spioenkop (24 January 1900) and Vaalkrans (7 February 1900).

British soldiers in the trenches at Ladysmith

THE FACTS OF WAR

The Anglo-Boer War of 1899–1902 is still spoken of as 'the last of the gentleman's wars' and as 'a white man's war'. It was neither of these. Thousands of women, children and old men, Boer as well as black, died of disease in badly run British concentration camps. Thousands of homes and farms were deliberately destroyed. A small number of black workers accompanied their Boer employers to the war, mostly as wagon drivers. On the British side, about 30000 black and coloured men were armed to fight against the Boers.

From left: Colley, Kitchener, Baden-Powell and Buller

BRITISH GENERALS

Sir George Pomeroy-Colley was the British commander in Natal during the first Anglo-Boer War. He was killed at Majuba.

Sir Redvers Buller commanded all British forces at the outbreak of the second Anglo-Boer War. The early battles were a disaster for the British.

Lord Frederick Roberts succeeded Buller as commander of the British forces. He led them to victory by capturing Bloemfontein and Pretoria.

Lord Horatio Herbert Kitchener succeeded Lord Roberts in November 1900. He was criticized for establishing concentration camps and for burning Boer farms.

Lord Robert Baden-Powell became a national hero during the 217-day siege of Mafeking. He went on to found the Boy Scouts movement.

On the Western Front

Kimberley was besieged by the Boers on 4 November 1899. On their way to relieve the town, British troops from Cape Town encountered Boers at Belmont, Graspan and Modder River, but the Battle of Magersfontein on 11 December was a complete catastrophe for the British. The day before, British forces had been crushed at the Battle of Stormberg. This week is recorded in British history as 'Black Week'.

Roberts in Command

On 15 February 1900, Kimberley was freed by British troops under the command of **Field Marshal Lord Roberts**. Twelve days later, 4 000 Boers encamped at Paardeberg surrendered after fighting 40 000 British soldiers for two weeks. On 13 March, Roberts took control of Bloemfontein, and thereafter marched on to take Johannesburg on 31 May and Pretoria on 5 June, without a single shot being fired. The siege of Ladysmith ended on 18 February and on 17 May Mafeking was relieved.

CTAR

Guerrilla Warfare

But the war was not over. Boer forces made extensive use of guerrilla tactics; those who went into hiding ambushed British troops, looted stores, blew up railway lines and cut telegraph wires. They were led by Generals De la Rey, Botha and the brilliant De Wet. Boers who surrendered were considered traitors and known as Hands-uppers or **hensoppers**. They gave themselves up by holding their hands above their heads.

The Scorched Earth Policy and Concentration Camps

Early in 1901 the new British commander-in-chief, Lord Kitchener, decided to force the Boers to surrender by burning their farms. He claimed he was protecting the women and children, and their black employees, by sending them to concentration camps. About 50 000 people of all races died in the camps.

The Peace of Vereeniging

With their farms destroyed, their families in concentration camps and their forces split, the Boers surrendered. They met the British leaders at Vereeniging to discuss the armistice terms. On 31 May 1902 a peace treaty was signed at Melrose House in Pretoria. The Boers had lost, but independence was granted only eight years later when the Union of South Africa came into being.

From left: Botha, Smuts, De Wet and Joubert

BOER GENERALS

Louis Botha succeeded General Joubert as commandant-general of the Transvaal commandos. Botha became the Union of South Africa's first Prime Minister in 1910.

Jacobus (Koos) de la Rey distinguished himself at the Battle of Modder River. He introduced trench warfare at Magersfontein and later also fought in the guerrilla war.

Petrus (Piet) Joubert was twice President of the ZAR and a commandant-general of the Boer forces in the first Anglo-Boer War.

Jan Christiaan Smuts helped plan the guerrilla phase of the second Anglo-Boer War, and served as a commander in the field. He was twice Prime Minister of the Union of South Africa.

Christiaan Rudolf de Wet fought in the first Anglo-Boer War and was commandant-in-chief of the Orange Free State during the second. He organized many ambushes and daring escapes.

GK/GI

HORSES

British horses were not suited to the harsh South African climate. Out of 520 000 mounts supplied to British troops during the conflict, some 326 000 died – more as a result of disease and exhaustion than enemy fire. The public outrage in Britain at the suffering and **loss of equine life** led to a heightened focus on the Royal Army Veterinary Corp and ultimately to the passing of the Protection of Animals Act by the British parliament in 1911.

ABWM

'OOM PAUL'

Part of a Voortrekker family, the young **Stephanus Johannes Paulus Kruger** was a skilled hunter and soldier, who was always interested in politics. When the British took over the Transvaal in 1877, he became the Afrikaner champion. With Piet Joubert and Marthinus Pretorius, he governed the Transvaal after independence in 1880, becoming president in 1883.

PLACES TO SEE

- The site of the Battle of Magersfontein, Kimberley
- Kruger House Museum, Pretoria

South Africa's Peoples

OFFICIAL LANGUAGES
South Africa has **eleven official languages**, showing that we enjoy great cultural diversity. The official languages are: isiXhosa, isiZulu, English, Afrikaans, siSwati, Xitsonga, Setswana, Tshivenda, isiNdebele, Sesotho and Sesotho sa Leboa. There are many more languages of African, European and Asian origin that South Africans use to communicate with one another. More South Africans speak Zulu as their home language than any other, but the language that is in general use by most South Africans is Afrikaans, followed by English.

Say '**Hello**':
'Abusheni' (Xitsonga)
'Dumela' (Setwana)
'Hallo' (Afrikaans)
'Lumela' (Sesotho)
'Molo' (isiXhosa)
'Ndaa' or 'Aa' (Tshivenda)
'Salinonani' (isiNdebele)
'Sanibona' (siSwati)
'Sawubona' (isiZulu)
'Thobela' (Sesotho sa Leboa)

South Africa consists not only of people who were born here, but also of **immigrants** who left their country of birth to make South Africa their home. People of foreign descent form an important part of community life and contribute considerably to the country's economy and culture.

At the beginning of South African recorded history, the Khoikhoi came into contact with the Portuguese in 1488. The word Khoikhoi is thought to mean 'men of men'. These 'men of men' kept cattle and sheep, and the more cattle and sheep a clan possessed, the more powerful and influential it was thought to be.

In this way, the Khoikhoi differed from the San (sometimes called Bushmen) who kept no cattle or sheep and looked upon one another as equals. The San were nomadic and existed off the land. The Khoikhoi have probably died out completely. Many of them died of disease during the epidemics that broke out among the settlers at the Cape.

The Dutch, who came to establish a fort and trading post, didn't intend to stay at the Cape and expected to return to Holland after a few years. But many of them did stay. Many Germans, too, came to the Cape as soldiers of the Dutch East India Company, and a group of Huguenots – French Protestants – settled here in 1688 because they were being persecuted for their religious beliefs in Catholic France.

Other people were brought here against their will. These were the slaves, first from Angola and, later, from elsewhere in Africa, from India and the East Indies. Many slaves, especially those from the East, became fine craftsmen and so we owe much of the beauty of the old Cape houses and furniture to their skills. The faith of Islam was introduced to South Africa through these slaves.

South Africa did not grow only from the settlement at the Cape, but also from other places to the north and east, where people had settled for hundreds of years before the arrival of the Dutch. These included the Nguni-speaking people who were farming in the Eastern Cape area as early as 700 AD. Others settled in KwaZulu-Natal. These farmers, who were also hunters, were the ancestors of the people whose present language is isiXhosa, and includes groups such as the Mpondo, Bomvana and Thembu.

By the time of the Dutch settlement at the Cape, other people had arrived in the South African interior after travelling from somewhere in central Africa or splitting off from the people already settled along the coast. This group is made up of the present Sotho-speaking people. Most of these, including the BaSotho, Tswana and Pedi, as well as many smaller sub-groups, live north of the Orange River, which some early South Africans called the Gariep, or 'great river'.

About 400 years ago, some of the people who had settled in KwaZulu-Natal moved to the interior. Their descendents are now known as the Ndebele. The Tsonga people of the Limpopo Province Lowveld moved almost 200 years ago from Mozambique and came under the influence of the Nguni-speaking Ndwandwe clan from the area now known as KwaZulu-Natal.

In the 18th century, some of the Karanga-Rozwi people of Zimbabwe moved across the Limpopo River to settle in the far Limpopo Province. Most of their descendents, now known as the Venda, still live there.

Throughout the country, many different people made war on the San, whom they accused of stealing their cattle. In the end, to escape their enemies, the San

42

of British warships landed British soldiers in False Bay. This was to prevent France seizing the Cape, which was of great importance on the sea route between Europe and the East Indies.

This was the start of the British or English influence. The first big migration of British people to South Africa took place in 1820, when about 4 000 new settlers landed at Algoa Bay. They were placed on small farms in the Eastern Cape, on land that had been taken away from the Xhosa. Some of them stayed, but others drifted to the towns.

Indians began to arrive in Natal (now KwaZulu-Natal) from 1860. After 10 years, they could choose whether to accept a paid passage back to India, or stay in KwaZulu-Natal on small grants of land. Most stayed, and more came from India at frequent intervals. Other Indian settlers came as traders or professionals. Most South Africans of Indian descent still live in KwaZulu-Natal, but many others live in Gauteng.

About 40 years after Indians began arriving in South Africa, a number of Chinese people also came to live here. They were brought in to work on the gold mines by the government of the time. By 1907, over 63 000 Chinese had made their home in this country.

THE LEMBA

The Lemba, who number about 70 000, are an Nguni-speaking people who live in Limpopo Province. They are often called 'the black Jews of South Africa' and trace their ancestry to Senna in the Yemen. Renowned South African geneticist Dr Himla Soodyall has established that Lemba males, particularly those from the Buba clan, display a high incidence of a particular Y-chromosome, called the Cohen Modal Haplotype, that is commonly found amongst Sephardi and Ashkenazi Jews. Dr Soodyall suggests that it is currently more accurate to use the term 'Middle Eastern' rather than 'Jewish' to describe the genetic signature of the Lemba.

moved to the drier parts of the interior, such as the far Northern Cape, and even further, to Namibia. They left behind many examples of wonderful rock art for modern visitors and scholars to admire and puzzle over today.

Events in faraway Europe in the 18th century also had an effect on the make-up of modern South Africa's people. After France invaded Holland, the Dutch appealed to Great Britain for help. So, in 1795, a fleet

THE BRITISH EMPIRE

In the world beyond South Africa, the language that is most widely used is English. This is probably because English was the language spoken throughout the British Empire. South Africa was once part of the British Empire, which was a large group of countries all over the world, controlled by Great Britain. South Africa became a part, or colony, of Great Britain after the Second British Occupation of 1806. This was when the British army and navy defeated the Cape army, which was made up of Dutch and local people of all colours, near the beach at Bloubergstrand, very close to Cape Town.

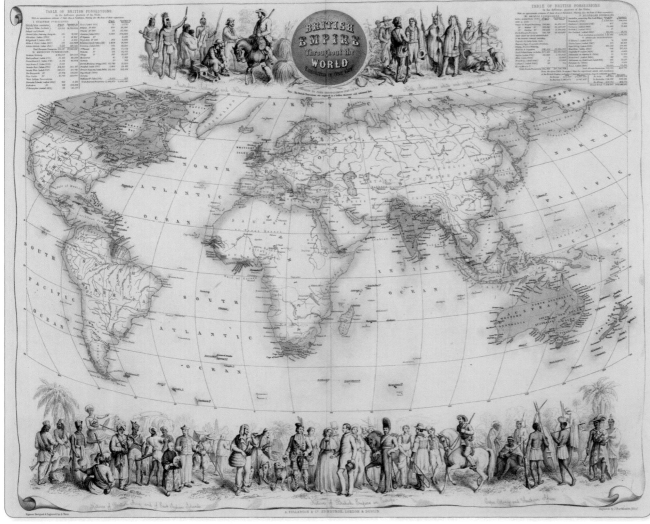

The British Empire, circa 1850

Facts and Figures

WORLD HERITAGE SITES
South Africa is home to eight World Heritage Sites that were proclaimed between 1999 and 2007. They are Robben Island (1999), iSimangaliso Wetland Park (Greater St Lucia Wetland Park) (1999), the Cradle of Humankind (1999), uKhahlamba Drakensberg Park (2000), Mapungubwe (2003), the Cape Floral Region (2004), the Vredefort Dome (2005) and the Richtersveld Cultural and Botanical Landscape (2007).

STERKFONTEIN
South Africa is sometimes described as the **Cradle of Humankind**. The Cradle of Humankind World Heritage Site, which is located just north of Johannesburg, contains the fossil remains of both extinct animals and a number of hominins. At the heart of this site is Sterkfontein Cave. Robert Broom found the famous hominin skull 'Mrs Ples' (first classified as *Plesianthropus transvaalensis*, now known as *Australopithecus africanus*) at Sterkfontein in 1947. It was also at Sterkfontein that Ronald Clarke found 'Little Foot' in 1997.

According to the 2011 mid-year population estimates (or census) compiled by Statistics South Africa, South Africa has a population of 51.7 million people made up of approximately 42 million Africans (79.6%), 4.6 million coloureds (9%), 1.3 million Indian/Asians (2.5%) and 4.6 million whites (9%). Pretoria is the executive capital, Cape Town is the legislative capital and Bloemfontein is the judicial capital of South Africa. Johannesburg (including Soweto) is the largest city, with an estimated population of around 3.9 million, followed by Cape Town, which has an estimated population of 3.4 million. The nation's main exports are gold, diamonds, metals and minerals, cars and machinery.

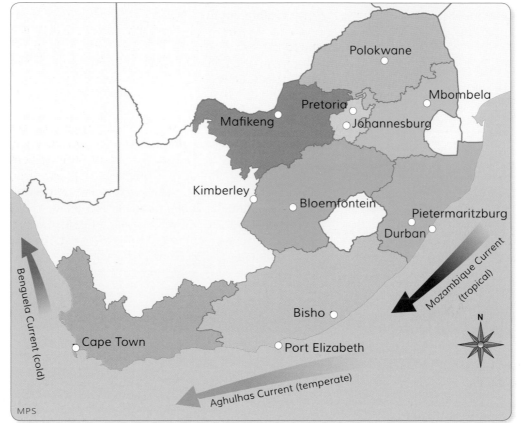

Provincial estimates indicate that Gauteng has the largest share of the population (23.7%), followed by KwaZulu-Natal (19.8%) and the Eastern Cape (12.7%). The Western Cape is home to 11.2% and Limpopo to 10.4% of the population. The provinces with the smallest populations are Mpumalanga (7.8%), North West (6.8%), the Free State (5.3%) and the Northern Cape (2.2%).

ESTIMATED POPULATION FIGURES BY PROVINCE

Province	Former name* and homelands	Capital	Area (km²)	Population (2011)
Eastern Cape	Cape Province*, Transkei, Ciskei	Bhisho	169 580	6.56 million
Free State	Orange Free State*, QwaQwa	Bloemfontein	129 480	2.74 million
Gauteng	Transvaal*	Johannesburg	17 010	12.27 million
KwaZulu-Natal	Natal*, KwaZulu	Pietermaritzburg	92 100	10.26 million
Limpopo	Transvaal*, Venda, Lebowa, Gazankulu	Polokwane	123 900	5.40 million
Mpumalanga	Transvaal*, Kwadabele, KaNgwane, Bophuthatswana, Lebowa	Nelspruit (Mbombela)	79 490	4.03 million
Northern Cape	Cape Province*	Kimberley	361 830	1.14 million
North West	Transvaal*, Cape Province, Bophuthatswana	Mafikeng	116 320	3.50 million
Western Cape	Cape Province	Cape Town	129 370	5.82 million

Almost 80% of the population are Christians. Other religious groups are Hindus, Muslims, Buddhists and Jews. A minority of the population do not belong to any major religions, but regard themselves as traditionalists with no specific religious affiliations.

THE NUMBER OF INDIVIDUALS BY RELIGION ACCORDING TO THE 2001 CENSUS
(The 2011 census did not include religious adherence)

Religion	%
Christian	79.7
African Traditional Religion	0.3
Judaism	0.2
Hinduism	1.2
Islam	1.5
Other	0.6
No religion	15.1
Undetermined	1.4

The Land
South Africa occupies the southernmost part of Africa, covering an area of roughly 1.2 million square kilometres. It has common borders with Namibia, Mozambique, Botswana, Zimbabwe, Swaziland and Lesotho.

The Ocean
South Africa is surrounded by water on three sides and has about 3 000 kilometres of coastline. The coastline is swept by two major currents: the warm Agulhas Current flows south-westwards along the east coast, reaching as far south as Cape Agulhas, and the cold Benguela Current sweeps northwards along the west coast, reaching as far north as southern Angola.

The contrast in temperature between the Agulhas and Benguela currents partly explains the difference in climate and vegetation along the west and east coasts. These currents also account for differences in marine life. The cold waters of the west coast are much richer in oxygen, nitrates, phosphates and plankton than the east coast, which is why the South African fishing industry is based on the west coast.

Climate
South Africa has an average rainfall of 450 mm. The world average is 860 mm. About 65% of the country receives less than 500 mm per year, which is considered the minimum required for arable farming. About 21% of the country, mainly the arid west, receives less than 200 mm per year.

The Economy
The United Nations classifies South Africa as a middle-income country and it is ranked 25th in the world in terms of Gross Domestic Product (GDP)*. It has an abundant supply of natural resources and a modern infrastructure. Effective communications and well-developed financial, legal, energy and transport sectors ensure an efficient distribution of goods to major urban centres throughout the region.

Gross Domestic Product is the total market value of goods and services produced by both workers and capital within a nation's borders during a given period – usually one year.

Agriculture
South Africa has a large agricultural sector and is a net exporter of agricultural products. Primary agriculture is estimated to provide about 7% of formal employment and contributes about 3% of the nation's GDP. However, only about 12% of land can be used for crop production and only about 3% is considered 'high potential' land, that is, land that can be used for intensive, high-yield, arable farming.

Mining
South Africa is a leading producer of precious metals such as gold and platinum, as well as a number of base metals (manganese, chrome, vanadium etc.) and coal. It is the world's fourth-largest producer of diamonds and was the world's largest gold producer until 2007, when it was overtaken by China. It has been estimated that South Africa possesses about 90% of the world's platinum reserves, 80% of the manganese, 73% of the chrome, 45% of vanadium and 41% of the gold reserves. Only crude oil and bauxite are not found here. Mining is crucial to the national economy. In 2009 coal became the largest component of the mining industry, followed by platinum and gold. In that year it was estimated that the mining industry contributed about 8.8% towards the nation's GDP (plus another 10% indirectly). The mining industry is also South Africa's biggest employer, employing about 500 000 people directly and another 500 000 in ancillary industries.

Open-cast coal mining

THE CAPE FLORAL KINGDOM
The **Cape Floral Kingdom**, which is sometimes called the Fynbos Biome, is a small and fragile ecosystem that contains over 8 600 species of plant, nearly three-quarters of which are found nowhere else in the world. This area – a crescent-shaped area stretching from Nieuwoudtville in the north-east to Port Elizabeth and Grahamstown in the south-east – is one of six floral kingdoms world-wide and is among the richest regions on Earth in terms of floral biodiversity.

Black nationalism and the liberation struggle

THE FREEDOM CHARTER

At a meeting at Kliptown, outside Johannesburg, in June 1955, 3 000 people adopted the Freedom Charter. It urged the establishment of a democracy that would represent everyone and in which there should be equal rights, and equal job and educational opportunities. The charter was signed by various political organizations, but the government of the day banned the publication of the document until 1984.

To many black people, the 19th century meant a series of bitter wars in which land was taken from them and, in some places, their social system collapsed. Black people wanted to share in the running of the country. But the terms of the Peace of Vereeniging, drawn up by the British and Boer leaders in 1902, made no provision for them to be represented in Parliament.

The Beginnings of the ANC

On 31 May 1910, the Union of South Africa came into being. Black people were denied the right to vote. Only the Cape Colony allowed coloured people, and certain 'qualified blacks', to remain on the voters' roll.

Black leaders felt that something positive needed to be done. In January 1912, the South African Native National Congress (SANNC) was formed at a meeting in Bloemfontein. Its aim was to achieve justice for black people and to work in peace and freedom. Its members believed that the 'perseverance, patience, reasonableness, the gentlemanly tendencies of Africans and the justice of their demands' would break down colour prejudice. The SANNC did not approve of violence.

In 1923 the organization changed its name to the African National Congress (ANC). It was banned in 1960. The ban was lifted in 1990 and, nine years later, the ANC won 266 of the 400 seats in the first democratically elected Parliament of South Africa.

PP/GTY/GI

Nelson Mandela casts his vote in a General Election

HVH/IOA

ROBBEN ISLAND

Robben Island was first used as a place of banishment (for any Khoikhoi suspected of theft) in the 1650s and has been used mainly as a prison ever since. (It has also been used as a hospital for people with leprosy and the mentally ill (1846–1931), and as a military training and defence station (1939–1945). The South African Navy handed over control of the island to the Prison Services in 1961, when a maximum security prison was established. Political prisoners were incarcerated on the island between 1961 and 1991. It is now a World Heritage Site and tourist destination.

SOME BLACK SOUTH AFRICAN LEADERS

TS/GTY/GI MPE/GTY/GI GI/AFP GI/BD/RB GI/AFP

From left: Sisulu, Biko, Mandela, Tambo and Luthuli

John Dube (1871–1946) Zulu clergyman and teacher, first president of the SANNC.

Clements Kadalie (1896–1951) Founder of the Industrial and Commercial Workers' Union of Africa the biggest trade union in South Africa in the 1920s.

Albert Luthuli (1898–1967) Became president of the ANC in 1952. He was awarded the Nobel Peace Prize in 1961.

Robert Sobukwe (1924–78) The Founder of the Pan Africanist Congress (PAC).

Steve Biko (1946–1977) Founder and president of the South African Students' Organization and 'father' of the black consciousness movement in South Africa. He died in police custody in 1977.

Nelson Mandela (born 1918) A lawyer, joined the ANC in 1944. He was found guilty and sentenced to life imprisonment at the Rivonia Trial in 1964. He was released in February 1990 and, as leader of the majority party in the 1994 election, became President of South Africa until 1999.

Walter Sisulu (1912–2003) An active member of the ANC from 1940, he was found guilty of sabotage and sentenced to life imprisonment at the Rivonia Trial in 1964. He was released in October 1989.

Oliver Tambo (1917–1993) Acting president of the ANC at the time, he left the country when the organization was banned in 1960. He continued to lead it in exile, but returned to South Africa in 1990.

Mangosuthu 'Gatsha' Buthelezi (born 1928) A prince of the Royal Zulu House and the founder and president of the Inkatha Freedom Party. He was Minister of Home Affairs from 1994 to 2004.

Opposing the Unjust Laws

During the eleven years of the SANNC's existence, several new laws caused increasing discontent. One of them sent black people in towns to jail if they did not carry a 'pass'. Another restricted black mineworkers to the humblest and worst-paid of jobs; skilled work was reserved for whites. Black people had to live in reserves, mainly in northern KwaZulu-Natal and in the former Transkei and Ciskei. Those working in the towns had to rent slum accommodation in 'locations'. The SANNC protested against these laws, but with no success.

During the 1920s, movements such as the Industrial and Commercial Workers' Union of Africa organized strikes in the towns and on farms. There were 'pass-burning' protests and marches, and people died. Despite this violence, the ANC continued to believe in passive resistance. In 1936 when black people were no longer allowed to vote in the Cape, some ANC members began to change their attitude.

Black protestors burn their 'passes' in defiance of the law

Official Apartheid

In 1948, the general election brought the National Party into power. From then onwards, the word 'apartheid' was constantly heard. Although laws already existed that made life difficult for blacks, they had always been able to share beaches, trains, post offices and other public amenities if they wished. In the Cape, 'coloured' people often lived in small communities within white suburbs. And, if they chose to do so, South Africans could mix with and marry people of any race or colour.

After 1948, new laws made these things a crime. The vote was taken away from the 'coloured' people. They had to move out of their homes in areas such as District Six to bleak townships on the Cape Flats. By 1952, the feeling of bitterness among people affected by the new apartheid laws had caused the ANC membership to rise from 7000 to 100 000. The ANC launched a defiance campaign against the carrying of passes.

The ANC Goes 'Underground'

ANC members remaining in South Africa now had to operate in secret or 'underground'. A military branch, called Umkhonto we Sizwe ('spear of the nation'), embarked on a campaign of bomb attacks against government buildings and installations.

On 11 July 1963, 17 ANC members were arrested at Rivonia in Gauteng while planning to overthrow the government. Among the eight later found guilty of sabotage and sentenced to life imprisonment were Walter Sisulu and Nelson Mandela.

Policemen stand guard at the court during the Rivonia trial

Black Nationalism Triumphs

Despite government pressure, black nationalism strengthened over the next 25 years. On 16 June 1976, police opened fire on protesting schoolchildren in Soweto, and hundreds of people were killed. Nation-wide unrest followed.

In 1977, black activist Steve Biko died of brain injuries inflicted while in prison. The government reacted to the outcry by banning 17 organizations and two newspapers. But the spirit of nationalism could not be subdued. In 1986, the government repealed the pass laws and the Mixed Marriages Act.

In 1989, the new State President, FW de Klerk announced the release of Walter Sisulu and seven other political prisoners. Soon after, the repeal of more laws meant that all people could use the same public places, such as beaches and parks, and could live in any area they wanted. Final victory for the ANC seemed certain when, on 11 February 1990, Nelson Mandela stepped out of prison as a free man.

Soweto pupils demonstrate during the 1976 protests

SHARPEVILLE

Younger members of the ANC opposed the element of 'white communism' in the ANC and in 1959 formed the Pan Africanist Congress (PAC). In 1960 they organized a nationwide protest against the pass laws. When scuffles broke out at a demonstration at Sharpeville outside Vereeniging, the police opened fire; 67 black people were killed and 187 wounded. After this, both the ANC and the PAC were banned and their leaders fled into exile outside the country.

ATTITUDES IN BLACK NATIONALISM

In the struggle for freedom, there were two attitudes among Africans, the first being that of the Charterists, who promoted the principles set out in the **Freedom Charter**. They included the **ANC**, the **UDF**, **COSATU** and **COSAS**. But **COSAS** also agreed with the attitude of the **Black Consciousness Movement (BCM)**, which declared that everyone in South Africa who was not black was a 'settler' or an 'imperialist'. They felt strongly that the country should return to its original inhabitants, the black people. Political groups that shared this opinion were **AZAPO**, the **PAC**, the **BCM** and **APLA**.

PLACES TO SEE

- When visiting Cape Town, look for the area previously known as District Six at the foot of Table Mountain
- In Johannesburg, visit the Apartheid Museum

Government and Politics

South Africa is a country of many people who have different ideals and viewpoints. For a long time, the country was governed by the white minority. In the first democratic election, in April 1994, the African National Congress (ANC) gained the majority of votes to head the Government of National Unity. Nelson Mandela was installed as the first black President of South Africa in May 1994. This was the beginning of a new era in politics, because the government now represented most South Africans, and not just the white minority.

OUR NATIONAL COAT OF ARMS

The new coat of arms was shown for the first time on 27 April 2000. The motto, in Khoisan language, *!ke e: / xarra //ke* means 'Different people unite'. The main features include ears of wheat (for agricultural progress), elephant tusks (for wisdom and strength), a shield (for defence), two San rock art figures (for unity and heritage) and a rising sun (for knowledge, good judgement and willpower).

THE CONSTITUTION

The Constitution of the Republic of South Africa Act, 1996, came into effect on 4 February 1997. This is the highest law in South Africa and no other law or government action can overrule the Constitution or be in conflict with it. Chapter 2 of the Constitution contains the **Bill of Rights**, which is the cornerstone of democracy in our country. It protects everyone's rights and affirms the democratic values of human dignity, equality and freedom. Protecting and upholding the Constitution is the job of the eleven judges of the Constitutional Court.

Parliament building, Cape Town

Parliament

Every five years, the people of South Africa get the opportunity to cast their votes in a General Election and choose a new parliament. The people they select to represent them – the Members of Parliament – act as the voice of the people who voted for them.

During a General Election, all adult South Africans have three votes: one for the National Assembly, one for the government of the province in which they live, and one for their local government or municipality. This means that if the voters are unhappy with the government or their local representatives, they can vote them out of office at the next election.

The Two Houses of Parliament

Parliament consists of two Houses, called the National Assembly and the National Council of Provinces. The National Assembly consists of 400 elected representatives who meet at the Houses of Parliament in Cape Town. During these meetings, issues of national importance are debated and discussed, and laws are made.

The National Council of Provinces consists of 54 permanent members and 36 special delegates from the nine provinces. Their job is to represent the interests of the various provinces and bring them to the attention of Parliament. The Members of the National Council of Provinces do this by discussing provincial issues and then taking part in debates in the National Assembly. (Each province also has its own provincial parliament and administration.)

What Parliament Does

The main job of Parliament is to make and pass laws. The National Assembly also chooses the President and debates issues that are of importance to the country. The National Council of Provinces is responsible for dealing with the needs and interests of the provinces.

The Cabinet

The Cabinet is appointed by the President and is responsible for seeing that the laws passed by the National Assembly are put into effect. The Cabinet consists of the President, the Deputy President and a number of Ministers. Ministers and Deputy Ministers are drawn from the National Assembly and represent a specific area of government. For example, the Minister of Education is responsible for drawing up educational policy and for seeing that schools, colleges and universities run efficiently, and the Minister of Health is responsible for all health-related matters. The President decides who will be in charge of each ministry.

MAX/MCSA

How a Law is Made

A draft law (called a Bill) is first introduced into Parliament. This is done by a Minister, a Deputy Minister, a parliamentary committee or an individual Member of Parliament. Where a Bill is introduced by a Member of Parliament, and not a Minister or Deputy Minister, it is called a Private Member's Bill. In most cases, Bills are drawn up by a government department under the direction of the relevant Minister or Deputy Minister.

The Bill then goes to the Cabinet for approval, after which it is introduced to Parliament where it goes to the relevant Committee. (By law, a number of Parliamentary Committees have to be set up for things like finance, defence, education and so on.) The Committee in question will discuss and debate the bill, make changes to it if necessary, and even arrange public hearings so that people outside Parliament have a chance to express their opinions about the proposed law.

When the Committee is happy with the Bill, it is sent back to Parliament, which must then decide whether or not to pass the Bill into law. Parliament may even refer the Bill back to the Committee for further work, if this is thought necessary. Members of Parliament then vote on the Bill.

If the Bill is passed, it goes to the National Council of Provinces for approval. When the Bill has been passed by both Houses, it is sent to the President for signature. After a Bill has been signed by the President, it becomes an Act of Parliament – the law of the land.

A parliamentary debate in progress

Political Parties in Parliament

The 1994 election brought about momentous changes in the composition of Parliament. For the first time, the members of the House of Assembly became representative of the majority of South African people and not just the white minority which, under the National Party (NP), had held power since 1948. In other words, in 1994 a number of new political parties entered Parliament, some of which had previously been banned.

The number of votes that a political party receives during an election determines how many seats it receives in the National Assembly or Provincial Councils. For example, if a party receives 50% of all votes cast, then it receives 50% of the seats that are available. This system is called proportional representation.

OUR NATIONAL FLAG

Our brightly-coloured flag was officially introduced on 27 April 1994. The central design begins as a 'V' at the flagpole, then comes together in the centre of the flag as a single horizontal band. This represents the coming together of all South Africans, in keeping with the motto on the national coat of arms (see page 48).

GOD BLESS AFRICA

Nkosi Sikelel' iAfrika, meaning 'God Bless Africa', is a hymn composed by Enoch Sontonga in 1897. Its first verse, with a verse from *Die Stem van Suid Afrika*, is the official national anthem of South Africa.

Nkosi Sikelel' iAfrika is also the national anthem of other African countries, including Zimbabwe, Namibia, Tanzania and Zambia. It is sometimes sung with a fist clenched as a sign of respect for Africa's traditions, culture and fight for freedom. One translation reads as follows:

God bless Africa,
let its banner be raised,
hear our prayers,
and bless us
Descend, O Spirit, descend,
O Spirit, descend,
O Holy Spirit.

HEALING THE LAND AND ITS PEOPLE

Government was hurtful to most South Africans during the apartheid years. It kept people in poverty and failed to develop the economy fully. The Reconstruction and Development Programme (RDP) was an attempt by the government to ensure that all South Africans enjoyed the benefits of citizenship. The RDP had five main principles:

1. To meet basic needs such as land reform, job creation, health care and social welfare, and the provision clean water, sanitation and electricity.

2. To develop human resources through better education for all, and by support for arts, culture and sport.

3. To build the economy by creating new industries to provide more jobs.

4. To democratize the state and society, so that people would know how government works and what it does.

5. To change South African society for the good of all people – this is a long-term aim that has received special consideration.

In 1995, the Truth and Reconciliation Commission (TRC), led by Archbishop Emeritus Desmond Tutu, was established to promote national unity through an understanding of the cruel things that had happened during apartheid. Although it was not a criminal court, the Commission was empowered to grant amnesty to people whom it believed had made full disclosures of their acts. The report of the Commission was handed to former President Nelson Mandela in 1998.

PLACES TO SEE

ⓘ Visits to Parliament are allowed by prior arrangement (ask your teachers to arrange a visit)

Milestones in South African History

SOUTH AFRICA IN TWO WORLD WARS

In August 1914, Germany went to war against Russia and France and then invaded Belgium. In support of the Belgians, Britain declared war on Germany on 4 August. The Union of South Africa was part of the British Empire and Prime Minister Louis Botha supported Britain's decision to go to war. Armistice was signed on 11 November 1918, ending the War, and on 16 January 1920 the League of Nations was formally established. But the League of Nations was unable to keep peace for long. On 1 September 1939, Adolf Hitler ordered his troops to invade Poland. Two days later, Britain was again at war with Germany. In the South African parliament, Prime Minister JBM Hertzog proposed that the Union should not take part in the war, but he was outvoted. General Smuts took over as Prime Minister and on 6 September 1939 South Africa declared war on Germany.

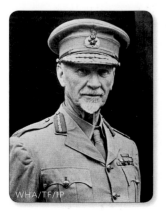

Jan Christiaan Smuts

2 000 million years ago A meteor impact results in the VREDEFORT DOME.

5 million years ago TAUNG CHILD – *Australopithecus Africanus* – roamed Gauteng.

3.3 million years ago 'LITTLE FOOT' – *Australopithecus* – roamed Gauteng.

2.5 million years ago 'MRS PLES' – *Plesianthropus transvaalensis* – roamed Gauteng.

200 000 years ago MODERN HUMANS – *Homo sapiens* – first appear.

3 000 years ago Ancestors of the KHOISAN living in South Africa.

1 700 years ago BANTU-SPEAKING FARMERS move south of the Limpopo River.

Circa 1200 MAPUNGUBWE at the height of its power.

1400–1600 THULAMELA at the height of its power.

1487 BARTOLOMEU DIAS reaches Mossel Bay.

1652 JAN VAN RIEBEECK establishes a refreshment station at the CAPE on behalf of the DUTCH EAST INDIA COMPANY.

1658 The first SLAVES arrive at the Cape.

1688 The HUGUENOTS arrive at the Cape.

1795 BRITAIN seizes control of the CAPE COLONY from the Dutch.

1803 The DUTCH (The Batavian Repubic) regain control of the CAPE COLONY.

1806 BRITAIN reconquers the CAPE COLONY.

1816–1828 THE ZULU KINGDOM under SHAKA rises to prominence (The Mfecane).

1820 BRITISH SETTLERS arrive in the CAPE COLONY.

1835–40 THE GREAT TREK.

1779–1878 NINE WARS, over land ownership in the Eastern Cape, take place between European settlers and the Xhosa.

1867 DIAMONDS discovered in Griqualand-West.

1886 GOLD discovered on the Witwatersrand.

1899–1902 THE ANGLO-BOER WAR.

1910 THE UNION OF SOUTH AFRICA founded.

1912 The SOUTH AFRICAN NATIVE NATIONAL CONGRESS (SAANC) formed; this later becomes the African National Congress.

1913 THE LAND ACT reserves homelands for black people.

1914–1918 WORLD WAR I OCCURS IN EUROPE.

1915 South Africa occupies GERMAN SOUTH WEST AFRICA (later to become NAMIBIA).

1920 The newly formed LEAGUE OF NATIONS makes SOUTH WEST AFRICA a South African PROTECTORATE.

1923 The SAANC changes its name to the AFRICAN NATIONAL CONGRESS (ANC).

1930 White South African WOMEN get the VOTE.

1939–1945 WORLD WAR II.

1948 The NATIONAL PARTY wins the General Election. APARTHEID becomes official policy.

1958 HF VERWOERD becomes Prime Minister.

1960 Police fire on demonstrators at SHARPEVILLE. ANC and PAC banned. British Prime Minister Macmillan warns of 'WINDS OF CHANGE' blowing through Africa.

Archbishop Emeritus Desmond Tutu

1961 SA becomes a REPUBLIC on 31 May. CR SWART becomes first State President.

1963 NELSON MANDELA and WALTER SISULU, along with 15 others arrested at Rivonia. Mandela, Sisulu and six others are later sentenced to life imprisonment.

1966 Prime Minister HF VERWOERD assassinated. BJ VORSTER becomes Prime Minister.

1967 Professor Christiaan Barnard performs the world's FIRST HEART TRANSPLANT OPERATION at Groote Schuur Hospital in Cape Town.

1974 SA Defence Force launches attack in ANGOLA.

1976 Serious UNREST begins in SOWETO. TRANSKEI granted independence.

1977 Opposition PRP becomes PROGRESSIVE FEDERAL PARTY (PFP). Black Consciousness leader STEVE BIKO dies in detention. USA forbids sale of armaments to SA.

1978 BJ VORSTER becomes the State President and PW BOTHA becomes the Prime Minister.

1982 The CONSERVATIVE PARTY and the NATIONAL UNION OF MINEWORKERS (NUM) are formed.

1983 REFERENDUM: white voters approve tri-cameral proposals. UNITED DEMOCRATIC FRONT (UDF) formed.

1984 New constitution establishes the TRI-CAMERAL SYSTEM. Blacks not represented. Intense opposition to system. SA and Mozambique sign NKOMATI ACCORD.

1985 STATE OF EMERGENCY declared. CONGRESS OF SA TRADE UNIONS (COSATU) formed.

1986 PASS LAWS and laws forbidding MIXED MARRIAGES and IMMORALITY abolished.

1987 GENERAL ELECTION. Conservative Party becomes official opposition. OVERSEAS SANCTIONS CAMPAIGN against South Africa strengthens.

1988 Many ANTI-GOVERNMENT ORGANIZATIONS (such as the UDF) RESTRICTED. Sanctions campaign increases.

1989 PW BOTHA replaced by FW DE KLERK. WALTER SISULU released. Many protest marches take place.

1990 MANDELA released from prison. BAN ON ANC, PAC and SACP lifted. SA Government NEGOTIATES with ANC. State of Emergency is lifted. Increased political VIOLENCE in townships. OLIVER TAMBO returns to SA.

1991 SA re-enters INTERNATIONAL SPORT. First meeting of CODESA (Convention for a Democratic South Africa).

1992 SA returns to OLYMPIC GAMES (Barcelona), the first time since 1960.

1993 Communist Party leader, CHRIS HANI, assassinated. The INTERIM CONSTITUTION is agreed upon. De Klerk and Mandela receive NOBEL PEACE PRIZE.

1994 Walvis Bay reincorporated into Namibia. ANC wins first DEMOCRATIC GENERAL ELECTION. PRESIDENT MANDELA installed in ceremony in Pretoria. South Africa rejoins the British Commonwealth and the United Nations General Assembly, and becomes a member of the Organisation of African Unity (OAU).

FW de Klerk   *Nelson Mandela*

1995 SA wins RUGBY WORLD CUP. The TRUTH AND RECONCILIATION COMMISSION (TRC) begins its work.

1996 Josiah Thugwane wins marathon at ATLANTA OLYMPICS and swimmer Penny Heyns takes two gold medals. National soccer side, Bafana Bafana, wins AFRICA CUP OF NATIONS.

1997 SA troops, as part of a SOUTHERN AFRICAN DEVELOPMENT COMMUNITY (SADC) action, invade Lesotho to help put down troubles in that country.

1998 The publication of the TRC REPORT.

1999 Second DEMOCRATIC GENERAL ELECTION. Thabo Mbeki elected President.

2000 TROPICAL CYCLONE ELINE causes severe flooding in Mozambique and northern parts of SA.

2004 Third DEMOCRATIC GENERAL ELECTION. At the Athens Olympic Games, Lyndon Ferns, Ryk Neethling, Roland Schoeman and Darian Townsend win gold for the 4x100 metres freestyle swimming event.

2009 Fourth DEMOCRATIC GENERAL ELECTION. Jacob Zuma becomes President.

2010 South Africa hosts the football World Cup.

2012 At London Olympics, Oscar Pistorius becomes first para Olympian to participate in an able-bodied event.

A NEW ERA FOR SOUTH AFRICA

Since the early 1990s, South Africa has been playing a greater role in world affairs. It joined the United Nations General Assembly in 1994, and became a non-permanent member of the highly influential UN Security Council in 2011. In April 2011 South Africa joined forces with four of the world's most powerful developing nations – Brazil, Russia, India and China. These nations, previously known as the BRIC group, are now called BRICS. The International Monetary Fund believes that, by working together, BRICS will account for 61% of global growth by 2014.

PRIZES FOR PEACE

Several South Africans have received, or been nominated for, the Nobel Peace Prize during the 20th Century. The first to receive this honour was Albert Luthuli who was awarded it in 1961 for his efforts in trying to convince people that change in South Africa should take place through negotiation rather than violence. Archbishop Emeritus Desmond Tutu received the Nobel Peace Prize in 1984, and in 1993 President FW de Klerk and Mr Nelson Mandela were awarded the prize jointly for their efforts to bring about peaceful change in South Africa.

PLACES TO SEE

ⓘ Visit the Union Buildings in Pretoria

Traditional South African Crafts

CLAY POTS

Most Tsonga pots have necks but those made by Nguni-speaking people seldom do. Zulu pots are round and typical Swazi pots are bag-shaped, while Xhosa people shape theirs like barrels. **Clay pots** vary in size and are used for cooking, brewing beer and holding food.

LOVE MESSAGES

Although beads are mostly just decorative, Zulu girls sometimes express their feelings with **bead letters**. Each colour may carry a message. Red beads mean passion or jealousy; blue shows that her thoughts fly to her loved one like a dove. White means purity and black beads mean that she longs to wear the black leather apron, which symbolizes marriage. A girl will ask a friend to deliver the bead letter to her chosen young man.

Many rural African people are skilled crafters, creating beautiful objects, ornaments and material requirements. Their methods are handed down from one generation to another and the styles, shapes and colours of their clay pots, baskets and intricate beadwork differ from area to area.

Pottery

Traditionally, the woman is the potter. Her clay pots are used for cooking, storing and serving food, and brewing beer. She collects clay from her own 'hole' in a river-bank, ant-hill or swamp, and prepares it by pounding and kneading it. She then shapes her pots with her hands. Some potters start with a lump of clay and hollow out the centre with their thumbs. Others make coils and wind them round to form the pot's walls. The potter smoothes the pot with a shell, a large pod or the rind of a calabash and then leaves it to dry. She may decorate the pot by drawing a design on the dry pot with a thorn or pin and colours it with black graphite or orange, red or white ochres ground from earth or clay.

The pot is then fired by placing it in a hollow in the ground. It is surrounded by fuel such as wood or cattle dung, which burns slowly. Pots are blackened with smoke, sometimes shone with boot-polish, or decorated with enamel paint. Today, many African people make pots for sale and may use modern methods such as potters' wheels. Many men have become as skilled in pottery as women.

Baskets and Wickerwork

In rural areas, many people use reeds, grass or palm leaves to weave baskets. Patterns, techniques and colours differ from area to area. The Zulu weave beads into an article as a decoration and sometimes to give it a special meaning. Sleeping-mats are woven from reeds, in beautiful patterns. During the day, the mat is conveniently rolled up and stored away, and at night the owner unrolls it and lies on the floor. These mats are also used as floor coverings, for sitting on and for drying flour in the sun. If the owner travels, he always takes his reed mat with him.

Baskets serve many purposes and are woven in a variety of shapes and sizes. The Sotho people weave enormous baskets that are used for storing grain and food, for carrying goods, for separating flour from bran and for straining sorghum beer.

Traditional basketwork

A Man's Work

The familiar cone-shaped Basotho hat may be a copy of the *toering* worn by Cape Muslims over a century ago. Traditionally men are the hat-makers and woodworkers. With simple tools, they make wooden spoons, dishes, mugs and buckets. They also carve beautiful smoking pipes and headrests for the women so that their elaborate hairstyles are not crushed. A pattern is burnt into the wood with a red-hot iron tool.

Traditional crafts are often sold at the roadside

Beads for All Ages

Beads are used for decoration, especially among the Zulu and Southern Ndebele, and give status to the owner. The colours and designs may have a hidden meaning. Some are for special occasions, while others symbolize the different stages of a person's life. Most African babies wear few or no clothes. A Ndebele baby will wear a necklace even before it wears clothes. Young children wear bracelets and anklets. Girls have a tiny beaded apron and boys wear a loin-cloth of either beads or animal-skins.

DECORATION

Before their initiation ceremony, Ndebele girls prepare beaded hoops, fringed headbands and dancing sticks, and learn the skill of mural design and painting. They also make beaded fertility dolls, while their mothers make leather aprons embroidered with beads. Hoops and brass rings are used as adornment for their limbs and neck.

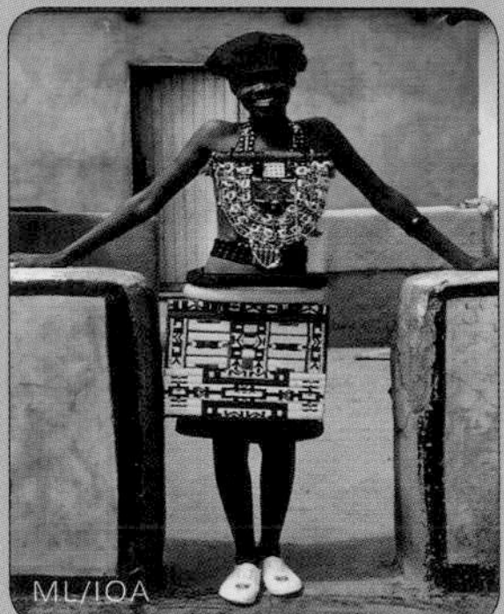

DRESSED FOR MARRIAGE

African brides often wear traditional clothing and ornaments. A Zulu bride may have an elaborate hairstyle woven with colourful beads. She shows respect for her husband's parents by shading her eyes with a veil of beads or beaded cloth. Huge bead-encrusted hoops encircle her neck and she wears a bead-embroidered blanket. Ndebele brides wear a beaded leather apron and brass ankle rings.

If a Zulu bridegroom is from an important family, he may wear a leopard-skin cape and the head-ring of a married man. However, many bridal couples choose to wear western-style clothes.

Rickshaws

Rickshaws on Durban's beachfront display spectacular beadwork. They were introduced to South Africa from Japan in the late 19th century by the sugar magnate, Sir Marshall Campbell. They were pulled by Zulu men who leapt and whistled dramatically. The men took tremendous pride in their colourful beaded costumes, elaborate horned headdresses and brilliantly decorated vehicles. During the 1930s, Durban had about 1000 rickshaws and their pullers enthusiastically paraded in the annual competition. After World War II the rickshaws became less popular, but numbers have recently risen due to an increase in tourism.

HOLES IN THEIR EARS

The beautiful beaded earrings worn by the **Zulu** vary from simple studs to enormous rings. Young boys and girls usually have their ears pierced with a reed, as many people still believe that by piercing the ears, the mind is opened to understanding.

WINDMILLS AND WAGONS

Wire toys on sale at roadsides are often made by children who have great fun playing with them. Made from cans, wire and scrap metal, these intricate and **accurate working models** of wagons, cars, bicycles and windmills have wheels and other moving parts.

Markets are a good place to buy locally made crafts

Weaving

Weaving on a loom is not a traditional craft in southern Africa, but many people are skilled in making beautiful fabrics, carpets and other textiles today. High-quality mohair from angora goats is woven in traditional patterns, and carpet-weaving has become an important industry in Lesotho. Woven textiles are also produced, each area having its own designs. Hand-woven South African textiles are sold throughout the world.

The Blanket People

African blankets are not only worn for warmth, but may indicate social position. A baby is tucked into a blanket tied to its mother's back. In some groups, a bride shows respect to her father-in-law by covering her face with a blanket. The red-ochred blanket is characteristic of the Xhosa. Animal skins worn as cloaks were first replaced by blankets imported from the East by a German trader. In the 19th century, the British introduced the 'Victoria' blanket with a bold design of crowns and other royal emblems, which became particularly popular with the people of Basutoland (later Lesotho). Today, the colours, patterns and sizes of the 'Basotho blanket' vary from year to year, depicting important events or the animal symbols of the group. Traditionally, men wear their blankets pinned on the right shoulder, while women pin theirs across the neck or chest.

PLACES TO SEE

ⓘ Durban Art Gallery Durban

ⓘ African Art Centre, Durban

ⓘ Vukani Zulu Cultural Museum, Eshowe, KwaZulu-Natal

Art in South Africa

CTAR

South Africa's very first artists were the San who decorated their rock overhangs with paintings and engravings depicting trance images.

Famous Professional Painters

The watercolours and pencil sketches of the British painter **Thomas Bowler** (1812–1869) accurately record places and events in the 19th century. Besides being a painter, **Thomas Baines** (1820–1875), was a well-known British explorer. He painted seascapes, battle scenes and animals, and also some of the earliest pictures of the Victoria Falls. The detailed and realistic works of these artists, and others such as **Frederick Timpson l'Ons** (1802–1887), are not only of artistic value, but also historically important.

IZ/AMO

Table Mountain from Bloubergstrand by Thomas Bowler

Artists from Holland

Trained at the Rotterdam Academy, **Anton van Wouw** (1862–1945) (pictured right) sculpted the statue of President Paul Kruger in Church Square, Pretoria. He is famous for his true-to-life bronze figures. **Frans David Oerder** (1867–1944) joined

NM/AMO

the Boers and sketched battle scenes during the Second Anglo-Boer War, but is most famous for his portraits. The best works of **Pieter Wenning** (1873–1921) are his winter landscapes of the Cape, although many of his still lifes are influenced by Japanese art. **Tinus de Jongh** (1885–1942) made etchings of buildings, and realistic oil paintings of Cape mountains and sunsets.

British Painters in South Africa

Robert Gwelo Goodman (1871–1939) is best known for his Cape landscapes and homesteads, and his exhibitions in London made British people aware of South African art. **Sydney Carter** (1874–1945) trained at the Royal College of Art and is known for his trees painted in watercolour. **Edward Roworth** (1880–1964) was a portraitist, landscape artist and professor at Cape Town's Michaelis School of Art.

Other Immigrant Artists

Trained in Germany, **Nita Spilhaus** (1878–1967) was one of the first female artists in South Africa. Two German-born artists who painted Namibian wildlife were **Adolph Jentsch** (1888–1977) and **Fritz Krampe** (1913–1966). **Jean Welz** (1900–1975) and **Alfred Krenz** (1899–1980) were Austrian. Welz's work includes landscapes, portraits and nude studies, while Krenz painted in strong, bold colours. **Moses Kottler** (1892–1977), born in Lithuania and trained in Jerusalem, was a painter and a sculptor in wood, stone and bronze. Italians **Armando Baldinelli** (1908–2002), **Edoardo Villa** (1915–2011) and **Giuseppe Cattaneo** (born 1929) are experimental artists who work with paint, stone, wood, steel, bronze and scrap-iron.

Russian-born artist, **Vladimir Tretchikoff** (1913–2006) is known for his popular art. At one time, more reproductions and prints of his work were sold than the work of any other living artist in the western world.

MA/AMO

Vladimir Tretchikoff

RHS

Edoardo Villa's sculpture, The Knot

20th Century Artists

Art in South Africa developed a special identity in the 20th century. One of the earliest South African-born artists was **Jan Ernst Abraham Volschenk** (1853–1936). He had no formal art training but is particularly well known for painting the beautiful scenery of the south-western Cape in minute detail.

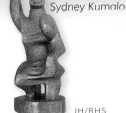

The Blessing by
Sydney Kumalo

JH/RHS

Hugo Naudé (1868–1941), who studied art in Britain, Germany and France, was influenced by Impressionism. He often painted southern Cape landscapes, but became famous for his portraits, especially of young people. His house in Worcester is now an art gallery. Along with Naudé, **Ruth Prowse** (1883–1967) brought European Impressionism to South Africa. She was a member of the New Group. Her home is now the well-known Ruth Prowse College of Art and Design in Woodstock, Cape Town.

JH Pierneef (1886–1957) was famous for his 'Transvaal' and Bushveld scenes. He studied under Frans Oerder and became internationally known. Pierneef's works include the giant murals commissioned for the Johannesburg railway station.

Irma Stern (1894–1966) studied in Germany and was influenced by Expressionism, which aims at expressing emotions in art. She is known for the rich colours and bold lines of her oil paintings, many of which depict rural black people. **Maggie Laubser** (1886–1973) was also influenced by Expressionism after studying in Britain and Germany, and is most famous for the powerful human figures and brilliant colours depicting the Cape countryside where she spent her childhood.

Landscape with Sheep by Maggie Laubser

Later South African Artists

Son of a well-known political cartoonist, **Gregoire Boonzaier** (1909–2005) studied art in London and was strongly influenced by Pieter Wenning. His works include paintings of District Six, the Bo-Kaap and cottages of the Boland. He jokingly referred to himself as a 'house painter' and was a founder member and chairman of the New Group. Lithuanian-born sculptor **Lippy Lipshitz** (1903–1980) trained as a wood-carver in Cape Town and then studied sculpture in Paris. He also joined the New Group, and became a professor of Fine Arts at the University of Cape Town. He emigrated to Israel in 1978.

The colourful murals in the Provincial Administration Building, Pretoria, are by **Alexis Preller** (1911–1975), whose figures and images were often inspired by Biblical history or mythology.

THE NEW GROUP

Founded in 1937, the New Group opposed the conservative style of established South African artists. The Group, whose members included Walter Battiss, Gregoire Boonzaier, Lippy Lipshitz and Cecil Higgs, had a strong influence on local art. The Group's last exhibition was in 1953 before it disbanded.

Gerard Sekoto (1913–1994) trained as a teacher but left the profession to concentrate on his painting. He is best known for his colourful paintings of township life.

Bettie Cilliers-Barnard (1914–2010) studied in Paris and Antwerp and started her career as a realistic painter. She is regarded as the first woman in South Africa whose work was truly abstract.

Internationally successful **Cecil Skotnes** (1926–2009) developed a distinctive style influenced by his work at the Polly Street Art Centre in Johannesburg for black artists in the city. He is best known for his award-winning woodcuts and wood panels.

Esias Bosch (1923–2010) specializes in pottery. He is well known for his mural at Johannesburg's OR Tambo International airport.

Painters **Louis Maqhubela** (born 1939) and **Ephraim Ngatane** (1938–1971) took lessons from Cecil Skotnes at the Polly Street Art Centre. Maqhubela is known for his large, abstract works, while Ngatane concentrated on township life.

SAP

Peter Clarke (born 1929) is known for his drawings of the Cape Coloured people, while the work of graphic artist and painter, **Leonard Matsoso** (born 1949), centres around African myth.

Especially known for a mural painting she did in Paris for an exhibition at the Pompidou Centre, **Esther Mahlangu** (born 1938) uses the traditional Ndebele wall-painting techniques in her work.

Mmakgoba Helen Sebidi (born 1943) is a painter and potter devoted to teaching children.

William Kentridge (born 1955), one of South Africa's best-known artists, is famed for his charcoal drawing stop-frame animations.

From the Land Carrying Food by Helen Sebidi

AEL

SCULPTORS

The first South African-born sculptor was **Fanie Eloff** (1885–1947). He trained in Paris and worked in bronze and marble. One of his best-known sculptures is the *Discus Thrower*.

Coert Steynberg (1905–1982) studied at the Royal College of Art, London. His works include the woman in the Huguenot Monument.

Lucas Sithole (1931–1994) and **Michael Zondi** (born 1926) work in wood and stone; both concentrate on human figures.

Sydney Kumalo (1935–1988) studied with Cecil Skotnes and Edoardo Villa. His human and animal forms have gained international acclaim.

Danie de Jager (1936–2003) is world famous for his sculptures of animals in motion.

Jane Alexander (born 1959) creates figures that are often eerie and difficult to interpret.

WK

PAINTING THE WALLS

Traditionally, **Ndebele** women paint the walls of their houses with bright colours and detailed patterns. Triangles, squares and other geometric shapes cover the walls, and spaces are filled with letters or numbers.

PLACES TO SEE →

ℹ️ Visit the many excellent art galleries in our major cities and towns

55

The Performing Arts

BP/AL

FESTIVALS OF THE ARTS
A National Arts Festival, with emphasis on the English language, is held every year in Grahamstown in June and July, while the predominantly Afrikaans Klein Karoo Nasionale Kunstefees is held in March and April at Oudtshoorn. Both festivals promote the performing and visual arts, attracting hundreds of presenters and many thousands of visitors.

OUR FIRST BALLET
The first truly South African Ballet was based on NP van Wyk Louw's poem, *Raka*. This meaningful story, choreographed by Frank Staff and performed to the music of Graham Newcater, was filmed in 1967.

**THE BAXTER
THEATRE CENTRE**
Throughout apartheid the Baxter Theatre Centre's doors and stages remained open to all, and today its Zabalaza Theatre Festival has become one of the most important development theatre platforms in the country.

Before the days of cinema and television, plays, operas and ballets were usually performed by amateurs, but professional companies sometimes toured South Africa.

Early Days
Cape Town's first theatre, the African Theatre, was opened in Riebeeck Square in 1800. Plays were in Dutch or English and sometimes in French. Performers, especially in a pantomime, were men and children because it was improper for women to appear on the stage. When Weber's *Der Freischütz* was performed in 1831, Capetonians enjoyed a full-length opera for the first time. Unfortunately, church authorities thought stage performances were wicked and, in 1839, the African Theatre closed and was converted into a church, which is a National Heritage Site today.

Plays continued to be performed during the 19th century. The diggers on the newly opened diamond and gold mines were entertained by actors, singers, dancers and circus performers in sheds and warehouses. Theatres were later built in all the big towns.

The 20th Century and Beyond
The invention of the cinema resulted in less interest in the stage, and foreign productions and performers were brought to South Africa to attract audiences. Afrikaans plays were also being staged. After the Second World War, several independent companies were formed and, with government assistance, the National Theatre Organization (NTO) was gradually developed until 1960.

In 1960 the government founded four performing arts councils to direct theatre, opera and ballet in the country's (then) four provinces. However, with the division of the country into nine provinces in 1994, the existing councils were given notice that state subsidies would decrease until, by 2000, only the councils' core infrastructure would be financed. This meant that theatre groups would increasingly have to fund their own activities. State funds are distributed by a National Arts Council (NAC), which promotes all art forms and

the free and creative expression of South Africa's cultures. The main State-sponsored theatres are the State Theatre in Pretoria, Artscape in Cape Town, The Playhouse in Durban and the Performing Arts Centre of the Free State. Councils have become more community-orientated by widening the range of productions and using mobile theatre.

Many of the plays written by and about black people in South Africa reflect the harsh life under apartheid, but many also express the humour and music of both authors and performers. Some plays that have been successfully staged overseas were once banned in South Africa. Productions include *uMabatha*, a play by Welcome Msomi based on Shakespeare's Macbeth, and Woza Albert. A film of the musical *Sarafina* stars Whoopi Goldberg.

BX

Janet Suzman and Khayalethu Anthony in Lara Foot's Solomon and Marion, staged at the Baxter

BX

The cast of Lara Foot's multi-award-winning Karoo Moose, staged at the Baxter

THE DREAM FACTORY
In a large theatre, such as the opera house at Cape Town's Artscape, the **backstage** area, where the scenery is kept, is up to four times the size of the visible stage. The **stage manager** watches what happens on stage on as many as four television monitors, and tells the **stagehands** when to take down or **strike** the movable scenery, known as **flats**. The **flymen** control the curtains and **props**, which need to be lifted from or lowered onto the stage from flying bars overhead. **Mechanists** control the machinery that places entire sets in position. The **lighting director** decides on light effects and tells the **lighting technician** where to focus the spotlight. Sound effects, such as thunder, gunshots or tinkling glass, are provided by the **sound technician**, while the **special effects** person creates mist, flames or smoke. This split-second timing demanded from stagehands and cast takes place in semi-darkness, and everything has to be carefully rehearsed before the **director** calls 'Curtain up!'.

The Independent Theatres

Among many privately run professional theatres and stage companies are The Baxter Theatre at The University of Cape Town, the 1820 Monument Theatre in Grahamstown, the Breytenbach Theatre in Pretoria, the Market Theatre complex in Johannesburg, Pieter Toerien's Theatre on the Bay at Camps Bay, Cape Town, The Fugard in Cape Town and the Montecasino Theatre in Johannesburg. Universities also present shows in their own smaller theatres.

Stage Personalities

Some of the country's top singers include **Miriam Makeba** (1932–2008) and **Johnny Clegg**, as well as opera stars **Mimi Coertse, Sibongile Khumalo, Marita Napier, Deon van der Walt** and **Aviva Pelham**. Because there are no permanent opera companies in South Africa, younger stars such as **Elizabeth Connell, Johan Botha** and **Pretty Yende** have not yet starred in their own country.

The University of Cape Town Ballet School was founded by **Dulcie Howes** (1908–1993), herself a prima ballerina. The most celebrated ballet duo was probably **Eduard Greyling** and **Phyllis Spira** (1943–2008). The Cape Town City Ballet is the country's only remaining permanent ballet company.

Television personality Shaleen Surtie-Richards

The list of successful stage actors includes **Andre Huguenet**, leading actor of the NTO; **Anthony Sher**, particularly successful as a Shakespearean actor in London, and the award-winning **John Kani**. Actors who have had successful film careers in Hollywood and the UK include **Marius Weyers, Richard E. Grant** and, more recently, **Sharlto Copley**.

Among the best-known South African actresses are **Charlize Theron**, who won the Best Actress Oscar in 2004, **Janet Suzman**, an internationally acclaimed Shakespearean actress, and **Alice Krige. Michelle Botes, Sandra Prinsloo, Fiona Ramsay** and **Shaleen Surtie-Richards** have performed on stage and television.

The late **Yvonne Bryceland** was famous for her roles in the plays of **Athol Fugard**, South Africa's most famous

English playwright. Fugard's work reflects the country's political and social problems. **Percy Mtwa** is an actor who successfully turned to producing and writing and, with other dramatists, produced such masterpieces as *Woza Albert* and *Bopha*. **Maishe Maponya** and **Gibson Kente** have written about life in the townships.

Other noted playwrights are satirists **Pieter-Dirk Uys**, whose best-known creation is Evita Bezuidenhout, and the late **Robert Kirby. David Kramer** and **Taliep Petersen** (1950–2006) wrote musicals romanticizing District Six.

A scene from the record-breaking District Six – The Musical

RADIO AND TELEVISION

The South African Broadcasting Corporation (SABC) was formed in 1936. Many people felt that, especially in its news broadcasts, the SABC was biased on the side of the former government, so a non-profit statutory body, the Independent Broadcasting Authority (IBA), was created in 1993 to be independent of government. The IBA has the authority to control and promote the public broadcasting service, community broadcasting and private broadcasting. It licenses new radio and television stations, may renew the licences of existing stations and acts as an industry 'watchdog'.

Independent television channels include M-Net and its satellite service DSTV, and free-to air e.tv.

TRADITIONAL DANCE

Zulu dancing is an expression of joy and is performed for special events such as weddings, the birth of a child, victory in battle or hunting, and the inauguration of a king. Dancers are dressed in traditional clothing and display remarkable agility.

Gumboot dancing developed in the mines and was traditionally performed by mineworkers wearing their work gumboots, which form an integral part of the dance in terms of the rhythms created.

Volkspele were first performed in 1914 at a picnic at Boshof, in the Free State, when pupils of Dr Henri Pellissier performed Swedish folk dances to the music of popular Afrikaans songs. Today they are still danced at some Afrikaans cultural festivals.

THE FILM INDUSTRY

South Africa has a vibrant film industry that is becoming increasingly competitive overseas. For example, in 2006, the film *Tsotsi* won the Academy Award for best foreign language film. *Yesterday*, a film about an HIV-positive mother, was also nominated for an Oscar in 2005, and *U Carmen E Khayalitsha*, a Xhosa language film, won the Golden Bear Award at the 2005 Berlin Film Festival.

Musical Medley

South African music ranges from the single-stringed **gorah** of the San hunter and the harmonies of African workmen to the grand piano and opera soprano. Symphony orchestras perform in cities, while the townships echo with the throb of **mbaqanga**.

Music of the San and Khoikhoi

San people used natural materials to make their musical instruments and even tied seed pods around their ankles, which rattled as they danced. The San shooting-bow was adapted and used as a musical instrument with a resonator temporarily attached, and played by beating the string with a light stick. Today they also use commercially manufactured materials such as paraffin tins and brass wire.

The Khoikhoi played on flutes made of different lengths of reeds. They also made 'drums' by stretching animal skins over clay pots or large metal containers, which acted as resonators, and were beaten with the hands. The Khoikhoi learnt to use the San music bow, called a gorah. This unique instrument is a 'wind bow' and is sounded by breathing.

Khoikhoi musician playing a gorah

> ### TRADITIONAL INSTRUMENTS
> The word **xylophone** comes from the Greek words for 'wood' and 'sound'. Xylophones are wooden slabs or 'keys' of different lengths that are struck with hard-headed hammers. There are two types: free-key and fixed-key instruments. Sometimes, hollow calabashes are attached beneath the wooden slabs to increase the sound volume. The fixed-key xylophone was traditionally used by the Venda and the Tsonga.
>
> Many African people play **horns** in ensemble in the same way that reed flute players interact. These instruments are made from the horns of various types of antelope, and are usually side-blown.

African Drums

Drums and drumming are not as widespread in Africa as commonly thought. In South Africa the Venda, Pedi and Tsonga are the only peoples who have traditional drum ensembles. The Nguni-speakers had no traditions of drums and drumming. The Zulu accompanied their war songs by beating their ox-hide shields with weapons or by beating their shields on the ground. After colonization the Nguni-speakers took to making their own double-skin drums, modelled on the western military drum and played with two beaters.

Nguni-speakers made drums styled on western military drums

Among the Classicists

During the days of the Dutch East India Company, ceremonies at the Cape were accompanied by military music played on trumpets, other wind instruments and drums. Organs were played at church services. In wealthier homes, children were expected to entertain guests on the harpsichord, violin, flute or harp.

Entertainment at the Cape was often provided by British soldiers. Operas and musicals were later staged at the garrison theatre on Riebeeck Square. A music academy was founded in Cape Town in 1826. After gold and diamonds were discovered, visiting musicians performed in Kimberley and Johannesburg. The Stellenbosch Conservatoire of Music was opened in 1905 and the SA College of Music was founded in Cape Town in 1910, both producing many talented musicians.

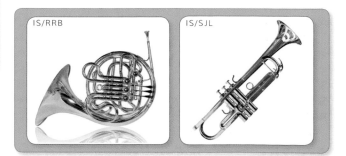

THE CHILDREN'S ORCHESTRA
Composers have written especially for the young musicians of the **South African National Youth Orchestra**. The orchestra has been conducted by world-famous conductors and has taken part in a number of international music festivals around the world. The South African National Youth Orchestra Foundation awards scholarships to promising young players.

THE DRAKENSBERG BOYS' CHOIR
The boys of the renowned Drakensberg Boys' Choir enjoy special choral training and the benefits of country life, as well as having ordinary school lessons. It was founded by John Tungay in 1967 and draws boys with musical interests from all parts of South Africa. The choir is composed of three different age groups, and the mpre senior choirs, which are of international standard, have travelled widely.

South Africa's Orchestras

Among the professional orchestras in South Africa are the Cape Philharmonic and the KZN Philharmonic. Before 1994, provincial theatre groups and several cities had their own orchestras, but sponsorship in many cases has been diverted to other projects, and orchestras are able to exist now only if they pay their own way or obtain private sponsorship.

The former Cape Town Symphony Orchestra in rehearsal

Music of a New Generation

Marabi music emerged in the 1920s and 1930s as a distinctive style with appeal to the urban African working-class. It blended African and Western traits and Cape Coloured musicians also contributed, introducing Cape Afrikaans and African-American music.

Mbube was an African all-male choral blend of Zulu, Swazi, Western, Afrikaans and African-American music. The name was derived from the title of a song by Solomon Linda, and the music was usually sung without accompaniment. Linda's *Wimoweh* became popular overseas, and was sung by Miriam Makeba.

Kwela was the popular urban style associated with young boys and their penny whistles in the late 1940s. Later, a guitar was added, and perhaps a string bass. Kwela was the first South African style to receive international recognition, and was successfully reinterpreted by the group **Mango Groove**.

Mbaqanga blends African jazz, kwela, older traditional music and American swing. Jive is a strong feature and the music is played on electric guitars, accordions, drums and violins. Among the great performers were 'Groaner' Mahlatini and the Mahotella Queens.

Kwaito dates from the 1990s and is a mixture of 1920s marabi, 1950s kwela, bubblegum disco music of the 1980s and *imibongo* (praise poetry). Its development was influenced by performers such as Miriam Makeba, Chicco Twala and Brenda Fassie (1964–2004). The name is from the Afrikaans word *kwaai* (angry). Kwaito is part of the proud, assertive image of township youth, with *isicamtho* or township slang.

Afrikaans Folk Music

The accordion and concertina were popular among Boers, who played them at dances, and **Boeremusiek**, at first based on popular European dance tunes, came into existence. Guitar or banjo added to the music's character and, by the 1930s, the **vastrap** (hop-dance)

had become fashionable. The **tiekiedraai** was a quick dance. A couple turned around on a spot said to be no bigger than a tickey coin.

NOTABLE SOUTH AFRICAN MUSICIANS

Ladysmith Black Mambazo, who performed on Paul Simon's *Graceland* album, have won three Grammys: 1987, 2005 and 2009. **Johnny Clegg** learnt the Zulu language, customs and dances, and formed **Juluka**. Clegg's later group, **Savuka**, became famous for their blend of Zulu chants, mbaqanga and rock 'n roll, accompanied by energetic dancing. International singing star, **Miriam Makeba** (1932–2008) began her highly successful singing career in the 1940s as a choir singer. In 1947 she sang for the visiting British royal family and later with township jazz groups. She also took part in a documentary film entitled *Come Back Africa* and was a spectacular success in *King Kong*. An active civil rights campaigner, Ms Makeba was awarded the Dag Hammarskjöld Award of the Diplomatic Academy for Peace in 1985. Trumpeter, **Hugh Masekela** (pictured) played in a group called the Black Epistles, the first local jazz band to make a record. He arranged the music for *King Kong*, recorded a number of internationally successful songs and wrote the music for *Sarafina* in 1987. Formerly known as Dollar Brand, jazz musician **Abdullah Ibrahim** is famous for his combination of jazz techniques and traditional South African rhythms. He was among many prominent South African musicians who returned to the country of their birth from self-imposed exile.

A Famous Musical

King Kong was first performed in 1959 and gave white audiences the opportunity to appreciate the talents of black actors and musicians. The musical, by Stanley Glasser, was about the life of a boxer in Sophiatown, and combined African, black American and European styles and featured the music of Todd Matshikiza. After successful performances in South African cities, the show went on to tour London. In the 1970s, the musical, *Ipi Tombi*, enjoyed similar success.

The lively folk songs sung by the **Cape Town Minstrels**, are a mixture of mainly Afrikaans, English and African-American ballads. Their New Year celebrations, centred around the Minstrel Carnival, are enjoyed by locals and tourists alike. At this time of year, the Cape Town Minstrels traditionally stream through the centre of Cape Town in brightly coloured costumes.

CITY DRUMS

A lively beat is often heard in the cities where street musicians use old oil-drums as instruments.

PLACES TO SEE

ℹ Go to a performance by a symphony orchestra and see how many instruments you are able to recognize

Books and Newspapers

SA/IOA

THE DEWEY DECIMAL CLASSIFICATION

In most libraries, books are arranged by a number system called the **Dewey** Decimal Classification. The numbers used are:

000–099 – **General works**
All encyclopaedias and catalogues.

100–199 – **Philosophy**
How we think and what we think about.

200–299 – **Religion**
Religious books such as *The Bible, The Koran,* etc.

300–399 – **Social sciences**
The way we live, law and government, education, etc.

400–499 – **Language**
Dictionaries, grammar, etc.

500-599 – **Pure science**
Physics and chemistry, geology and wildlife, astronomy, biology, etc.

600-699 – **Applied science**
Engineering and building, cookery, medicine, farming, etc.

700–799 – **The arts**
Music, sport, hobbies etc.

800-899 – **Literature**
Poetry, plays. Also all fiction, although this is kept on separate shelves arranged in alphabetical order according to the name of the author.

900–999 – **History, geography, biography**
People and places of all countries and times. For example, 968 is the number for a book about South African history.

You are reading a book right now! Do you ever wonder how books started? Ever since man first began to communicate, he has shared stories and information with friends and, through his drawings (and later by writing), he has kept these stories and other information alive.

The First Books

The first 'books' in Africa were probably cave paintings and engravings done thousands of years ago by the San. Today, we can still 'read' about their hunting expeditions and warfare in these beautiful paintings.

LH/IOA

Lending Libraries

When Europeans came to live in South Africa, some brought books along with them. In 1761, Joachim von Dessin provided 4 565 books to form the very first free library in the country. In 1829, the South African Library opened in Cape Town. People who could not afford an education could borrow library books, from which to learn. Today there are over 1 600 public libraries around the country, and you are allowed to borrow books (print and digital), CDs and DVDs. There are also special library services that supply books to people in hospitals, old-age homes, prison, and audio books for those with sight problems. Special 'book buses' visit remote villages and communities that do not have libraries.

BP/AL

Interior of a lending library

BP/AFS

The National Library in Cape Town

Newspapers and Publishers

Much of our knowledge comes from the written word. When a book is published, many copies are printed, so that people can share their ideas. The first South African printing presses published only newspapers and pamphlets, and today newspapers are still important sources of information for the public.

Thomas Pringle, one of the 1820 British Settlers, was the editor of *The South African Commercial Advertiser* (1824), the first independent newspaper in the Cape. Pringle was a keen supporter of 'freedom of the press' and believed that newspapers should be completely free of official control.

The Publishers Association of South Africa has about 120 members, twelve of whom are classed as 'large', seven as 'medium' and the remainder as 'small'. Books on a variety of topics are published in all eleven official languages. Publishers (both trade and educational) include Random House Struik, Penguin Books South Africa, Jonathan Ball Publishers, Juta, Pearson, Oxford University Press, Ravan Press, Nasou Via Afrika and Shuter and Shooter.

Authors

Well-known South African literary writers include two winners of the Nobel Prize for Literature, Nadine Gordimer (1991) and JM Coetzee (2003), as well as André P Brink, Damon Galgut, Es'kia Mphahlele, Mongane Wally Serote, Njabulo Ndebele, Can Themba, Breyten Breytenbach, Antjie Krog, Olive Schreiner, Alan Paton, Adam Small, Herman Charles Bosman, Sol Plaatje, Zakes Mda, Achmat Dangor, Rian Malan, Uys Krige, C Louis Leipoldt, Doris Lessing, Stephen Black and CJ Langenhoven (who was also responsible for one verse of the words of the national anthem.

Popular local novelists include Deon Meyer, Mike Nicol, John van der Ruit, Jassy Mackenzie, Daleen Mathee, Wilbur Smith, Ivan Vladislavic, Marlene van Niekerk, Marita van der Vyver, Diane Awerbuck, Imraan Coovadia, Henrietta Rose-Innes and Pamela Jooste.

South African Books for Children

One of the most famous books for young people in this country is *Jock of the Bushveld*, written by Sir Percy FitzPatrick and first published in 1907. The FitzPatrick Award is presented to the author of a South African children's book of outstanding quality, but has been awarded only a few times.

For many years, South African readers relied on books published in England or America. In the past, children's books by local authors, such as Freda Linde, Hester Heese, Elsabé Steenberg, and Rona Rupert, were only available in English or Afrikaans, but nowadays many children's books are being published locally, often in a number of languages. Popular children's authors include Marguerite Poland, Lesley Beake, Maretha Maartens, Dianne Case, Peter Slingsby, Cicely van Straten, Beverley Naidoo and many others. South Africa also has many fine book illustrators, including Niki Daly, Alida Bothma, Cora Coetzee and Joan Rankin.

Royalty and Copyright

Every time a book is published, an agreement called a **contract** is made between the author and the publisher. This means that the publisher promises to pay the author a **royalty**, which is usually a percentage of the shop price of each book. The more copies that are sold, the more money the author makes.

When a text is published, the author is protected by the law of **copyright**, which means that nobody may copy the work without the author's permission. If you see this sign, ©, the work is protected by copyright.

A reading lesson in progress

HOW A BOOK IS MADE

A book starts with an idea in the mind of the author. Once the author has written the story, the manuscript is sent to a publishing house where the publisher decides if it is good enough to be published. The editor makes corrections and the pages are planned and laid out by a book designer. By this stage, the costs of producing the book have also been worked out. Nowadays, publishing companies use computers to edit and design books and an electronic copy is sent to a printer. After being printed and bound with its cover, the finished book then goes to the bookseller so that you can buy it.

E-READERS AND TABLETS

E-Readers and tablets are hand-held electronic reading devices that can download digital versions of books (ebooks), newspapers and magazines from the Internet cheaply and easily. A typical e-Reader, for example, can store the equivalent of about 3 500 printed books.

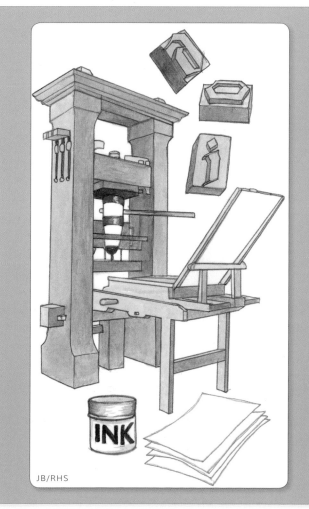

MOVEABLE TYPE

In earliest times, books were written by hand. This meant that making multiple copies of a book was a laborious process that could take many years. Later, books were copied using wood blocks. This process involved making a copy of every page by taking a sheet of wood and cutting away the background, leaving the print or illustration to be copied as raised text. The wood block was then inked and sheets of paper pressed onto it to make a copy.

Johannes Gutenberg of Mainz, Germany, usually described as the father of modern printing, invented the **moveable type printing press** in about 1450. Gutenberg's press used interchangeable metal type (made up of individual letters and punctuation) which could be easily produced using moulds rather than by carving them from wood. This invention changed the world. For the first time, books became available to the masses. The first book produced by Gutenberg was The Bible.

PLACES TO SEE

- ℹ The Centre for the Book in Cape Town
- ℹ The National Library in Cape Town and Tshwane (Pretoria)
- ℹ The Albany Museum in Grahamstown

Homes and Houses

PUNTJIE

About 70 **kapstyl** houses are clustered on a high outcrop overlooking the sea near Riversdale in the southern Cape. About 60 years ago, a Mr FJ de Jager built these little houses in the style used by trekboers. Kapstyl houses consist of little more than a roof structure placed directly on the ground.

A Khoikhoi hut

South Africa has many different peoples and their houses have changed considerably since the cave homes of the people from the Stone Age. Owing to technological advances, architects today design homes and offices that differ considerably from the simple clay houses of long ago.

Indigenous Houses

Because the San were nomadic and did not stay in one place for long, they never built permanent homes but slept in caves or rough shelters made from branches. The Khoikhoi were also wanderers, so their huts were light enough to be rolled up and carried. Young trees (saplings) were bent inwards to form a beehive-shaped frame that was covered with overlapping grass mats. These **matjieshuise** may still be seen in Namaqualand. Some Nguni people lived in circular stone huts probably thatched with reeds. Traditional Zulu and Swazi houses were dome-shaped frameworks of saplings thatched with grass. Many people live in **rondavels**, which are round huts of clay or brick and have cone-shaped, thatched roofs.

A circular rondavel with a traditional thatched roof

PINELANDS – THE FIRST GARDEN CITY

Pinelands in Cape Town was planned so that there are many parks and every house has a garden. The idea originated in Europe after the First World War. Parliamentarian Richard Stuttaford donated £10 000 for a similar scheme in Cape Town.

Early Cape Houses

Jan van Riebeeck's Fort of Good Hope was made of clay and stone. The Dutch colonists first lived in small wooden shelters inside the fort, but soon built their own houses. Most had three rooms and walls of clay or rubble bound by mortar made from seashells. The roofs were thatched with reeds.

The Gable Appears

The earliest type of gable was known as a **dormer** or leg-o-mutton gable and a small window provided light for the loft. The gable also stopped rainwater flowing from the roof onto the stoep. If a fire broke out, the gable would prevent burning thatch from falling onto people standing below.

In later years, gables became taller and had moulded edges. These were **holbol** gables. Stars, animals, fruit and flowers were sculptured onto the face of the gable. These mouldings, probably the handiwork of Eastern slaves, were later replaced with triangular pediments with plaster urns on either side. This was the **neoclassical** style.

Holbol gable   *Neo-classical gable*

The Alphabet Plans

As families grew, a kitchen was added at right angles to one end of the house and an extra room at the other. Most townhouses took on this **U**-shape. In the country, a single wing was sometimes added to the centre of the back of a house, so that it looked like the letter **T**. Sometimes, farmers added a third section across the end of the T so that the house looked like an **H**.

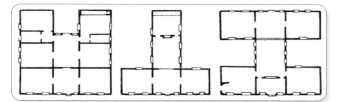

U-shape, T-shape and H-shape floor plans

Fire! Fire!

Fires spread easily in thatch-roofed homes so, by the end of the 18th century, people in Cape Town built flat-roofed, often double-storeyed, houses. The **Cape Dutch** style was inspired by styles seen in Holland, Germany and Indonesia and was used until about the middle of the 19th century.

Boer Houses

Most trekboers lived in simple thatched houses. Saplings were set in two parallel rows and bent over so that their tops touched. The walls were filled in with stiff reeds, or *harde biesies*, which may be why the house was called a **hartbeeshuisie**. The **kapstylhuisie** was really only a thatched roof on the hartbeeshuis ground, rather like an 'A-frame' house.

Hartbeeshuis frame

Hartbeeshuis

The Voortrekkers used whatever materials they could find to build their first homes. Most houses were made of stone and had a single room with an open fireplace at one end. The windows were holes in the walls.

Sir Herbert Baker

HOMES OF THE PAST

Many historical homes are now museums and monuments. **Koopmans de Wet House** in Cape Town's Strand Street is typical of an early Cape-Dutch city house.

Melrose House in Pretoria is an example of late Victorian architecture. It is here that the Peace of Vereeniging, ending the Anglo-Boer War, was signed.

Koopmans-de Wet House

Brick-faced **Bertram House** in Cape Town is an excellent example of late Cape Georgian architecture. It is now a museum.

Bletterman-huis, now part of the Stellen-bosch Museum complex, and wine farm **Meerlust**, both have *holbol* gables. One of the Cape's most famous gabled houses is Governor Wilhem Adriaen van der Stel's **Vergelegen**, near Somerset West.

Bertram House

Melrose House

The British Influence

When the British took over the Cape, King George III was reigning and English architecture was known as **Georgian**. When the double-storeyed style was copied by Cape settlers, it became **Cape Georgian**.

English **Regency** architecture (1811–1820) is similar to Georgian, but rather more elaborate. It included wrought- and cast-iron balconies, railings and fanlights with carved wooden frames. Wrought iron was also popular during the reign of Queen Victoria (1837–1901), when many roofs were of corrugated iron.

The Work of Sir Herbert Baker

Architect Sir Herbert Baker (1862–1946) undertook the remodelling of Groote Schuur, which had been bought by Cecil John Rhodes, then prime minister of the Cape. In restoring Groote Schuur, Baker used local stone, wood, thatch and tiles and his craftsmanship was of the highest standard. Rhodes Memorial, the Union Buildings in Pretoria and many Anglican churches are other examples of his work.

Buildings Between the Wars

In the late 1920s and 1930s, the **Art Deco** style became popular. Examples are the Voortrekker Monument in Tshwane (Pretoria) and the former Old Mutual Building in Darling Street, Cape Town. Art Deco, introduced in Paris in 1925, featured sharp angles, block-shaped patterns, mosaic floors of enamel tiles and intricate chrome and bronze decorations.

South Africa's Cities Today

Some of Pretoria's finest buildings were designed by Norman Eaton (1902–1966), whose simple designs suited the South African environment. He used local materials and insisted on fine craftsmanship. The 222-metre high Carlton Centre in Johannesburg, built in 1973, is the tallest building in the country, with 57 floors, including seven underground. Nowadays, South African architects and builders make use of all the modern technology at their disposal.

The Housing Shortage

South Africa has a serious shortage of housing. In 2011, it was estimated that some 12 million people were without adequate housing. Despite concerted attempts to provide basic houses, the backlog of housing units stands at between two and three million.

Many people who arrive in the urban areas build homes from whatever materials they can find. Large informal settlements can be seen on the outskirts of most towns. Most of these settlements have very poor sanitary facilities, and fire is a constant danger. Providing housing and upgrading informal settlements with water and sanitation is a government priority.

An informal settlement

PIETERMARITZBURG – THE VICTORIAN CITY

Red brick and ornate Victorian design can be seen in many of this city's public buildings. Maritzburg College was designed by architect Philip Dudgeon, who also designed the old Standard Bank as well as Durban's old Town Hall, now the Post Office.

The Standard Bank Building in Cape Town's Adderley Street, is a fine example of Victorian architecture

CHIMNEY TAX

Chimney sparks, fanned by a strong south-east wind, often destroyed rows of thatch-roofed houses in old Cape Town. To fund a fire fighting service, house owners had to pay a tax of two shillings per chimney in their house.

PLACES TO SEE

Look out for gables in the Western Cape. Note the different styles in the Eastern Cape, KwaZulu-Natal and Limpopo Province

Sport and Recreation

SURF'S UP!
Surfing started in South Africa after World War I. The pioneer surfers used very long boards made from wood that were heavy and not very manoeuvrable. Since then, boards have got smaller and lighter and surfing styles have evolved. South Africa has produced many world-class surfers such as **Shaun Thomson**. **Jordy Smith**, one of the current stars on the world surfing circuit, grew up in Durban. **Jeffreys Bay**, near Port Elizabeth, one of the top surf spots in the world, hosts a Billabong Pro event each year.

DRUGS IN SPORT
Some competitors take performance enhancing drugs that help them to develop their strength and stamina. Competitors who are found to have been taking drugs are usually disqualified. The Department of Sport and Recreation, in conjunction with the National Olympic Committee of South Africa (NOCSA) has established a drug testing facility at the University of the Free State. With accreditation from the International Olympic Committee (IOC), South Africa has the first accredited laboratory on the African continent for the testing of human tissue for the use of forbidden substances by athletes.

South Africa's sunny climate is ideal for sport and outdoor activities. The National Olympic Committee (NOCSA) and South African Sports Confederation and Olympic Committee (SASCOC) represent aspects of South African sport and recreation.

Athletics
South Africa has a long tradition of sporting excellence. Olympic athletes include **Esther Brand** (Gold medal, high jump, Helsinki 1952), **Josia Thugwane**, (Gold, men's marathon, Atlanta 1996), **Caster Semenya** (Silver, 800 metres, London 2012). Other notable athletes are **Bruce Fordyce** and **Frith van der Merwe** (ultramarathon), **Hestrie Cloete** (high jump), **Elana Meyer** (10 000 m) and **Hezekiel Sepeng** (800 metres).

THE COMRADES MARATHON
This world-famous ultramarathon (±89km) is run annually between Durban and Pietermaritzburg. The record for the fastest time is held by Russia's Leonid Shvetsov, who completed the course in a time of 5:20:49 in 2007. The fastest woman, Frith van der Merwe, achieved a time of 5:54:43 in 1989. Bruce Fordyce won the race a record nine times.

Cricket
After beating Australia in 1970, South Africa was regarded as the world's cricket champions, but the sports boycott soon kept the team out of international competitions. This isolation ended in 1991 when we played a one-day game against India at Calcutta. In 1994 our cricket team scored a resounding victory over England at Lords, and in the same year we won the first competition for the Mandela Trophy, beating Pakistan in the final match. Recent cricketing greats include Shaun Pollock, Jonty Rhodes, Alan Donald, Makhaya Ntini, Jacques Kallis, Mark Boucher, Gary Kirsten, Dave Richardson and Lance Klusener. In 2003, against England at Edgbaston, Graeme Smith set a new South African record in only his 15th test innings with a score of 277. Smith became South Africa's youngest-ever captain at the age of 22. In 2012 South Africa was ranked the Number 1 team in the world for Test Cricket and Hashim Amla the Number 1 One Day International (ODI) batsman in the world. Also in 2012, Dave Richardson was appointed the president of the International Cricket Council (ICC).

Soccer
No game in South Africa attracts more players and spectators than soccer, also known as Association Football. The game was first played in the country in the late 19th century and professional soccer was introduced in 1959. After years of isolation, South Africa was readmitted to international soccer in 1992. In 1996 the national team, Bafana Bafana, won the Africa Cup of Nations. Locally, teams compete for the South African National Championship and the PSL, hotly contested by popular sides such as Orlando Pirates, Kaizer Chiefs, Mamelodi Sundowns and Supersport United. Great names in soccer include Lucas Radebe, Jomo Sono, Mark Fish, Doc Khumalo and Benni McCarthy. In 1999 a players' union was formed. In 2010 South Africa hosted a highly successful FIFA World Cup.

Bafana Bafana

Swimming
South Africa has produced some outstanding Olympic swimmers. Joan Harrison won gold at the 1952 Helsinki Olympics, Penny Heyns won two gold medals at the 1996 Atlanta Games. The 4 x 100 m freestyle relay team (Ferns, Neethling, Schoeman and Townsend) won gold at the 2004 Athens Olympics. At the 2012 London Olympics, Chad le Clos (200m butterfly) and Cameron van der Burgh (100m breaststroke) won gold medals.

Chad le Clos, Olympic and Commonwealth Games champion

Tennis

The South African Lawn Tennis Association was established in 1903, but the first national colours for tennis were awarded only in 1908. Since the 1970s, many foreign players have participated in the SA Open Championships. Although no South African has won a singles title at Wimbledon, some have won doubles titles, and Kevin Curren reached the finals in 1985. South African women won gold at the All-Africa Games in 1999. In 2000 Amanda Coetzer and Wayne Ferreira won the Hopman Cup in Perth, Australia. Many South African players follow the international Grand Slam circuit.

Hockey

Hockey was first played in South Africa by British troops at Newlands in 1899. The game is now very popular among men, women and children. In fact, South Africa has one of the highest percentages of women hockey players in the world. The men's and women's hockey teams won gold at the All-Africa Games in 1999, the year in which the women's team reached the finals of the Telstra Challenge in Australia. In 2012, both the South African men's team and the South African women's team were ranked 12th in the world.

SA women's hockey team vs India at London Olympics 2012

Sports Development

Sport in South Africa gives full-time employment to 35 000 people, part-time work to 6 000 and also involves 8 000 volunteers. It is government policy that equal sporting facilities are available to all who want to use them and our national teams are expected to be representative of the population as a whole. The South African Sports Confederation and Olympic Committee (SASCOC) was formed in 2004. Its main functions are to promote and develop high performance sport, and act as the controlling body for the preparation and delivery of Team South Africa at multi-sport international events such as the Olympics, Commonwealth Games, World Games and All-Africa Games.

Road Cycling

The Cape Argus/Pick 'n Pay Cycle Tour in Cape Town, the largest timed cycle event in the world, attracts 40 000

entrants, and the Momentum 94.7 Cycle Challenge in Johannesburg attracts about 30 000 entrants. Because of their popularity, many cycling road races attract valuable sponsorships, and South African events, particularly the long-distance events, are well known overseas. Mountain biking, or cycling over fairly rough paths, is a popular family pastime. Competitive road cycling and track racing are challenging sports, and competition in big races can be fierce.

OUR MAGNIFICENT PARALYMPIANS

The Paralympic Games date from 1948 when Sir Ludwig Guttmann organized competitions for World War II veterans with spinal injuries at Stoke Mandeville, England. The first official Paralympic Games, in Rome in 1960, attracted 400 athletes from 23 countries. A total of 4 200 athletes from 166 countries competed at London 2012. At Beijing in 2008, South Africa was sixth on the medal table with 30 medals, including 21 gold. In 2012, South Africa won 29 medals, including eight gold. Swimmer **Natalie du Toit**, the first amputee to qualify for and compete in the 'normal' Olympic Games, won five gold medals in Beijing and three in London. Sprint runner **Oscar Pistorius**, the 'Blade Runner', a double amputee, won three gold medals in Beijing and two in London; he also competes in able-bodied athletics and took part in the 4 x 400 m relay in London.

Natalie du Toit

Rugby

Paul Roos led the first national team, **De Springbokken**, on their first international tour to Britain in 1906. Dawie de Villiers, Naas Botha, Danie Craven, Morné du Plessis, Francois Pienaar and John Smit are among our most memorable Springbok captains. At a local level, provincial teams compete for trophies in the ABSA Currie Cup, and against teams from Australia and New Zealand in the Vodacom Super 15 Series. The South African Rugby Football Union (SARFU) was established in 1992 and paved the way for South Africa's readmission to the international arena after eight years of isolation. Since 1992, South Africa has won the Rugby World Cup twice – in 1995 and 2007.

THE CAPE EPIC MOUNTAIN BIKE RACE
The Cape Epic, one of the biggest and most prestigious mountain bike races in the world, takes place every year around March/April. All entrants for this eight-day race, over some of the most beautiful and challenging terrain in Africa, must compete as part of a two-rider team.

AMATEUR OR PROFESSIONAL?
What is the difference between being an amateur or professional sportsman? 'Amateur', in this sense, means that a person plays or participates for pleasure only and is not paid, while a 'professional' is paid for playing sport. Most sporting bodies have codes that decide a player's amateur or professional status.

PLACES TO SEE →

The Comrades Marathon Museum in Pietermaritzburg

Towns and Cities

CITY OR TOWN?

English and Irish cathedral towns are traditionally called cities. After the British took control in southern Africa, towns in which Anglican cathedrals were established were known as cities. These included Cape Town, Pietermaritzburg and Grahamstown. Other large towns were later granted city status by the government.

THE TOWN THAT MOVED AND MOVED

The Tlhaping people lived in a flourishing settlement near the Moshaweng River. It was called **Lattakoo**. In 1802, the town was moved closer to the Kuruman River. When Chief Molehabangwe died in 1806, his son, Mothibi, moved the settlement back to the Moshaweng River again. In 1817, missionaries persuaded Mothibi to move his town to the Kuruman River once more. Today the town is known as Kuruman.

The first people to live in what is now South Africa were the San and the Khoikhoi. Later, the Nguni-speaking people arrived and built the first permanent settlements. Thereafter, the Dutch established a small outpost at the Cape. The Dutch and, later, British settlers introduced their own styles of building and forms of government. South Africa's cities and towns grew from these varied and humble beginnings.

Villages and Towns

Many centuries ago, Nguni-speaking people built the first villages, long before the Europeans arrived and settled. Coastal towns developed around safe harbours, while inland towns sprang up near mines and along roads and railway lines. The most highly concentrated industrial area in South Africa is the Pretoria-Witwatersrand-Vereeniging complex that makes up the province of Gauteng. Other areas of dense urban settlement are Cape Town, the Port Elizabeth/Uitenhage area and the Durban/Pinetown area.

Urbanization and Growth

Some towns and villages develop into cities. People move to cities to find both employment in the many industries, as well as good schools for their children. This movement is called urbanization. People living in urban areas need houses, hospitals, schools and churches. Services such as roads, electricity, water and sewerage are also required.

The Urban 'Explosion'

The rapid development and growth of our towns began after the discovery of gold and diamonds, when people flocked to the mines in search of work. South African towns and cities are growing so quickly that, in most cases, the local authorities are unable to provide proper services for all the people arriving to live in their areas. This is a feature of almost all countries in which an industrial economy develops from an rural, agriculture-based economy. However, in South Africa it is more obvious because it has come about so suddenly.

Under the system of apartheid, the government controlled the movement of black people through the **'influx control'** system. This was abolished in 1986 so that anyone who wants to live or work in a town is free to do so. New arrivals can't always be provided for and so many people build shacks on the edge of towns: these are called 'informal settlements'.

Money Matters

Town and city administrations are responsible for providing services for their citizens. The money for providing these services comes from rates and taxes paid to the local authority by all those who own property or who use the services. Money paid for traffic fines, and entrance to swimming pools and sports grounds also contributes to the local authority's funds.

Why They Began

Most of South Africa's cities and towns have grown as the result of industrialization. South Africans of all colours came to the towns to find jobs and to build homes. Black workers, however, were paid very little and so could not afford to live in the white areas. Many black workers built houses outside the white towns, in 'townships'. The parallel and unequal growth of town and township can be seen all over South Africa.

Soweto (**SO**uth **WE**stern **TO**wnships) consists of 26 black 'townships' that developed near Johannesburg. In 1984 it was the first black residential area to be classified as a city, and today houses over four million people.

Cape Town, the 'Mother City', was established in 1652 as a refreshment station on Table Bay, which was a convenient place for ships to anchor. Further inland, **Stellenbosch** was founded in 1679 as an 'agricultural colony', with crops watered from the Eerste River.

Durban (Port Natal) started in 1824 as a trading post and later became an important harbour. Today, it is Africa's busiest port and the largest container terminal in the Southern Hemisphere.

Port Elizabeth was named by the Acting Governor, Sir Rufane Donkin, after his wife, Elizabeth. During the Wars of Dispossession, British troops landed at the Buffalo River mouth, and East London, South Africa's only river-harbour, was established in 1850.

Grahamstown, **Queenstown** and **King William's Town** are Eastern Cape towns that were established as fortified centres in the 19th century.

Important inland towns were often set up on trade routes, where water and wood could be found. **Bloemfontein** became the capital of the Orange River Sovereignty in 1848. **Pietermaritzburg** was founded as the capital of the Voortrekker Republic of Natalia. **Pretoria**, the capital of the Zuid-Afrikaansche Republiek, has been the administrative capital of South Africa since 1910.

Where fortunes may be made, towns will be established. **Kimberley** began after the discovery of diamonds in 1871. A tent town sprang up when gold was discovered on the Witwatersrand in 1886. This became **Johannesburg**, and the Witwatersrand has since produced nearly half of the world's gold.

NAME CHANGES

The South African Geographical Names Council is responsible for standardizing the names of towns, cities and geographical areas. A number of the larger metro councils have adopted new names for the relevant local authority but the names of the cities remain for everyday use. Examples of these are Mangaung (Bloemfontein), Nelson Mandela Bay (Port Elizabeth) and Tshwane (Pretoria). Some of the better-known towns that have undergone name changes include Pietersburg (Polokwane), Warmbaths (Bela-Bela), Louis Trichardt (Makhado), Umtata (Mthatha), Stanger (KwaDukuza) and Piet Retief (eMkhondo). By 2012, some 57 000 name changes were under consideration, although these include rivers, mountains and street names as well.

Map of South Africa showing provinces: ZIMBABWE, BOTSWANA, NAMIBIA, LIMPOPO (Polokwane), MPUMALANGA (Mbombela), GAUTENG (Pretoria, Johannesburg), SWAZILAND, NORTH WEST, FREE STATE (Bloemfontein), KWAZULU-NATAL (Pietermaritzburg, Durban), LESOTHO, NORTHERN CAPE (Kimberley), WESTERN CAPE (Stellenbosch, Cape Town), EASTERN CAPE (Grahamstown, Port Elizabeth)

PLACES TO SEE

Mini Town on Durban's beachfront

Rescue Services and Road Safety

SCHOLAR PATROLS

Scholar patrols are organized by traffic departments. Each school has four patrol members for every crossing, and a captain who organizes the patrols and makes sure his teams have the necessary warning and stop-sign boards, whistles and uniforms. Patrols are trained by the traffic officials before they go on duty.

Every year many people are hurt or killed in senseless accidents. But the greatest number of casualties actually results from road accidents: each year there are approximately 500 000 road accidents! Fortunately, the network of rescue services is fast and efficient.

Emergency!

In an emergency, telephone 082 911 or 10177 (landline) or the South African Police Service's (SAPS) flying squad at 10111. The flying squad cruises city streets day and night, and help should arrive within minutes. The police will also contact the necessary rescue service. Ambulances arrive quickly and a doctor is always on duty at the hospital. Rescue teams have special equipment, such as the 'jaws of life' to remove victims from car wrecks. There are also privately run emergency and medical services in most large centres.

Fire Services

Almost every town has a fire brigade with full-time firemen on duty, but smaller towns depend on volunteers. Apart from extinguishing household fires, industrial fires and forest fires, the fire brigade also rescues animals and people from rooftops or tall trees for which a long ladder is needed.

Fire engines are equipped with long ladders and special hoses to help extinguish fires

Search and Rescue

The South African Search and Rescue Organisation (SASAR) rescues survivors of aircraft mishaps and accidents at sea. SASAR also co-ordinates search and rescue operations. In 2000 it was announced that a long-range Coast Guard was to be established. Major rescues took place in the floods of 2000 and in the sinking of the Greek cruise liner Oceanos (1993). In both incidents the helicopter showed itself to be a most versatile rescue vehicle.

A National Disaster Management Centre has been established to prevent human, economic and property losses by avoiding environmental degradation.

The NSRI

The National Sea Rescue Institute of South Africa (NSRI) was founded in 1967. It provides a 24-hour rescue service for accidents at sea up to 50 nautical miles (92.5 km) from the coast. NSRI crewmen are all volunteers who are excellent swimmers.

The NSRI has 32 coastal and three inland stations, including one on the Vaal Dam. It has a fleet of 92 rescue craft, 27 vehicles and access to a range of helicopters. The NSRI is a non-profit organization that depends upon donations for its survival.

NSRI rescuers rush to the aid of a vessel in distress

THE SOUTH AFRICAN RED CROSS

The Red Cross Society, the world's most famous rescue service, was brought to South Africa in 1896. Apart from social services, such as health and child care, education, housing, home nursing and first aid, the Red Cross also provides emergency and rescue services.

Disaster units in Johannesburg and Port Elizabeth are able to provide immediate aid in a crisis, such as a flood or earthquake, while two ambulances of the **air mercy services** in Cape Town can transport seriously ill people or accident victims. A doctor or nurse always accompanies the patient and the aircraft is fitted with the most up-to-date equipment. When municipal or provincial services are unable to provide transport, the Red Cross sends one of its **ambulances**. It also contributes to **hunger relief** when there is a shortage of food following disasters such as a drought or flood.

SSPL/GI

Surf Lifesavers Clubs

Life-saving training

A red and yellow striped flag flying at a beach that means volunteer surf lifesavers are on patrol. They are on duty at most of our beaches and some dams over holidays and at weekends.

Lifesavers are trained in water safety rescue methods such as 'the kiss of life' (artificial respiration) to people saved from drowning. Lifesavers are also trained to help victims of shark attacks. If someone is in trouble in the sea and there are no lifesavers on the beach, call the police and a doctor immediately.

The Mountain Club of South Africa

Volunteer rescue teams of the Mountain Club are always on stand-by and each team consists of expert climbers and often a doctor. Sometimes a helicopter is necessary to help rescue a climber who cannot be reached in any other way.

Mining Accidents

The mobile rescue equipment of the Chamber of Mines' Rescue Drilling Unit in eMalahleni (Witbank) can reach the nearest coal mine in less than half an hour. They are called out to drill large holes to reach men trapped underground.

One machine drills a narrow hole to locate trapped men and provide them with air and food. The other powerful machine drills a hole big enough to rescue the men. The unit is called out on practice runs to keep members alert and prepared. During a call-out, a team raced to the Cornelia Colliery, 250 kilometres away, and drilled a hole 47-metres deep – all in only 19 hours!

Look, Think and Stay Alive!

Every year about 10 000 people are killed and 150 000 are injured in about 500 000 accidents on South Africa's roads. The cost of these accidents is about R11 billion every year. Some 70 per cent of those killed or injured are pedestrians. Alcohol is a contributory factor in many accidents. The rate of accidents is fairly constant throughout the year.

To help reduce these figures, motorists and their passengers must, by law, wear safety belts. Motorcyclists (and their passengers) must wear crash helmets and keep their lights on even during daylight. Local authorities and the Road Traffic Safety Board organize projects to teach children about road safety. The government's Arrive Alive campaign was introduced in 1997, to reduce fatal road accidents.

ARRIVE ALIVE
www.arrivealive.co.za

RULES OF THE ROAD

Pedestrians should always
- Look right, left and right again to make sure no cars are approaching before crossing a road.
- Cross only at traffic lights or pedestrian crossings.
- Wait for the 'green man' to appear.
- Never play on or near the road, especially with balls, skateboards or scooters.
- Wear bright raincoats in wet weather and luminous belts or schoolbags at night.
- Make sure they are facing oncoming traffic when walking along a road with no pavement.

Cyclists should always
- Hold the handlebars with both hands.
- Keep left and ride in single file.
- Keep a safe distance when passing a parked car – a door might suddenly open.
- Avoid carrying a passenger.
- Give clear hand-signals.
- If you cross at the traffic lights, push your bike, don't ride it.
- Before you change lanes, look over your shoulder to see if cars are approaching.
- Stop at stop streets.
- Use a light and reflectors at night.

A rule for everyone:

KNOW YOUR ROAD SIGNS!

Our Busy Roads

Many existing road patterns in our towns were laid out in the days of carts and wagons that were pulled by horses or oxen. Not only was the pace of this traffic much slower than it is today, but there were also far fewer vehicles. Now, more than 17 million passengers use minibus taxis to commute between home and workplace every day. In addition, heavy transport and private cars add to the crush.

Peak-hour traffic

MIRACLE MACHINE

The first bicycle, called a **hobby-horse**, was designed in France in 1791. It was a small wooden horse fitted with two wheels. It had no pedals and the user had to move it forward by pushing with his left and right foot in turn. The rider could only move in one direction and could not turn.

GI/DB

EARTHQUAKE!

On 29 September 1969, a huge earthquake, measuring 6.4 on the Richter Scale, rocked a large area of the Western Cape, and was followed by two severe aftershocks. Eleven people were killed and many injured, veld fires raged, power and telecommunication services were disrupted and there was widespread panic in the area.

PLACES TO SEE

ℹ Ask your teachers to arrange a visit to your local traffic department and fire station

Caring for Others

LC/RHS

WHAT IS AIDS?

The body is protected by an immune system made up of white blood cells, which fight disease (1). The human immuno-deficiency virus (HIV) kills most of the white blood cells (2). The body cannot protect itself against disease (3). This results in the Acquired Immune Deficiency Syndrome (**AIDS**). The disease is spread almost entirely by sexual contact. There is no known cure and attempts to develop a vaccine have not been fully successful. At the end of 2009 it was estimated that about 5.6 million South Africans were living with HIV and AIDS and that just under 1 000 AIDS deaths occurred every day. The incidence of the disease among miners and transport workers, who are separated from their wives and families for long periods, is particularly high. People who have had sexual contact with an AIDS-infected person may test positive for the virus, but may develop the full disease only many years later. South Africa is thought to have the sixth highest incidence of AIDS in the world, with 16.9% of the population thought to be HIV-positive in 2008. Women face a greater risk of HIV infection than men. On average, about three women are infected with the virus for every two men infected. The different infection rates are greatest in the 15–24 age group, where about three women become infected for every one man infected.

Because many people lack access to clean water and sanitation, and have had little health education, great numbers suffer from diseases that are usually quite easy to prevent. Government health policy provides basic health care as a basic right, and concentrates on primary health care and preventive medicine rather than expensive treatment.

Primary Health Care

About 40% of South Africans are poor, and most of them live in rural areas. Public primary health care (PHC) facilities such as clinics and community health centres offer certain free services to patients who are not members of a medical aid scheme. The idea is to keep patients away from the large hospitals, which are used for the most serious cases only. PHC workers provide a service that includes immunization, maternity care, screening tests, health promotion and counselling, family planning, emergency and accident services. At most PHC clinics, patients are treated by nurses, although some of the clinics also have doctors.

Hospitals and Hospices

The National Department of Health ensures that health facilities are properly used. Provincial health authorities also provide health services and run public hospitals. Some sick people can be treated at outpatients' departments or at clinics.

Hospices care for people who are terminally ill. Specially trained staff provides advice and comfort.

A private hospital is run as a business, but most offer a wide and excellent range of services.

SU

NURSING IN SOUTH AFRICA

Nurses spend much of their time caring for others at hospitals or even at the patients' own homes. Some clinics, factories and schools may also have nurses. Some assist doctors in their consulting rooms, while others train student nurses.

Henrietta Stockdale, an Anglican nun, established the first nurses' training centre, in Kimberley in 1877. Nurses train at hospitals, nursing colleges or universities. **Cecilia Makiwane** became the first black South African woman to register as a trained nurse, in 1908.

For the Children

When children are neglected, abused or cannot be cared for by their own families, workers from the Department of Social Welfare arrange for babies to be adopted or temporarily placed with foster parents.

LT/IOA

The Department also controls and subsidizes homes for older children. The government pays for their upkeep, and welfare workers make sure that the best care is provided.

Care of the Elderly

Caring for old people is usually the responsibility of private welfare organizations, but most are subsidized by the government. It is important to care for elderly people who live alone, and to make sure that they do not feel lonely. Social workers visit them, arrange cooked meals, and organize helpers to assist with household tasks. Some welfare organizations take elderly people shopping or on outings.

Welfare organizations also run homes where people live together and have proper medical attention. Societies and clubs provide entertainment and activities such as exercise classes and bridge.

IS/AR

The Handicapped

Although the government subsidizes the care of the mentally and physically handicapped, most of these people are supported by voluntary organizations.

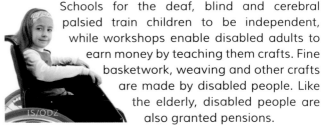

Schools for the deaf, blind and cerebral palsied train children to be independent, while workshops enable disabled adults to earn money by teaching them crafts. Fine basketwork, weaving and other crafts are made by disabled people. Like the elderly, disabled people are also granted pensions.

IS/ODZ

BP/AL

DISEASES

The most important and deadly disease in Africa is **HIV/AIDS**. In South Africa in 2009, the national average of pregnant women attending ante-natal clinics who were HIV-positive was 29.4% with the province of KwaZulu-Natal having the highest prevalence at 39.5% followed by Mpumalanga with 34.7%. It is estimated that between five and seven million South Africans have already died from AIDS. **Cholera**, which spread across southern Africa from Zimbabwe in 2008/9, is caused by bacteria found in dirty water. It occurs in overcrowded areas where sanitation is poor.

Malnutrition often leads to gastro-enteritis, which is a common cause of death among children in South Africa.

Malaria is caused by the bite of the *Anopheles* mosquito and symptoms include chills, fever and sweating. Attacks may recur from time to time.

Measles is caused by a virus and is very common among children. Symptoms include high temperatures, sore eyes and a rash, and the disease could lead to complications.

Meningitis is a serious disease in which the membranes covering the brain and spinal cord become inflamed, causing headaches and nausea. The patient may die if not treated immediately.

People bitten by infected animals may get **rabies**, so pets should be immunized.

Tetanus, or lockjaw, causes muscular spasms that clamp the jaws together. Tetanus bacteria are often found in the soil and enter the body through cuts and scratches.

Tuberculosis (TB) is highly infectious and usually affects the lungs. Symptoms are tiredness, weight-loss and a dry cough. Although TB can be cured, it is one of South Africa's most serious diseases. Cases increase by about 20% every year. Many TB cases are linked to AIDS.

Typhoid usually occurs near unhygienic sewerage systems. This bacterial infection of the tummy causes stomach cramps, a high temperature and diarrhoea. Typhoid is a serious problem, mainly because about three per cent of sufferers who recover remain carriers and pass it on to others.

Viral hepatitis, or jaundice, attacks the liver, and the skin and body fluids turn yellow.

Diseases such as **diphtheria**, **smallpox** and **poliomyelitis** (polio) were once common, but can be prevented by immunization.

Like malaria, **bilharzia** is a parasitic disease (caused by a tiny water worm). It attacks the liver, kidneys and bladder. **Congo fever** is also a parasitic disease, caused by a tick bite, and it causes high fever with bleeding under the skin. Other serious infectious diseases such as diphtheria, smallpox and poliomyelitis were once common, but have been controlled by immunization.

The Health Team

Specially trained health workers are vital to keeping up a high standard of national health. Although accurate figures are difficult to come by, there are currently about 25 000 doctors registered with the Health Professionals Council of South Africa (HPCSA). Foreign doctors have been brought in to help overcome the shortage. When new doctors qualify, they have to do a year of paid service at a state hospital. Many doctors specialize in particular diseases or disciplines after qualification, and may become physicians, cardiologists, gynaecologists or dermatologists among others.

There are about 4000 dentists and 1000 oral hygienists. Dentists train at hospitals connected to some of the larger universities.

Pharmacists make up and dispense medicines, and are trained at a university. There were 10 830 pharmacists in 2004, of whom 16% were employed in state or provincial hospitals.

Nurses and nursing auxiliaries make up the largest body of health workers. In 2009 there were only 115 372 working nurses, less than half the number required. Basic training as a nurse and midwife takes four years, and is offered at nursing colleges and at some universities. A midwife is a nurse who specializes in childbirth. A nursing auxiliary trains for one year.

The many other members of the health team include optometrists, who measure people's vision and fit them with spectacles or contact lenses; dieticians, who prescribe the best diet for various conditions; physiotherapists, who control physical mobility; radiographers, who operate X-ray and other diagnostic machinery.

PB/BI/GTY/GI

Health and hospitals

The first recorded hospital was a tent on the shores of Table Bay in 1652. Sailors who were treated here suffered from scurvy, caused by a lack of fresh vegetables while at sea. Cape Town's New Somerset Hospital is really very old. It was built in 1858 and is still in use. It was also the first teaching hospital for medical students, and houses the Cape Medical Museum. Chris Hani-Baragwanath, near Johannesburg, serves Soweto and is the largest hospital in Africa.

HAVE A HEART

Dr Chris Barnard performed the world's first heart transplant in South Africa. On 3 December 1967 the heart of an accident victim was transplanted into Louis Washkansky at Groote Schuur Hospital in Cape Town. In April 1969 Dorothy Fisher became the first woman to receive a new heart. She died 20 years later.

MEDICAL AID SCHEMES

There are about 150 medical aid schemes in South Africa, which, in total, provide private medical cover for about seven million people – about 14.5%, of the population. Many people cannot afford to pay for private medical cover and rely on state hospitals and clinics for their health care.

COPING WITH TB

It is estimated that about 1.7 million people died of tuberculosis (TB) worldwide in 2009 and South Africa is one of the world's worst TB areas. The South African National Tuberculosis Association (**SANTA**) was founded in 1947 to teach people how to avoid TB and how to recognize its early symptoms. It runs hospitalization centres that treat people with TB, and also helps the dependents of TB sufferers.

PLACES TO SEE

ℹ The Adler Museum of the History of Medicine, Johannesburg

The Star-spangled Sky

THE SOUTHERN CROSS
The first astronomer to examine the Southern Cross from South Africa was Guy Tachard in 1685. This famous constellation appears on the flags of both Australia and New Zealand. It is easy to see from South Africa on a clear night, but is not visible from Europe and most of North America.

New Zealand

Australia

Astronomy is the study of the heavens. Thousands of years ago, man grouped the stars in constellations and named the planets after gods and goddesses. Southern Africa's indigenous people believed that the Earth was carried on the back of a giant turtle swimming around the sun in the huge blue sea, and an ancient San cave engraving shows the five brightest planets circling the sun.

Early South African Sky-watchers
Portuguese navigators of the 15th century guided their ships by the stars, but the first scientific observations of the southern sky were made only in 1685 by a French priest, Father Guy Tachard. Twenty years later, astronomer Peter Kolb set up an observatory at the Castle. In 1751, the French mathematician, Abbé Nicolas de la Caille, plotted the shape of the southern hemisphere, and recorded more than 10 000 new stars, grading them according to brightness.

In 1869, David Gill took the first clear photographs of the moon. Ten years later, he measured the brightness and positions of nearly 500 000 stars, using a photographic atlas that he compiled of the southern sky.

Many amateur astronomers have contributed to our knowledge of the southern sky. Two new comets were named after Jack Bennett of Pretoria. In fact, one became so brilliant that, in 1970, it could be seen without the aid of a telescope.

South African Observatories
The SA Astronomical Observatory (SAAO) and the Hartebeesthoek Radio Astronomy Observatory are the major observatories in South Africa. SAAO was established in 1972 when the facilities of the Royal Observatory, Cape of Good Hope, and the Republic Observatory were combined. SAAO's headquarters are in Cape Town, but its four large reflecting telescopes are at Sutherland. HartRAO is the only major radio observatory in Africa. The telescope is a giant radio receiver with a moveable 'antenna'.

South Africa and Australia are to share responsibility for hosting the Square Kilometre Array (**SKA**) project, which will comprize about 3 000 linked radio telescopes that will give astronomers the best view of the uniververse ever. The MeerKAT (Karoo Array Telescope), the precursor to the SKA, is under construction in the Northern Cape.

Planetaria
A planetarium is a building with a domed ceiling against which lights representing the night sky are projected. Projectors at the planetarium at the Iziko South African Museum in Cape Town can reproduce the sky over Cape Town at any time, day or night. They also show how the stars looked 13 000 years ago and how they will look in the future. The Johannesburg Planetarium has a projector that can reproduce almost any part of the sky.

Satellites and Spacecraft
Satellites are objects that circle (or orbit) the Earth. The first manmade satellite, **Sputnik 1**, was launched in Russia (then part of the Soviet Union) in 1957. Today satellites provide weather information, send telephone calls and transmit television pictures worldwide.

In 1990 the **Hubble Space Telescope** was launched in the USA to send back data and pictures of distant space objects until 2008. Two unmanned roving vehicles named **Opportunity** and **Spirit** were landed on Mars in January 2004 and also sent back valuable information. Neil Armstrong was the first man on the moon, conveyed by **Eagle**, the landing module of **Apollo 11**, in July 1969. In 2002, South African Mark Shuttleworth became the first African in space, where he spent eight days.

METEORS AND COMETS
Meteors, also known as 'shooting stars', are large chunks of rock that circle the sun and are visible only when they reach the Earth's atmosphere. Some burn up completely, but others reach the Earth's surface before this happens. Once a meteor lands on the Earth, it is known as a meteorite. Meteorites have been found in various parts of southern Africa and some may be seen in the Iziko South African Museum in Cape Town. The world's largest meteorite was discovered in Hoba West in Namibia in 1920. It measures 2.7 by 3 metres and weighs almost 80 tons. **Comets** are balls of ice and rock particles from the furthest part of the Solar System and circle the sun. They can be seen in the night sky only when they near the sun. Sunlight causes the comet to release gases that glow, and the comet brightens and produces a tail. Encke's Comet is seen every 3.3 years whereas Halley's Comet – the most famous of all – appears every 76.03 years. It last appeared in 1986.

Astronaut walking on the surface of the moon

SPACE FACTS

The **universe** is so enormous that astronomers measure it in light years. A **light year** is the distance light travels in one year – 9.5 million million kilometres. Light travels at 300 000 kilometres per second. Astronomers can only see about 15 000 million light years into the universe.

Galaxies are families of stars held together by gravity. Earth's galaxy is the Milky Way, which measures about 950 000 million million kilometres across, and has about 100 000 million stars. There may even be more than 6 000 million other galaxies!

Stars begin as space dust that forms a ball of burning gas. As the gas is used up, the star swells up to 50 times its original size. Eventually it bursts or cools down, and then shrinks into a tiny star, which is commonly known as a white dwarf.

The **sun** is a star in the Milky Way. Nine planets circle the sun to form our **Solar System**. The temperature of the sun's surface is 6000°C. A pinhead of this temperature 150 kilometres away could kill a man. The sun measures 1 392 000 kilometres across – 109 times the Earth's diameter.

Moons are made of rock and circle most of the planets. In fact, Jupiter has at least 13 moons. Earth's moon does not shine on its own, but is lit up by the bright rays of the sun.

IA/RHS

ORION

Because the three stars of Orion's belt are in a straight line, this is possibly the easiest constellation to recognize in the southern sky. Orion is named after a famous hunter in Greek mythology. Some of the stars in the constellation form his sword. Seen from the southern hemisphere, he appears to be standing on his head!

WPK

The South African Astronomical Observatory at Sutherland

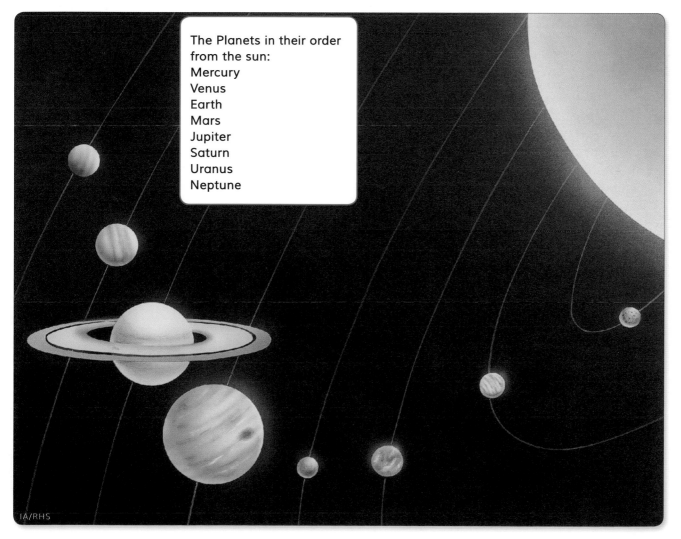

The Planets in their order from the sun:
Mercury
Venus
Earth
Mars
Jupiter
Saturn
Uranus
Neptune

IA/RHS

THE SUTHERLAND OBSERVATORY

Because city lights and increasing pollution make it difficult to observe the night skies, a new research complex was been built in the clear air at Sutherland in the Karoo. Scientists flocked to Sutherland to see the collision with Jupiter of the comet fragments known as Shoemaker-Levy-9 in 1994.

PLACES TO SEE

- Observatory Museum in Bathurst Street, Grahamstown
- The South African Astronomical Observatory, Cape Town
- The Johannesburg Planetarium, Johannesburg
- The Planetarium at Iziko South African Museum, Cape Town

Keeping in Touch

INTRODUCING THE POSTAGE STAMP

In 1840, penny postage was introduced in Britain. A stamp was stuck onto the letter before it was posted. In 1853, the first South African stamps were issued. They were triangular and were either red (worth a penny) or blue (worth fourpence). These were the first **triangular stamps** ever issued and are very valuable today.

Before the founding of the Cape settlement, many Dutch and English ships called at Table Bay for refreshment. Sailors left letters under large, engraved stones, hoping they would be found and delivered. Today, post and telecommunication services, including the Internet, have become much more sophisticated and efficient.

The Cape's Postal Service

After the settlement was founded, post office stones were no longer needed as ships stopped regularly at the Cape. In 1792, a new post office at Cape Town began to handle mail passing between Europe, the East Indies and the Cape. Official documents were also carried to landdrosts by Khoikhoi 'runners' – messengers running in relays between towns – but it was not until 1805 that the Cape had a regular inland postal service.

Sea-mail

From 1815 onwards, sailing ships travelling to and from India collected and delivered mail between England and the Cape on a monthly basis.

The 114-day voyage was reduced to 58 days when the first steamship, the *Enterprise*, arrived in Table Bay in 1825. In 1857, the Union Line took over the Cape's sea-mail service, and in 1900, the Union Line merged with the Castle Line to form the Union-Castle Mail Steamship Company. The last mail ship, the *Windsor Castle*, sailed from Table Bay for the last time in September 1977.

UNDER STONES

Sailors landing in Table Bay began placing their letters under stones on the beach in the hope they would be sent on. Soon there were many **post office stones** carved with the names of ships and their officers.

An old mail coach

Our First Post Offices

In 1849, the Orange River Sovereignty opened its first post office and the following year four were opened in KwaZulu-Natal. Gauteng's first post office at Ferreira's Camp (later Johannesburg) dealt with all the gold miners' mail. By 1899, all parts of South Africa were connected by routes taken by mail coaches. A regular postal service was started and a postal union was formed between what are now the nine provinces of South Africa and Mozambique.

Airmail

On 27 December 1911, Evelyn Driver piloted a Bleriot monoplane carrying 729 postcards from Kenilworth to Muizenberg in the Cape. But the public did not trust the new airmail service, which started between Durban and Cape Town in 1925, and it closed. Fortunately, in 1929 a new airmail service linked Cape Town, Port Elizabeth, East London, Durban, Bloemfontein and eventually Johannesburg. It ceased functioning when the Second World War broke out as all aircraft were needed for military service.

Postal Services Today

Today, letters and parcels are transported by road, rail and air – and sometimes even by bicycle. Mail is also delivered to privately owned boxes at post offices in South Africa. Machines sort up to 45 000 items in an hour. Because they sort according to numbers, a postal code system was introduced in 1973 and each post office has its own code.

THE FIRST POST BOX

South Africa's first letterbox was an old boot hung from a tree at Mossel Bay in 1501 by Pedro d'Ataide, a passing Portuguese sea captain. The letter in his boot was discovered by a sailor, who delivered it. Although there are no more old boots to be found, you may still find a few post-boxes bearing the initials of the reigning British monarch from colonial days.

The main post office in Durban was opened in 1895

Mass mail sorting machines

Telephones

RHS

South Africa's first telephone exchange opened in Port Elizabeth in 1882 with 20 subscribers. Callers had to crank a handle and ask the operator to connect their call. Automatic exchanges were later introduced, but it was only in the 1960s that most large centres were connected.

Today, there are millions of telephones in South Africa and a network of telephone lines links us to countries all over the world. A microwave network transmits thousands of calls by relaying them through antennae on high towers. In 1975, South Africa became a member of the International Telecommunications Satellite Organisation (Intelsat), which has **telecommunications satellites** circling the Earth 36 000 kilometres up in space.

Saucer-shaped antennae beam radio signals (which include TV) from Hartebeesthoek in Gauteng to other countries, and satellites relay radio signals from the rest of the world to South Africa. Cellular telephones operate through networks of radio transmitters serving areas known as 'cells'. The cellphone switches frequencies automatically as it passes from one cell to another.

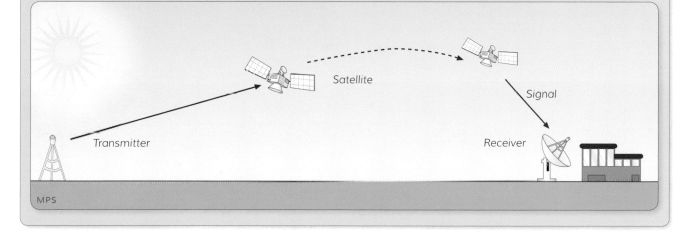

Satellite

Signal

Transmitter

Receiver

MPS

INTERNET CRIME

The **Internet** allows criminals to hack into computer networks to steal money and information from across the world. One such computer criminal, the American Kevin Mitnik, who was arrested in 1995, was found to have 20 000 credit card numbers at his disposal. Catching and prosecuting criminals who live in one country but who commit crimes in another is posing a serious problem to law-enforcement agencies.

THE SILICON CHIP

The silicon chip is a tiny slice of silicon only a few square millimetres in size. Its use in electronics was discovered only in 1958. A silicon chip contains hundreds of electric circuits and, once these have been programmed to work together, it can control almost any machine. Washing machines, telephones, automatic bank tellers, and television sets are some of the machines controlled by silicon chips.

From Telegram to Internet

The first local telegraph messages were sent between Cape Town and Simon's Town in 1860. A message tapped out on a hand-operated 'key' by the Morse code of dots and dashes was carried by electricity to its destination. There it was decoded, printed (as a telegram) and delivered.

From the 1920s the teleprinter slowly replaced the Morse code, sending a typed message from one post office to another. The word telex is made up from 'teleprinter' and 'exchange'. Telex machines were hired out by the post office to large companies such as newspapers and mining houses, which then had their own exchange for sending and receiving telegrams. The system was computerized in the 1980s, but has been replaced by the fax.

Fax machines operate through telephone lines and radio transmissions and are like long-distance photocopiers. The word 'fax' is short for 'facsimile', which means an exact copy. In the 1930s facsimile services sent pictures by landline or radio, especially for use in newspapers. Today, many private users have their own fax machines.

The fax, in its turn, is being overtaken by e-mail, which, with a personal computer and a digital scanner, is capable of sending and receiving not only text, but also accurate colour images. These can be sent all over the world, sometimes with a reply received in a matter of seconds.

The Internet is like an electronic library that can be accessed, via telephone links, through a personal computer. Organizations wanting to supply information maintain an electronic website that can be accessed by entering a code on the computer keyboard. The user is then able to 'browse' the website's electronic pages.

SMS

The **Short Message Service** is one of the options offered by cellular phones, and allows subscribers to send text messages, which appear as written words on the cellular phone screen. One advantage of the SMS is that it can be used to send text messages overseas, which is not always possible with a conventional call. The SMS is cheaper than phoning.

Storing Information

Information can be stored on paper, but it often takes a long time to sort through books and files to find the required facts. Then, in the 1940s, computers were invented and made by using valves. They could store vast amounts of information, but were very big and clumsy. However, when the silicon chip was invented it became possible to make smaller, more powerful computers. They do calculations and store information that can be instantly retrieved. Today, many bank transactions can be carried out from the safety of home by means of a personal computer.

PLACES TO SEE

ℹ The Telkom Exploratorium at Cape Town's Waterfront
ℹ Iziko Old Slave Lodge Museum, Cape Town

Lighting up the Land

Eskom, or the Electricity Supply Commission, was established in 1923 and is one of the top 20 utilities in the world by generation capacity. It generates about 95 per cent of the electricity used in South Africa. The most abundant source of energy in the country is coal and thus Eskom is dependent on coal for 90 per cent of its electricity, producing over 90 million tons of coal per annum. However, it also owns one nuclear power station.

Eskom's Power Network
Power lines from Mpumalanga stretch 250000 km to reach all parts of South Africa and the neighbouring states. Almost half of Eskom's electricity is sold to local authorities, which resell it to individual users. Additional power stations (including Medupi and Kusile) and major power lines are to be built to meet South Africa's rising demand for electricity. Some older coal-fired power stations are also being recommissioned.

An electricity generating plant

IS/BK

THE LIGHTS GO ON
South Africa's **first electric lights** were turned on to illuminate the streets of Kimberley in 1882 – even before London had streetlights. In 1886 the Rand Central Electrical Works erected a power station at Brakpan to have electricity available for gold mining. Johannesburg installed its first generating plant in 1891, Pretoria in 1894 and Cape Town in 1895.

The Gautrain runs on electricity

Hydro-electric Power
The word **hydro** means 'water', and hydro-electric power is electricity generated by the force of falling water. Some countries use their rivers to generate hydro-electric power, but because South Africa has few rivers that flow strongly throughout the year, it is unable to do this. Instead, Eskom harnesses water flowing from the country's big dams and reservoirs. Hydro-electric power is a very important part of several impressive water-storage schemes. The Orange River scheme has hydro stations at the Gariep and Vanderkloof dams. They are on standby in case of failure at coal-fired stations.

A pumped storage scheme is a special kind of hydro station that can supply electricity at peak periods, such as early morning and late afternoon. There is a pumped storage scheme on the Palmiet River near Grabouw in the Western Cape and another is the Drakensberg project. When excess energy is available, usually at night, it is used to pump water up to a higher reservoir. When extra power is needed, the water is released into the Kilburn dam, generating electricity as it rushes through the tunnels.

The Lesotho Highlands Water Project is designed to irrigate farmlands and to double the supply of water to Gauteng before the year 2020. At the same time, an enormous hydro-power plant will increase the supply of electricity to South Africa's most active industrial area.

The Power of the Atom

South Africa entered a new technological age when the country's first nuclear power station at Koeberg, 30 kilometres north of Cape Town, generated electricity for the first time in April 1984. Instead of using coal or water, power was created by splitting the atom in a process called **nuclear fission**.

Koeberg was built close to the beach where sea water could be pumped into the power station for cooling purposes. In this way, 100 million litres of fresh water are saved every day. Instead of burning 200 million tons of coal a year, the power station uses 50 tons of enriched uranium fuel. One kilogram of uranium supplies the same amount of energy as would have been supplied by three million kilograms of coal.

Every nuclear power station has a nuclear reactor. There are also turbines and generators. The medium used to rotate the shafts of the generators is steam. When the nucleus of the uranium atom is split in the reactor, energy is released in the form of heat. This heat is used to boil water, and steam drives the turbines. The turbines turn generators, and produce electricity.

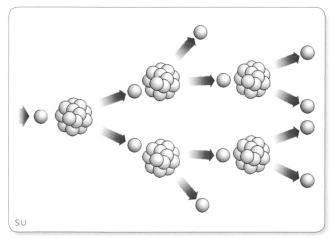

SU

The splitting of a uranium atom causes a nuclear reaction

KEEPING KOEBERG SAFE

There have been three serious accidents elsewhere in the world involving the release of radioactive material at nuclear power stations – Three Mile Island in the United States in 1979, Chernobyl in Russia in 1986 and Fukushima in Japan in 2011. These leakages can be dangerous even for people living quite far away. Can this happen at Koeberg? The design of Koeberg is inherently safe. The fuel is in the form of a dense ceramic material and encased in zirconium tubes. The stainless steel reactor vessel is 25 centimetres thick and contained in a two-metre thick concrete shield. The nuclear steam supply system is housed in a one-metre thick reinforced concrete structure that cannot even be destroyed by an earthquake. Precautions are taken to prevent exposing staff to radiation. If an accident should happen, an emergency plan will come into operation immediately.

ENERGY AT HOME

Although many people live in isolated areas that are not provided with electricity, those who live in towns and cities use electricity all day. But each household appliance uses a different percentage of the monthly electricity account.

IS/PPT

IS/PC

Television set: 2%

IS/BSK

Refrigerator: 16%   Microwave oven: ±2%

IS/SW

IS/MD

Washing machine: 2%   Vacuum cleaner: 2%

IS/GR

Small household appliances: ±2%

WHERE DOES ALL THE ELECTRICITY GO?

Eskom sells most of its electricity to the mines and factories of Gauteng and the Free State. Of the electricity supplied to the various local authorities, towns in the Gauteng province are the highest consumers. Houses in the Western Cape use more electricity than any others in the country, but transport here uses less electricity than the trains of Gauteng, KwaZulu-Natal and the Free State.

MORE POWER NEEDED

South Africa faces an ever-increasing demand for electricity. At the moment, Eskom's reserve capacity – the amount of electricity needed for surges in demand – is about 8%. The internationally accepted minimum reserve capacity is 15% of total demand. Having a relatively small amount of capacity in reserve usually leads to power cuts when electricity demand is high.

RHS

BUILDING ON THEIR EXPERIENCE

The French construction companies that built the Koeberg power station had 30 years' experience in this field. France generates more than 73% of its electricity at nuclear power stations. The first commercial nuclear reactor was opened in 1958 at Calder Hall in Britain. Britain was also a pioneer in nuclear energy and by 1970 its nuclear power plants generated more electricity than was generated in the rest of the world together.

PLACES TO SEE

ⓘ Koeberg Power Station at Koeberg, Western Cape

ⓘ Eskom Visitors' Centre at Lethabo in the Free State

Transport

BREAKING THE 8-HOUR BARRIER

On 23 April 1989, British Airways **Concorde** Alpha Foxtrot landed at London's Heathrow 7 hours and 46 minutes after leaving Cape Town's international airport. Although the supersonic dash had included an hour-long stop at Monrovia in Liberia, about 14 minutes had been clipped off Concorde's record. The aircraft's average speed was about 2 000 kilometres an hour. After a fatal crash near Paris in 2000, Concorde services were withdrawn.

SA/IOA

MINIBUS TAXIS

Minibus taxis are the most popular mode of transport for the majority of South Africa's population because they are affordable and convenient. Since the mid-1980s, the industry has grown dramatically and now comprises more than 20 000 owners and 200 000 employees. Of the 36 lives that are lost in motor vehicle accidents every day, three are killed in taxi-related incidents.

South Africa's harbours and busy industrial areas are often far apart. Because the country has no suitable rivers for ships to carry cargoes inland, we rely heavily on roads, railways and airports.

Early Roads

San and Khoikhoi followed animal tracks through the mountains, and the same routes were taken by later settlers from Europe, who found that crossing the mountains with their wagons was a terrifying experience. No good roads were built during the Dutch period, and it was only after Colonial Secretary John Montagu introduced convict labour, in the 1840s, that conditions improved. Scottish immigrant Andrew Geddes Bain, and his son, Thomas, proved to be skilful surveyors and road-builders. Among the many mountain passes they built are Bain's Kloof, Montagu Pass and the soaring Swartberg Pass – all of them are still used today.

Before the modern age of powerful construction machines and reinforced concrete, road-builders followed the line of least resistance. If there was a tree or a boulder in the way, it was usually quicker to go around it rather than remove it.

When taking a road across a mountain, the gentlest slope was chosen, even though this made the journey much longer. Examples of this can be seen from the Outeniqua Pass with its deep cuttings, between George and Oudtshoorn, and the views of the nearby Montagu and Cradock Kloof passes.

Wagons and carts

The sturdy trek wagon, pulled by teams of up to 16 oxen, was suited to the rough roads of South Africa. It was the trekkers' home on wheels and could carry a load of several tons. Even heavier freight wagons, with iron axles and wide wheel-rims, were later built to carry loads such as coal and even copper ore.

A few high officials rode in smart coaches pulled by horses, and, as the towns developed, other wealthy people used a range of smaller vehicles. A favourite was the two-wheeled **kapkar**, so called because its folding roof resembled a woman's bonnet. It became known as the Cape cart. The hansom cab (named for its designer) served as a taxi in Cape Town until the 1960s, and others included the dogcart, spider and buggy.

The Mail Coach

Post wagons and post carts began a regular service between Cape Town and Simon's Town in 1801, and by 1838 the post route had already reached Swellendam. The first mail coach, a much morecomfortable vehicle, began running in 1844 between Grahamstown and Port Elizabeth.

After the discovery of diamonds, and then later of gold, mail coach services grew quickly, carrying diggers from the coast to Kimberley and the Witwatersrand in just a few days.

On the Road

The first motor car or 'horseless carriage' sent to South Africa was driven in Tshwane (Pretoria) in 1896. Today there are 6.6 million vehicles on our roads and 150 000 of them are minibus taxis. About 65% of urban passenger trips are by minibus taxi, 20% by bus and 15% by rail. About 80% of all freight transported in South Africa is done using road transport and just under 7% of the Gross National Product is spent on freight haulage.

MA

The first cars were commonly known as horseless carriages

THE HUGUENOT TUNNEL

The Huguenot toll tunnel, which carries the N1 between Paarl and Worcester, was opened in March 1988. By cutting through the mountain, it reduces the distance over Du Toitskloof by eleven kilometres. The four kilometre-long tunnel is one of the most sophisticated in the world. It is lit throughout, has emergency telephones and parking bays, fire extinguishers, television monitoring cameras, traffic lights, service vehicles, and even access to local radio stations.

HEADLAMPS ON DIP / HOOFLIGTE OP DOMP

THE FIRST BUSES

South Africa's first horse-drawn omnibuses were introduced between Cape Town and Wynberg in 1838. By 1863, single- and double-decker horse-drawn trams were running on iron rails between the city and Green Point. They were replaced by electric trams in 1893, but Kimberley claims to have introduced electric trams in 1887 already.

On the Track

The country's first steam locomotive, 'Blackie', was displayed on Cape Town Station for many years. This Scottish-built (1859) engine arrived at the Cape with its driver, William Dabbs, and was used from about 1861 between Cape Town and Eersterivier. By the end of the century, railway tracks extended over 7000 kilometres, linking the country's main centres. In 1925, a few electric trains began to replace steam trains in KwaZulu-Natal and today over 1000 electric locomotives cover many kilometres annually. The diesel-electric locomotives also cover huge distances. Until recently, steam engines were fairly common. As they are expensive to run they have been withdrawn, but a few 'specials' remain, including the Apple Express between Port Elizabeth and the Langkloof, the Outeniqua Choo-choo between George and Knysna, and the Banana Express in southern KwaZulu-Natal. A private company operates steam trains between Johannesburg and many other towns.

'Blackie' – the first steam locomotive to arrive in South Africa

In the Air

In 1875, John Goodman Household's homemade glider flew over 200 metres in KwaZulu-Natal. But 34 years passed before South Africa's first powered flight was made when Frenchman, Albert Kimmerling, piloted his 'Flying Matchbox' six metres over East London. In 1911, John Weston flew the first South African-made aircraft over Kimberley.

Today, much of South Africa's domestic air traffic is handled by South African Airways, but there are also smaller airlines in existence. About 44 foreign airlines operate services to the international airports at Cape Town, Johannesburg and Durban. SAA carries out maintenance work for most of these airlines. Airports previously owned by the State are now controlled by a private organization called the Airports Company.

An SAA aircraft with its distinctive tail livery

South Africa's Seaports

Industrialization and expansion in South Africa depended heavily on sea traffic for many of its needs, but it was only in the mid-1800s that a serious effort was made to make harbours safer. In Table Bay in 1865, despite a new breakwater, 18 ships were wrecked in a fierce gale. Our modern harbours are safe and important refuelling bases for the world's ships.

Durban harbour handles sugar as well as exports and imports for Gauteng. **Cape Town** is our main fruit-exporting and fishing port. **Richards Bay** handles over 100 million tons of dry bulk goods, such as coal, every year. **Port Elizabeth** handles wool and all products of the agricultural Cape Midlands. **East London** is our only viable river port and exports grain, as well as copper from Zambia and the DRC. **Saldanha** is our largest natural harbour and has been developed to export iron ore and steel. **Mossel Bay** is a shallow harbour for the south coast fishing fleet and nearest port to the offshore oil-drilling platforms.

South Africa's harbours handle a wide variety of goods

THE GAUTRAIN

The Gautrain travels at speeds of around 160 km per hour, linking Tshwane (Pretoria) to Johannesburg, and OR Tambo International Airport to Sandton. This rapid-rail transport system carries over 100 000 passengers per day and was constructed to relieve pressure on the N1 Freeway, the most congested highway in the country.

TOLL ROADS

Building new roads and keeping old roads safe, is very expensive. One way of raising money is by building toll gates on new roads and tunnels. South Africa's first tollgates were set up in 1812 at the two main entrances to Cape Town. A toll, or fee, had to be paid for every wagon and cart entering the town, and on every sheep being driven to market.

> **PLACES TO SEE**

Arms and Armour

THE SANDF
The South African
National Defence Force
(SANDF) is one of Africa's best-equipped military forces. The four branches of the defence force are the Army, Air Force, Navy and Military Health Service, and all have their headquarters at Tshwane (Pretoria). The head of each branch reports to the Chief of the SANDF, who in turn reports to the Minister of Defence.

WOMEN IN THE SANDF
The South African Military Nursing Service was raised in 1915. In World War 2, 25 000 volunteers joined the women's services. The SA Army Women's College, offering a 12-month training course, was started in 1971. These days, women serve in all sectors of the SA National Defence Force, with many reaching the highest ranks.

During World War 2, ammunition and armoured cars were manufactured on a large scale in South Africa for the Allied forces. This was done under franchise and was the country's first involvement with armaments production, which has since developed into a multi-billion rand industry. Today South Africa produces world-class military vehicles, communications equipment and weapons.

Our Defence Force
The South African National Defence Force (**SANDF**) is a volunteer organization in which Army, Navy, Air Force and Military Health Service make up 'one force'. The **Regular Force** of each component is made up of highly trained soldiers, sailors or airmen who form the core of our defence system. Supporting them is the **Reserve Force**, which is made up of former part-time or Citizen Force units. In 2007, the Minister of Defence reported that there were approximately 11 000 Reserve Force members. In the past these were supported by several thousand members of the **Territorial Reserve**, but these units were disbanded in 2009.

In recent years, the SANDF has assisted with rescues during floods, notably in Mozambique in 2000. It delivered food, accommodation and clean water and set up treatment centres in Limpopo and KwaZulu-Natal during the 2008/9 cholera outbreak. SANDF contingents have also served in the Democratic Republic of Congo, Burundi and Darfur (Sudan) as part of the United Nations Peacekeeping Force.

A large military organization requires food, clothing, transport and other specialized equipment to operate.

The Armaments Industry
After World War 2 ended in 1945, South Africa stopped making weapons. In 1962, to show opposition to apartheid, the United Nations banned the sale of arms to South Africa. Parliament then established a Munitions Production Board, which was the basis of the modern South African arms industry.

Armscor (Armaments Corporation of South Africa), a state-owned corporation, serves as the acquisition agency for the SANDF, procuring armaments from a number of different sources. **Denel**, also a state-owned

A Rooivalk attack helicopter

entity, makes arms and equipment for the SANDF and for export. The arms industry employs many thousands of people and is worth billions of rands.

Many people believe that guns encourage aggression, while others claim that South Africa's possession of modern weapons will discourage other states or groups from using violence against our country.

Military Products
The **Eland**, the first armoured car assembled by Armscor, was succeeded by the **Rooikat**. Other locally produced armoured cars designed to carry troops as well as to fight, are the **Ratel** and the **Buffel**. The **Badger**, the latest eight-wheeled infantry combat vehicle, designed by Denel, has a 60 mm long-range mortar.

The **G-6** artillery gun is one of the most powerful of its type in the world, and can be driven over almost any obstacles in a radius of 40 km. Another version, the **G-5**, is towed into action by lorries or special gun tractors.

The Badger

Rooikat armoured car

EVERYTHING ON WHEELS

Several pieces of equipment are available as trailers on wheels to support troops in the field. Meals for up to 250 people can be prepared in the field-kitchen trailer, which is fitted with an oven, water-boiler, two grill plates and three cooker-burners, which all work with gas.

The mobile medical post carries medical supplies, oxygen cylinders, stretchers, a gas stove and a pressure cooker. The mobile operating theatre is equipped with an operating table, operating lights, an anaesthetic machine, an ECG (heart) monitor, instruments and oxygen cylinders. There is even a mobile blood bank that can store 216 half-litre units of blood at a temperature of 4°C. It has two diesel generators to supply power when there is no other power available.

THE WAR IN THE AIR
During World War 2, the **South African Air Force** grew from 1500 men and 104 aircraft to 45000 men and women and 35 squadrons, each with ten to 18 aircraft. Bombers and fighters were active in East and North Africa and the Italian campaign. The SAAF also fought in Europe. Today, trainee SAAF pilots learn to fly in the Swiss-built Pilatus aircraft.

Corvettes Come Home

The first of South Africa's new Valour-class patrol corvettes, **SAS Amatola**, arrived in Simon's Town from Wilhelmshaven, Germany, in November 2003. It is described as a 'stealth frigate', difficult to detect at sea, 121 metres long with a top speed of over 30 knots and a crew of 117. It can carry 16 Umkhonto surface-to-air missiles, two helicopters as well as a range of other weapons. South Africa has ordered four of these swift, powerful warships and three modern submarines.

PROTECTING OUR HARBOURS
The Navy uses a locally developed patrol boat, the **Namacurra**, to protect our harbours. It is a twin-hulled vessel armed with machine guns and scare charges, which are dropped into the sea to scare off divers who might be sabotaging ships or harbour installations. The boats are stationed at all major ports in South Africa.

A Gripen fighter

Missiles can follow and hit a fast-moving target. The **Cactus**, the world's first low-level surface-to-air missile system, developed jointly by South Africa and France, is now out of service. Denel's **Umkhonto**, a vertically launched, infra-red homing surface-to-air missile, is fitted to the Navy's corvettes. Denel also makes the **Ingwe** missile and the **Mokopa** 10000 metre-range anti-tank missile for local use and for export. The **Umbani** guided bomb kit is a joint development with the UAE.

The SA Air Force used **Impala** jet aircraft for over 30 years, until 2000. French **Mirage** jets were the frontline fighters, and these supersonic aircraft (faster than the speed of sound) were locally updated. Known as the **Cheetah**, these fighter planes carry a full range of South African-made rockets and missiles.

An advanced South African twin-engine attack helicopter, the **Rooivalk**, can cruise at 260 kilometres per hour over a range of 700 kilometres. Other modern and sophisticated aircraft are the Swiss-made **Pilatus** training aircraft, the British jet-propelled **Hawk Mk120** lead-in fighter-trainer, whose cockpit and avionics were specially adapted for South Africa, and the Swedish **Gripen**, a supersonic front-line fighter.

SAS Amatola

The SAS Drakensberg

This was the first naval ship designed and built in South Africa, and the biggest ever built in a South African shipyard. The SAS *Drakensberg* is a replenishment vessel and can carry 5500 tons of fuel and 750 tons of supplies and ammunition for transfer to other vessels at sea. This increases the range and capabilities of smaller vessels, such as submarines and strike craft. The ship also has four desalination systems, which can produce 70000 litres of fresh water from the sea per day. The *Drakensberg* also carries two helicopters on board.

PLACES TO SEE

- ℹ The South African National Museum of Military History, Johannesburg
- ℹ The Military Museum in the Castle of Good Hope, Cape Town
- ℹ The Maritime Centre Museum at the V & A Waterfront, Cape Town
- ℹ The South African Naval Museum, Simon's Town

Mining Gold and Minerals

Krugerrands, bearing the portrait of President Paul Kruger, were introduced in 1967 to give people the opportunity to invest in gold. There are four sizes: the largest coin contains one ounce of pure gold, and the smallest one-tenth of an ounce. As pure gold is soft, the coins contain some copper to harden them.

BARGAINING POWER
The **National Union of Mineworkers** (NUM), the first all-black union for mineworkers, began in 1982 and is affiliated to COSATU. It negotiates with bodies such as the Chamber of Mines of South Africa on matters such as wages, productivity and working conditions. Its first general secretary was Cyril Ramaphosa.

South Africa has some of the richest mineral deposits in the world, and gold and other mineral exports earn the country billions of rand every year. Mining has become extremely important and is becoming more and more technologically advanced. Today, computers are used to predict rock-bursts, detect fires, and assist mining engineers to design mines that extend many kilometres underground.

The Story of Gold
Gold bowls and ornaments found in Limpopo Province prove that people living there 700 years ago knew how to mine gold. Travellers from Europe found small quantities of gold in the Magaliesberg and at the Orange River mouth, and in 1871 a mine was opened at Eersteling near Mokopane (Potgietersrus). Later, more gold was discovered, especially around Lydenburg, Barberton and Pilgrim's Rest. Barberton soon became the centre of a gold rush and 20 000 fortune hunters crowded into the new town.

Working Underground
Miners work in unpleasant conditions deep under the ground. In spite of strict safety precautions, from time to time rocks burst, fires break out, and there are gas explosions and sudden floods. Cool air is pumped into the mines, which would otherwise be unbearably hot because of high rock temperatures. Miners drill holes into the gold-bearing rock deep underground with jackhammers. The holes are then filled with explosives and the resulting blast loosens the gold-bearing rock that is brought up the shafts in skips.

On the Surface
When the gold-bearing rock reaches the surface, it is taken to the reduction plant to be washed, sorted, crushed, chemically treated, filtered and poured into moulds. Each bullion bar contains 88 per cent gold, 9 per cent silver and 3 per cent impurities, and weighs just over 31 kilograms. The silver and other impurities are later removed at the Rand Refinery in Germiston. Here refined gold bars, which are 99.6 per cent pure gold, are produced.

Most of these refined gold bars are bought by the South African Reserve Bank for sale to banks, gold-dealers and private buyers all over the world. The price is set by the London Bullion Market. Some of the gold is sold to gold jewellers in South Africa.

Gold mines pay high taxes and provide hundreds of thousands of jobs. Large amounts of money are spent on improving mining methods, establishing new mines and making working conditions safer.

JOHANNESBURG
In 1886, George Harrison and George Walker, diggers and handymen on the Witwatersrand's Confidence Reef, discovered a rich gold deposit on the farm Langlaagte. This was the very large Witwatersrand Main Reef. A stampede of prospectors followed; within months a 'tin town' housing 3 000 people had sprung up. This was the beginning of Johannesburg, our biggest city and financial centre. It was later found that the Witwatersrand's rich goldfields stretched into the Free State, Mpumalanga and North West Province.

An underground rock driller

The Chamber of Mines of SA
Three years after gold was discovered on the Witwatersrand in 1886, the Chamber of Mines was founded to protect the interests of the gold-mining industry. It later expanded to represent all mining concerns in South Africa. It recruits mineworkers, draws up safety standards and organizes research into mining and safety methods. It also negotiates wages and productivity with trade unions representing the mineworkers.

Asbestos consists of very strong fibres that are resistant to heat and to most chemicals. However, it is no longer mined in South Africa because it has been shown to cause severe lung disease and some forms of cancer. Because of the environmental and health risks, world production has declined. Safer alternatives have been found for most asbestos-based products.

Nguni-speakers mined **copper** at Phalaborwa in Limpopo Province over 1000 years ago. Van der Stel's expedition searched for copper in the Namaqualand mountains and found copper-bearing rock eleven kilometres east of where the town of Springbok is now. In 1966 a large open-cast operation was started at Phalaborwa. Copper is also mined in the Northern Cape, the Free State and the North West Province. Copper has many uses in industry. It is an excellent conductor of electricity and is used in electrical fittings and wiring.

Most of the world's **chrome ore** is found in South Africa, in the North West Province. It is used for making stainless steel tools.

Iron ore is used to manufacture many things. After the giant Iron and Steel Corporation (Iscor) (now ArcelorMittal South Africa) opened outside Pretoria in 1934, there was a steep rise in iron production for overseas and local use. About half of South Africa's iron ore deposits are at the Sishen mines in the Northern Cape, and others are around Phalaborwa and Thabazimbi in Limpopo Province. The principal ports for the export of iron ore are Richards Bay in KwaZulu-Natal and Saldanha Bay in the Western Cape

Manganese is essential in the manufacture of high-grade iron and steel. It was discovered near Postmasburg in the Northern Cape in 1922. South Africa is third among leading manganese producers, and produces about 15% of the world's total output.

Six metals form the platinoid group. **Platinum** is valuable and people buy it not only for jewellery but also as an investment in the hope that its value will increase. Platinum is used for refining petroleum, making fertilizers and pollution-free car exhausts. Southern Africa has most of the world's reserves of platinum group metals, which are mined in Limpopo Province, Mpumalanga, the Northern Cape and the North West Province.

South African farmers use large quantities of fertilizer containing **phosphates**. Until phosphate deposits were discovered in Limpopo Province (at Phalaborwa) in 1951, phosphate was imported, but now South Africa exports it to other countries.

Uranium, a radioactive metal used to generate nuclear energy, was first detected in gold-bearing rock on the Witwatersrand in 1923. Research into nuclear energy was only started in the 1940s. Today, over 20 companies recover thousands of tons of uranium as a by-product of gold mining.

Silver is mined on the Witwatersrand as a by-product of gold; South Africa produces close to 150 tons annually, ranking 15th on the list of producers. South Africa is also the world leader in the production of vermiculite, alumino-silicates, vanadium and ferro-chromium. It ranks second as an exporter of zirconium and titanium.

Iron ore

Chromite, chrome

Copper

Asbestos   Manganese

GOLD REEF CITY

At Gold Reef City, near Johannesburg, you can go down a shaft to explore the underground workings of a gold mine. The venue also features an old-fashioned newspaper office, an early version of the Johannesburg Stock Exchange and many examples of how people lived and worked during the gold-rush era in what is today Johannesburg.

TRANSFORMING THE UGLY DUMP(LING)S

Over the years, trees and grass were planted on Johannesburg's dusty mine dumps to make them less of an eyesore. But the dumps are now being put through mills again to extract the tiny amounts of ore left over after the first extraction process. Considerable amounts of gold can be recovered in this manner.

PLACES TO SEE

- The Gold Reef City complex in Johannesburg
- The City Museum of Roodepoort near Johannesburg

Turning Our Wheels

A SWAMPY BEGINNING
Coal started forming in swamps about 200 million years ago. Plants, from tiny algae to enormous trees, flourished in the warm, moist atmosphere. When they died they sank to the bottom of the swamps and rotted. Layers of rock pressed them down firmly and chemicals then gradually changed the plant matter into coal, anthracite and graphite.

150 YEARS OF FUELS
Industry developed rapidly in the first half of the 19th century. Great quantities of fuel were needed for the new factories. Much of it was coal, which can produce thick, black, polluting smoke. Today, industrialists are concerned about the effects of acid rain and other pollution caused by burning fossil fuels and are researching alternatives which will keep the air clean.

Aeroplanes, cars and trains all need energy to run their engines. Industries and homes need light, heat and power, and all this requires energy. Much of that energy comes from oil and coal. South Africa has huge coal reserves, but imports oil. Scientists are developing ways to make oil from coal, as well as from gas deposits found under the sea floor.

Black Gold
Coal provides about 85% of South Africa's fuel and is its main source of power. Power stations use about 33% of the total coal production. About 25% of the coal output is exported, bringing in close to R24 billion per year (2007). After gold, coal is South Africa's largest money-earner abroad. Some of the remaining coal is converted into synthetic oil; the rest is used in industry.

South Africa's Coalfields
Centuries ago, South Africa's early inhabitants used coal to smelt iron. After gold was discovered on the Witwatersrand in 1886, many mining-related and other heavy industries needed coal in order to operate. Several coal mines opened on the East Rand and at Vereeniging. Today, mines are found in northern KwaZulu-Natal, the Free State and Mpumalanga. Almost half our coal is found around eMalahleni (Witbank) in Mpumalanga. Deposits are found as deep as 400 metres underground although the seam may only be two to five metres thick in places. To date no coal mining goes deeper than 200 metres. Many of the major collieries use the open-cast mining system. It is believed that there are about 55 000 million tons of economically extractable coal deposits under South Africa's soil.

An open-cast coal mine in the eMalahleni area

Oil from Coal
Sasol, founded in 1950, was the first company to make liquid gas and oil from coal, and today it is still the world leader in the manufacture of petrol and petroleum products from coal. Situated in the northern Free State, Sasol One is close to a large coalfield in the Vanderbijlpark, Vereeniging and Sasolburg area, as well as being close to Johannesburg and the Vaal River.

The town of Sasolburg was established in 1954 to provide homes for Sasol workers. By 1963, about two-and-a-half million tons of coal were being processed to make petrol each year. Because of the crisis in the overseas oil industry in the 1970s, petrol became very expensive. More synthetic petrol had to be produced in South Africa, so two more Sasol plants were built. Sasol Two, in production since 1980, was erected in Mpumalanga and is served by the town of Secunda. Sasol Three was also built near Secunda.

At the three Sasol plants, coal is converted into gas which is processed to make petrol, diesel oil and other products such as ammonia, coal-tar, alcohol, paraffin wax and many chemicals that are currently also exported and which earn South Africa valuable foreign exchange every year.

The process columns of Sasol 2, Secunda, light up the night sky

CLEAN, SAFE AND NATURAL
Methane, one of the components of natural gas, can be used as fuel, and may help to rid the world of much of its air pollution. Currently, natural gas is used for heating and cooking, but scientists think that, in the future, it will also provide the energy for cars and trucks. Methane is clean, safe and plentiful. However, it takes up lots of space so cars powered by natural gas need huge fuel tanks. Garages will also have to install giant reservoirs. Although cars powered by methane do exist, no car manufacturer has started making them on a large scale.

THE SIMPLEST FUEL OF ALL

Many South Africans still depend on **wood** for fuel, and in some parts of Asia and Africa, timber provides 80 percent of the fuel needed for energy. Developed countries in North America, Britain and Western Europe, use an almost equal amount of gas and nuclear power.

OIL RIGS: MAN-MADE ISLANDS

Some oil rigs are needed for exploration. They are moved about so that the drills can probe parts of the seabed where oil might be found. But the base of the rig for the Mossgas project is firmly attached to the ocean floor, so the structure is as rigid as a man-made island. Every part has to be very carefully made as it has to work efficiently for many years while the waves and winds buffet it. The platform, which is raised above the waves, is bigger than a hotel. It has several decks that together equal the height of a 35-storey building. These decks have space for drilling apparatus, huge machinery, laboratories, offices, living- and sleeping-quarters, kitchens, and games rooms. Workers usually remain on the rig for two weeks at a time, and are flown back to shore by helicopter.

Oil rigs operate all day and night, and are very noisy. Labourers doing the heaviest work are commonly called 'roughnecks'; the 'drillers' are next and the most senior, or 'toolpushers', are responsible for the efficient operation of the rig. Also on board are a drilling engineer, a geologist, radio operators, medical and catering staff.

Oil Under the Sea

Sasol cannot provide all South Africa's oil, so in 1965 the Southern Oil Exploration Corporation (Soekor) was established to search for oil. No worthwhile quantities were discovered on land, but in 1980 Soekor located a source of natural gas under the seabed off Mossel Bay. From this, South Africa makes petrol and diesel oil.

In 1992 a fuel refinery – one of the largest in the world – was constructed a few kilometres to the west of Mossel Bay, and is connected by pipelines to a massive platform 85 kilometres out to sea. Three gas fields, namely F A, EM and Oribi, are currently in full production off the southern Cape coast.

RICHARDS BAY

The deep water harbour at Richards Bay in KwaZulu-Natal is home to the largest export coal terminal in the world. This 24-hour operation has a quay 2.2 kilometres long, with six berths and four ship loaders. Railway lines connect the inland coal mines to the port. An aluminium smelter is among the industries developed at Richards Bay to take advantage of the port. The safety of the environment has been taken into account in the development of the Richards Bay Coal Terminal and its industries. As bulk carriers sail in and out, you can still see hippo splashing in the nearby lagoon of the Mhlatuze River.

The drills of an oil-rig probe the seabed for oil

PLACES TO SEE

Chamber of Mines Coal Museum, part of the Talana Museum, Dundee

Diamond Mining

COLOURS OF THE RAINBOW

In their natural state, diamonds look like dull, rounded pebbles. But when they are cut into facets by experts, their true brilliance comes to light. The most common diamond is the beautiful blue-white, but it also comes in other colours such as yellow, pink, green, blue, brown, red and black.

GRIQUALAND WEST

Diamond discoveries in the Vaal-Orange River region led to a feud between the Cape Colony, the Orange Free State and the Transvaal republics and the Griquas. The area was the home of the Griquas, but suddenly everyone wanted to share the diamonds. Eventually the lieutenant-governor of Natal, Robert William Keate, recommended that Griqualand West should become a British crown colony. So from 1873 to 1877 the area was a crown colony. Despite the diggers' objections the Cape Colony took control in 1877.

Diamonds were first mined 2500 years ago in India. Until diamonds were discovered in Kimberley in the 19th century, South Africa had been a poor, farming nation. But once the glittering stones were recovered from the Northern Cape, wealth began to pour into the country. Over a century later, we still sell diamonds worth over two billion rand every year.

How Diamonds Are Formed

Billions of years ago, hot, molten lava was pushed upward through weak rocks from below the Earth's crust. Inside these volcanic 'pipes', lumps of carbon gathered under tremendous heat and pressure that transformed the carbon into diamonds – the hardest substance in the natural world. So diamonds were formed at great depths and brought to the surface as 'passengers' in molten rock or magma.

Over millions of years of ice ages, heavy rain and floods, the molten rock was eroded and, in some places, diamonds were washed out of the pipes and into the newly formed riverbeds. Some were swept out to sea; some were returned to the shore by tides and currents. These formed the diamond deposits of southern Africa's west coast. Other diamonds sank to the bottom of riverbeds while those still inside the pipes were covered by layers of soil and vegetation. In 1866, 15-year old Erasmus Jacobs found a 'pretty pebble' on the banks of the Orange River, near Hopetown in the Northern Cape, Schalk van Niekerk, a farmer, sent it to Grahamstown where it was found to be a diamond, worth R250000 today. It was named **Eureka** (meaning 'I have found it'). Three years later, a larger diamond was found by

a Griqua shepherd who exchanged it with Schalk van Niekerk for cattle, Van Niekerk sold the diamond, called the **Star of South Africa**, for £11 000. Soon prospectors flocked to the Vaal-Orange River area. By the end of 1870, fortune-seekers were prospecting near present-day Barkly West, where surface diamonds had been found in what was called 'yellow ground'. Then some diggers discovered diamonds on a hill on the De Beers brothers' farm, Vooruitzicht. They named the hill Colesberg Kopje, now known as Kimberley's Big Hole.

The first alluvial diggings on the Vaal River

1. The pressure of molten magma begins to crack the surrounding rock.

2. Eventually, the crack reaches the surface.

3. As the volcano erupts, a cone is formed.

4. When the eruption process is complete, the magma hardens.

5. Over time, the cone weathers and disappears.

6. The pipe is mined. Erosion has removed the cone and lowered the surface of the ground.

CARATS

A carat is the unit of weight in which diamonds and other gems are measured. One metric carat equals 200 milligrams. The uncut Cullinan diamond weighed more than half a kilogram before it was cut up and incorporated into the British **Crown Jewels**.

Kimberley and De Beers

So many diggers flocked to Colesberg Kopje that it was called New Rush. Most of the stones were found in kimberlite, commonly called 'blue ground'. This was the richest source of diamonds yet discovered. Colesberg Kopje was soon shovelled away and a huge hole took its place. Tents and shacks were erected and a small town began to form; it was named after the British colonial secretary, Lord Kimberley. Among the diggers was Cecil John Rhodes, who later became prime minister of the Cape and founder of De Beers Consolidated Mines.

The Board of Directors of De Beers, September 1891

As prospectors dug deeper, buckets of rock were hauled to the surface by ropes. The rock was then broken up and the diamonds sifted out. As the different holes began to merge, roads between the claims began to collapse and it became difficult to separate claims. The diggers formed groups and groups merged into companies. Rhodes gradually bought all these companies and in 1888, he formed De Beers Consolidated Mines, and went on to become a powerful industrialist. Today, most diamond mining is still controlled by De Beers, one of the world's most important mining companies.

Alluvial diamond mining on the Namaqualand coast

Diamonds in the Sand

Many of the world's diamonds from kimberlite pipes are found in remote alluvial fields. In 1925, the first marine diamonds in South Africa were discovered by Captain Jack Carstens. Prospectors and geologists rushed to the area and two years later Alexander Bay's rich deposits were discovered. Today, diamonds are also recovered from the seabed off the coast of Namaqualand in the Northern Cape.

The Biggest and Brightest

South Africa is one of the world's top producers of gem diamonds. The Premier Mine, near Pretoria, was established on a large kimberlite pipe which is about 1200 million years old. This pipe was discovered by Percival Tracey and Thomas Cullinan in 1903.

Order of Merit

Six of the world's ten largest diamonds were discovered in southern Africa.

Rank	Carats	Name	Date	Place
1	3106.00	Cullinan	1905	South Africa
2	995.20	Excelsior	1893	South Africa
3	968.90	Star of Sierra Leone	1972	Sierra Leone
4	793.00	Great Mogul	1650	India
5	770.00	Woyie River	1945	Sierra Leone
6	726.60	Vargas	1938	Brazil
7	726.00	Jonker	1934	South Africa
8	650.25	Reitz	1895	South Africa
9	609.25	Baumgold Rough	1923	South Africa
10	601.25	Lesotho	1967	Lesotho

On 25 June 1905, the world's largest diamond was discovered in this pipe. Named the **Cullinan Diamond**, it was as big as a man's fist. It was bought for £125 000 (about R2 million) by the Transvaal government who presented it to King Edward VII. The diamond was cut into nine large stones and 96 smaller ones. The largest stone, the **Star of Africa**, was set in the royal sceptre, and the second biggest, the **Lesser Star of Africa**, became part of the Imperial crown. The other diamonds are in the royal regalia on display in the Tower of London.

Mining

There are two types of diamond mines: pipe or kimberlite mines, and alluvial mines. Until 1890, Kimberley's mines were 'open-cast', which means that open trenches were dug. As trenches became deeper, falling rocks and seeping water made digging dangerous, so shafts were sunk for underground mining. When World War I broke out in 1914, Kimberley Mine was closed. Today, diamonds are mined in Gauteng, Limpopo Province, the Northern Cape, North West Province, the Free State, Zimbabwe, Botswana and Namibia.

THE BIG HOLE

Kimberley's Big Hole was once a hill called Colesberg Kopje, but eager diamond prospectors dug away the hill, leaving a huge hole, one of the world's largest man-made craters. When work stopped in 1914, the mine shafts ran 1100 metres deep.

PLACES TO SEE

ℹ The Kimberley Mine Museum in Kimberley

South Africa at Work

WK/IOA

A GROWTH INDUSTRY

South Africa is a big, beautiful, exciting country, which explains why tourism is one of the fastest growing sectors of the economy. **Tourism** now contributes over 8% of the country's Gross Domestic Product (compared to about 4.3% in 1993) and provides employment for about 7% of the population.

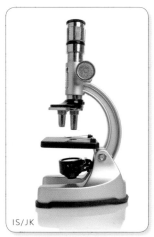

IS/JK

THE CSIR

The Council for Scientific and Industrial Research (CSIR) carries out research for various industries. It runs about 20 laboratories for research into building, chemicals, electronics, food, fuel, telecommunications, transport, engineering and other sciences. The CSIR awards various bursaries and scholarships to encourage research.

Following the shortage of manufactured goods from overseas during the World War II, South Africans began to make their own goods. More factories were built and soon local products were good enough to export. Besides being an agricultural and mining country, South Africa is the leading industrial nation in southern Africa today. People are also encouraged to start their own businesses and factories and so create more employment and wealth for the country.

ArcelorMittal South Africa

The Iron and Steel Corporation of South Africa (**Iscor**, now called ArcelorMittal South Africa) was founded in 1928. Ten years later, it had doubled its output. In 1950 a second steelworks was opened in the new town of Vanderbijlpark, and other steel plants were built in Newcastle (KwaZulu-Natal) and Saldanha Bay. Today, South Africa produces over 17 million tons of stainless steel per year, with many small mills producing copper and brass, chrome and other specialized metal products. Iscor was privatized in 1989, which means that the company is now run by the private sector. The State was paid R3 billion and Iscor shares were sold on the Johannesburg Stock Exchange.

WHERE ARE THE INDUSTRIES?

Factories should be situated near supplies of raw materials, labour, power, water and transport (roads, railways and harbours), and have access to machinery, equipment and packing materials. **Gauteng Province**, incorporating the Pretoria-Witwatersrand-Vereeniging triangle is the country's busiest industrial area. It is close to coalfields and mines, and there are wheat and maize fields, cattle, dairy and other farms in the area. Power is available from Eskom, and the Vaal River and Dam provide water. National roads and railway lines run through Gauteng and OR Tambo International Airport is nearby. Gauteng's industries include mining, machinery, cars, chemicals, clothing and food.

The farming, fishing, food-processing, wine and clothing industries are important in the **Western Cape**. Many of these goods are exported through Cape Town's harbour.

Sugar farming in **KwaZulu-Natal** led to the establishment of a sugar refining industry. Coal deposits in northern KwaZulu-Natal and Gauteng, have been exploited for the development of foundries and other heavy industries.

The Port Elizabeth-Uitenhage area in the **Eastern Cape** is the main centre of the automotive industry (cars and trucks). Many industries need secondary industries to supply them with raw materials or finished parts. Car manufacturing is a good example of one industry creating others, like factories that produce tyres, spare parts, paints, and electrical components.

BP/AL

ArcelorMittal South Africa's steelworks in the Western Cape

The Food Industry

Many foods are sold or exported fresh – that is, without being cooked or preserved in any way. However, a large part of our harvests is processed in a factory. Processing includes drying and juice extraction (fruits), freezing (poultry, vegetables) and canning (meat, fish, fruit, vegetables). The food processing industry employs over 20 000 people at the busiest season, when fruit is being harvested and brought to the factories. Factories or processing plants are always situated close to the products' source, such as the fish canning factories at St Helena Bay, fruit canneries at Grabouw and Ceres, and meat processing plants at Estcourt.

CK/M

Much of South Africa's fruit is packed for export

What Else Do We Make?

South Africa manufactures a wide range of products. One of the most important categories is chemicals, such as fertilizers, pesticides and medicines. Another is clothing. Textile manufacturers produce wool, cotton, synthetic fabrics and leatherwear. Most clothing factories and textile design studios are based in Cape Town and the surrounding towns.

South Africa's motor industry produces a wide range of motor vehicles. The automotive industry is one of our most important, and provides employment in many subsidiary industries.

Other important local industries include beverages (alcoholic and non-alcoholic), tobacco, wood products, printing, publishing and a wide range of machinery.

The Fishing Industry

Over 27 000 people are employed in the marine fishing industry, which is worth over R4 billion per year. The inland fishing industry is also an important source of income and recreation. The main fishing areas are the deep sea banks off the southern Cape coast and around St Helena Bay on the west coast. Many marine products, such as crayfish, are exported and bring in millions of rands. Catches are strictly controlled because of poaching and over-exploitation. There are twelve fishing harbours, from Lambert's Bay on the west coast to Still Bay on the south coast. In addition, most of our large harbours also have fisheries sections.

THE FISHING FLEET

Huge fishing vessels, called factory ships, process fish. Most of our fish is obtained by **purse seine fishing**. A dinghy is lowered from a trawler and surrounds a shoal with a net. The ends of the net are closed, forming a circle and a line at the base is drawn tight like a string purse. The trapped fish are pumped into the trawler. Most of the haul of pilchards, anchovies, mackerel and red-eye is processed into fishmeal, oil and canned fish.

Trawling brings in most of our fish. It takes place mostly between Saldanha Bay and Cape Point. A funnel-shaped net is dragged along the seabed to catch hake, kingklip, monkfish, horse-mackerel, and squid, which are sold fresh or frozen. The industry is controlled by law and the total allowable catch is strictly limited.

Trekking is sometimes called beach seine fishing. A small boat rows out from the beach drawing the net behind it to form a closed ring and the shoal, mainly of mullet, is netted inside it. Fish, such as kob, silverfish, geelbek and galjoen, are caught from boats by hand-line.

Some seafood delicacies, such as perlemoen, black mussels and oysters, are **farmed** sustainably. Perlemoen is canned or frozen and about 90 per cent is exported. The rock lobster (crayfish) catch is worth more than R250 million a year. Lobsters have to be a certain size before they may be caught.

FISH CARTS AND HORNS

In days gone by, horse-drawn carts took fresh fish from the fishing boats at Cape Town's harbours and delivered it to homes in the Peninsula. The driver would blow his little **tin horn** and customers would buy his fish. Fresh and frozen fish is now available in supermarkets, so the fish carts are no longer seen and the fish horn is silent.

Year	Tourists (million)
1997	5.2
1998	5.9
1999	6.0
2000	6.0
2001	5.9
2002	6.6
2003	6.6
2004	6.8
2005	7.5
2006	8.4
2007	9.0
2008	9.4
2009	9.7
2010	10.5

International tourist arrivals (1997-2010).
Source: Department of Tourism

TOURISM

The number of tourists to South Africa increased dramatically after 1994. In that year, 3.9 million tourists visited our country. By 2004, this figure had almost doubled to 6.7 million. Over 10 million tourists visited our country in 2010, the year of the Soccer World Cup, an increase of 8.5% compared to the previous year.

PLACES TO SEE

- Kalk Bay fishing harbour in False Bay
- The Hout Bay Museum in Hout Bay, Cape Town

In the Cape, many people rely on the sea for a living

Killing Our Planet

PLASTIC KILLS!
Because most plastic cannot be broken down by bacteria, plastic buried in rubbish dumps may, in fact, remain intact for thousands of years. Plants and animals can be trapped in plastic, and animals and birds may eat pieces of it and die. So much plastic is produced every year that it is enough to wrap the whole of the Earth.

KEEPING OUR WATER CLEAN
Many storage dams have purification plants to make water safe for drinking. Purified water supplied in pipes is free of **pollutants** and organisms that cause disease. Where large numbers of people live together with only open water available, the water source soon becomes polluted and may cause dangerous diseases such as cholera, which broke out in KwaZulu-Natal in 2000–2001.

It is only when the air becomes so impure that we find it difficult to breathe, or when water is contaminated or scarce that we discover how precious air and water are. Pollution is one of the most serious problems people and wildlife all over the world have to face today.

Breathing Polluted Air
The average person inhales about 15 000 litres of air every day. Whether we notice it or not, the air is almost certainly polluted in some way, particularly if we live in or near a city. Research shows that children living in highly polluted areas grow slowly, and the polluted air they breathe may also affect their ability to learn.

A filthy cloud, visible from many kilometres away, hangs over most of South Africa's cities. It consists of a mixture of soot, ash, dust and impurities ranging from gases and acids to other chemicals. Many people have to burn wood for cooking and heating, which pollutes the air indoors as well as outside. Large amounts of **fossil fuels**, such as oil and coal, are burned to make electricity for homes and factories. Fossil fuels, including petrol, pollute the air, mainly through the gases they give off. Car exhausts, for example, produce so much carbon monoxide that measurements in rush hour have shown that there is enough of this poisonous gas to damage the human brain. Lead is also present in exhaust gases. Other gases produced by factories and cars, such as sulphur dioxide and nitrogen dioxide, combine with moisture in the atmosphere and produce sulphuric and nitric acid. In this way the acid level of our rainfall is increased. This **acid rain** is very harmful to the environment as it destroys sensitive plant and animal life and even soil structure.

Rubbish is produced by factories and by private homes. Much of it is burned in furnaces, but **fire** creates pollution in the form of smoke. When chemical waste is burnt, harmful gases are often given off. Aerosols, such as spray paints, insecticides and deodorants, give off gases called freons, or **chlorofluorocarbons** (CFCs), which attack the ozone.

LIVING IN A GREENHOUSE
Many people in countries with long, cold winters grow vegetables and flowers in greenhouses. Sunlight passes through glass walls and heat rises from the Earth, but it is the roof of the greenhouse that traps the warm air and maintains the high temperature in which the plants grow.

Much the same happens on Earth. Warmth from the sun passes through the atmosphere, but heat rising from the ground cannot pass through the 'roof' of polluted water vapour and carbon dioxide. Heat is then radiated back and the Earth's temperature rises. Scientists believe this **greenhouse effect** is making the Earth hotter.

Above: Both man and industry damage our environment
Left: Only some aerosols are 'ozone friendly'

What Can We Do?

The Southeaster, which blows Cape Town's polluted air out to sea, is affectionately known as 'the Cape Doctor'. But nature cannot always help to combat pollution.

Tall factory chimneys would ensure that smoke is lifted well above the ground. This is particularly important where the air is usually very still, for example in towns in windless hollows or valleys.

Although economically it is best to keep them close together, **factories** should be **spaced apart** to avoid a concentration of pollution in the air.

Since the South African government passed the Atmospheric Pollution Prevention Act in 1965, inspectors have tried to **control** possible **sources** of air pollution. Scientists try to ensure that fossil fuels do not give off excessive amounts of harmful gases. Open fires are forbidden in certain areas, known as smoke-free zones.

The use of CFCs is banned in most countries, some of which compel motorists to fit anti-pollution converters to their motor vehicle exhaust systems. Some scientists say that the 'hole' in the ozone layer is getting smaller.

Water for Survival

Although water is often in short supply in South Africa, people still throw rubbish into rivers, which then wash it out to sea. Our beaches and rivers are littered with plastic bottles, cans and sweet wrappers.

Industry is often to blame. Factories dispose of their waste products in the sea or in nearby rivers. This not only destroys life in the river or sea, but also affects our drinking water, and water used for crop irrigation.

Mines, particularly those on the Witwatersrand, contain vast quantities of underground water that is high in acids. This, as well as equally destructive substances found on mine dumps, eventually finds its way to the country's drainage system.

Giant tankers carrying enormous quantities of crude oil pass the coast of southern Africa. If there is an accident, or if ships wash their tanks at sea, **pollutants** and **oil** spill into the ocean. Marine animals and plants become coated with oil and many die and oil washes ashore, polluting our beaches, killing sea-life on the shore and making swimming impossible.

SAVING THE OZONE LAYER

Pollutants called chlorofluorocarbons (CFCs) react with and destroy the ozone molecules in the Earth's outer atmosphere. This **ozone layer** absorbs the sun's ultraviolet rays. Scientists believe that increased amounts of ultraviolet radiation can cause skin cancer and kill certain fish and other sources of food.

OIL ON THE BEACH

About half the oil that ends up at sea comes from land-based activities, such as cars, heavy machinery and industry, about a third comes from oil-tanker spills and the rest from accidents at sea and offshore drilling. The **SANCCOB** sea bird centre in Cape Town has been saving oil-affected sea birds, penguins in particular, for over 40 years.

The wreck of the Seli 1 spilt oil onto Cape Town beaches in September 2011

PLACES TO SEE

Visit the SANCCOB Sea Bird Centre based at Rietvlei in Cape Town; birds are kept there until they have recovered and can be returned to sea

Working the Land

South Africa's earliest farmers sowed and reaped crops at Mzonjani near today's Durban as long ago as the Stone Age and, by the 10th century, people living in the broad river valleys between the Drakensberg and the sea grew crops and kept cattle and sheep. The remains of farming villages and kraals have been found on the Highveld.

European Settlers

The main task of the first settlers in South Africa was to plant a garden to supply fresh fruit and vegetables to the crews of passing ships. In the Company Gardens, they cultivated vegetables, grapes, apples and citrus fruit. They also planted wheat near Green Point, but the wind destroyed the young shoots.

In 1657, nine Free Burghers were granted farms in the Liesbeeck river valley on the sheltered eastern side of Table Mountain where they grew maize (mealies) and, later, vines. Their farming methods had remained unchanged for centuries. They worked the soil with spades and picks; oxen drew ploughs with wooden blades strengthened with iron, and scythes or sickles were used for hand-reaping crops. On threshing floors, horses trampled the grain, separating it from the husks. Slaves trod grapes in large wooden casks to extract the juice for wine-making.

Two Types of Farming

During the 18th century some farmers left Cape Town and headed east, over the Hottentots Holland mountains. They seldom grew crops, but kept sheep (for meat rather than wool) and cattle. Each farmer produced just enough food for his own family. This is known as **subsistence farming**.

Over the years, pastures in parts of the north-eastern Cape became scarce, particularly after long periods of drought, and farmers moved further afield. Some settled near present-day Grahamstown, while others crossed the Orange River and headed north. On their way, they met black subsistence farmers who had been in the area for centuries.

Meanwhile, farmers at the Cape had learned to manage their land efficiently and had prospered. Stock farming improved, especially after importing Merino sheep from Spain. By the mid-19th century, wool was doing well on the European market. Wine was another important export. Growing crops principally for sale or export is called **commercial farming**.

Merino sheep are the foundation of the wool industry

Farming Difficulties

By the beginning of the 20th century, many black farmers had been displaced from their land, and arable land became scarce and expensive. Farms that were destroyed during the Anglo-Boer War took years to recover. Droughts and other natural disasters turned fertile fields into wastelands and nothing was done to prevent soil erosion. Farmers seldom used fertilizers to enrich the soil and hadn't learnt how to control pests.

THE OLDEST TOOL

The **hoe** is probably the oldest farm implement still used today. A long-handled tool with a short, curved blade, it has been used for loosening and tilling the soil for thousands of years. Not even modern tractors are as efficient as the hoe in *skoffeling* the ground and removing weeds from among crops.

FARMING WITHOUT SOIL

Growing plants without soil is called **hydroponics**. The plants are usually grown in troughs of water with a layer of pebbles on which the roots can anchor themselves. Hydroponic farmers add nutrients to the water in which the plants grow. Plastic or fibreglass 'tunnels' are well suited to hydroponic farming.

Maize forms the staple diet for many rural black communities

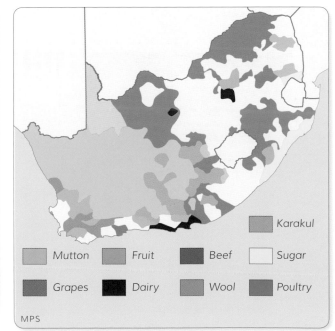

Mutton	Fruit	Beef	Karakul
Grapes	Dairy	Wool	Sugar
			Poultry

INCREASED FOOD PRODUCTION

South Africa's population is growing so fast that we may soon be unable to produce enough food. But increased production may be the solution. This means that we must make better use of farmland. The soil must be kept fertile and well watered. Modern farmers have to be efficient and labourers must be trained. Researchers are working on ways to improve the quantity and the quality of crops, animal fodder, meat and dairy products.

Modern farming

In a good year, our farmers are able to produce almost all the food South Africans need. Because of the many different climates and conditions found in South Africa, farmers grow almost every type of crop and rear all kinds of animals. Within our borders there are areas varying from sub-tropical to Mediterranean and from semi-desert to grassland. Each region is suitable for a particular type of agriculture.

When thousands of sheep and cattle died during the droughts of the 1920s and early 1930s, farmers planted grain instead. They grew wheat in the winter rainfall areas of the Western Cape, and maize on the Highveld, where it rains in summer. The state helped farmers by lending money, giving seed and equipment, and providing information on farming methods. Cheap tools and other necessities could be bought from co-operative societies, and agricultural committees ensured prices did not fall too low. Young farmers who once learnt by working with their fathers could study modern methods at the new agricultural schools and colleges.

Elsenburg College of Agriculture, Stellenbosch

Improved farming methods

Improved farming methods included the battery system of poultry and egg-production. Cows were milked by machine, animal breeding improved, and stock fed on scientifically balanced foods were healthier. Pests and diseases were controlled. One result was that sheep farmers prospered and South Africa became one of the world's most important wool producers. The country started to manufacture its own chemical fertilizers and other agricultural necessities. Huge water storage projects, such as those at the Gariep and Vanderkloof dams, were constructed, and the Orange-Fish River tunnel and other irrigation schemes were established.

IS/BGB

Hens are specially bred to produce good quality eggs

Quick and efficient machines were introduced. Tractors worked on almost every farm, and in the 1950s the combine harvester was introduced. These machines have taken over most of the hard labour of farming. Combine harvesters reap and thresh crops, and blow the grain into trucks, which take it to storehouses. Fields that were once weeded by hand are now sprayed from tractor-drawn tanks or low-flying aeroplanes. Electric pumps, boreholes and sprinklers have replaced water-furrows to irrigate the land.

IS/SF

Combine harvesters do the hard labour on crop farms

THE RISING COST OF FOOD

South Africa's **food production** has not kept pace with population growth over the last two decades. Between 1991 and 2007, food production is estimated to have increased by 10%, whereas the population grew by about 26% (from about 38 million to 48 million – not taking into account illegal immigrants). Adverse climatic conditions, the availability and quality of water, and a lack of investment in farming have all adversely affected food production, and food prices have also been driven up by rising demand from other countries. In June 2008, food prices were rising at 17.8%. In 2006, South Africa exported about R26.9 billion and imported about R20.5 billion in agricultural products. By 2007, these figures were R29.9 billion and R30.3 billion respectively, meaning that South Africa is beginning to import more food than it exports.

PLACES TO SEE

- Kleinplasie Open-Air Museum, Worcester
- Willem Prinsloo Agricultural Museum near Pretoria
- Bathurst Agricultural Museum, Bathurst
- Wheat Industry Museum, Malmesbury

Stock Farming

GAME FARMING

South Africa has more **game**, and more species, than most other countries in the world, and game farming is fast becoming an industry with great economic potential. Indigenous game is well adapted to survival in the arid conditions of southern Africa, although very large land areas are needed to provide enough grazing.

South Africa's earliest stock farmers were black people living in today's KwaZulu-Natal. They settled in villages, kept cattle and sheep and grew crops. The Khoikhoi of the Western Cape kept cattle and fat-tailed sheep. To both these groups, cattle were a sign of wealth and oxen were only slaughtered for special occasions.

Animals that help

When the Khoikhoi first encountered European settlers, they bartered with them, exchanging their cattle and sheep for copper bracelets, beads and pieces of iron. The Dutch settlers bred animals they bought from the Khoikhoi with cattle and sheep that they had brought with them from Europe. Their cattle provided meat and milk, and also drew heavy wagons.

In South Africa today, there are breeds of cattle descended from stock kept by the early stock farmers. Among them are the hump-backed **Red Afrikander**, which is resistant to many African diseases, and the **Nguni**. Both are bred for their high-quality beef.

Afrikander cattle provide good beef

HOW MUCH MEAT DO WE EAT?

Although South African consumption of pork has remained much the same over recent years, we now eat less mutton and beef than before. On average, one person eats just over three kilograms of **pork**, about four kilograms of **mutton**, and between 15 and 20 kilograms of **beef** each year.

Nguni are the indigenous cattle of Africa

Animal Diseases

In 1896 a devastating epidemic, called **rinderpest**, killed 2.5 million cattle in southern Africa. This fatal viral disease spreads by contact; today, cattle can be vaccinated against it. **Foot-and-mouth disease** is another fatal viral disease of cattle, sheep, goats and pigs. It is spread by contact and by contaminated fodder, and is controlled by the slaughter of infected animals and by strict quarantine. Many thousands of head of stock were killed after an outbreak of the disease in the KwaZulu-Natal Midlands in 2000.

Cattle for Meat and Milk

Today, it is estimated that there are over 13.6 million head of cattle on farms and dairies across South Africa. Afrikander, Hereford and Bonsmara cattle are bred for their meat. The most popular breeds for milk production are the black-and-white **Friesland** and the golden-brown **Jersey**.

The mechanized milking of cows

Friesland cows are used for milk

Sheep Farming

In 1789, the King of Spain presented the Cape Dutch government with two Merino rams and four ewes. This breed of sheep flourished at the Cape, yielding wool of excellent quality. More Merinos were imported and soon spread throughout South Africa. Today the Merino and its cross-breeds make up over 60% of the country's sheep farming.

Sheep are generally bred either for meat or for wool, but the **Merino** is prized for both. One of several mutton sheep in South Africa is the **Dorper**, which is a cross between the **Dorset Horn** and the **Blackhead Persian**. It was developed here in the 1930s and is widely distributed around the country. It is a hardy animal, well suited to the Karoo, which is South Africa's main sheep-farming region.

Today there are 28 million sheep in the country – the greatest part of our agricultural livestock. South Africa has become one of the world's top five wool producers. Annual wool auctions held in Port Elizabeth attract buyers from many other countries.

Goats

The **boerbok**, seen in many parts of South Africa, especially the semi-desert and mountainous areas, developed from indigenous animals kept by the country's first stock farmers. They are sturdy, short-haired animals that give good milk and meat.

More important for the economy is the long-haired **angora goat**, which is farmed mainly in the Eastern Cape. It is for the sake of this valuable breed that warnings of cold weather and snow are often broadcast on the weather forecast. Angora goats were originally imported from Turkey to improve the quality of local goat meat. Today they are kept for their soft, silky mohair. South Africa's 1.5 million angora goats produce six million kilograms of mohair every year, making this country the world's foremost mohair producer.

Angora goats are bred for their valuable hair

COLONEL GORDON'S MERINOS

When six Spanish **Merino** sheep arrived at the Cape in 1789, the military commander at the Castle, Colonel Robert Jacob Gordon, was delighted. He was anxious to start a wool industry and, to ensure that the breed did not cross with the local variety, he kept them in an enclosure at the outpost of Groenkloof (now Mamre). The Merinos flourished and produced wool of an excellent quality. After Gordon's death in 1795 they were put up for auction. Some were bought by men from a sailing ship that had called for provisions at Table Bay, and taken to Australia. This started what has become one of the richest industries in that country. Descendants of these original Australian Merinos were later imported back into South Africa to improve the breed in this country.

Pigs for Pork

Pigs were introduced to South Africa by Dutch settlers in 1652. At the beginning of the 20th century new breeds were imported from Europe and America and pig farming has since become increasingly scientific. Most of South Africa's pigs are kept in modern, hygienic housing systems. Fed a balanced diet, they grow so quickly that they are usually ready for the market by the time they are five months old.

Livestock, such as pigs, are slaughtered at an abattoir

Poultry

Until the 1940s, chickens, ducks and turkeys ran free in open pens. Hens hatched their eggs on straw nests and reared their own chicks. Today, chicks are hatched by the thousands in incubators. Some spend a brief life as **broilers**, raised in an environment in which temperature, lighting and other conditions are artificially controlled. After six weeks they are slaughtered and sold at supermarkets, or exported. Many hens are kept in batteries as **layers**. Breeding houses for chicks and broiler batteries are situated close to most big cities. Demand for free-range eggs and poultry is increasing.

Ostrich with chicks

METHANE

As part of their digestive process, **ruminants** – camels, sheep, goats, cattle and buffalo – generate **methane**, one of the gases linked to global warming. In fact, the number one source of methane worldwide is animal husbandry. It is estimated that there are approximately 1.5 billion cows on the planet, almost one animal for every four humans.

OSTRICHES

The ostrich, the world's biggest bird, thrives in the dry climate of the Little Karoo and on the lucerne grown there. Ostriches are indigenous to Africa and, although they cannot fly, they can run as fast as 48 km per hour. Oudtshoorn is the principal town of the ostrich farming industry. Every part of the ostrich is useable. The skin makes excellent leather and the meat is eaten fresh or as biltong, Ostrich eggs, which are equivalent to 24 hen's eggs, are emptied and sold as souvenirs, as are the two-toed ostrich feet. Feathers are now mainly used in feather dusters but also for fashion garments such as stoles or boas.

PLACES TO SEE

When travelling in the Karoo, see how many different types of sheep you can recognize

Crop Farming

MILHO, MBILA OR MEALIES?

Portuguese traders discovered maize in America, and introduced it to the people living along the east coast of Africa. The Portuguese called it **milho**, meaning grain. Nguni-speakers called it **mbila**. Voortrekkers called it **mielie**, sometimes spelt mealie. In the USA it is known as Indian corn. But its official name is maize.

DRYING OUR FRUIT

The **dried fruit** industry is well established in South Africa. Raisins are one of the most important dried fruit products. All dried fruit is processed according to size and quality, packed and then sold, especially to the overseas markets.

South Africa produces many different crops. With such a diversity of climatic regions, farmers can cultivate a variety of fruit, such as citrus, pineapples, berries, grapes apples and peaches, in different areas. Field crops like maize (mealies), wheat and other cereals, are grown in various parts of the country. Sugar flourishes in KwaZulu-Natal. Indigenous plants, such as *waterblommetjies*, are also cultivated, and chicory, an additive in instant coffee, thrives in the Eastern Cape.

Maize

Popcorn, mealie-meal porridge, samp or corn, which we call mealies, all come from the same plant: maize. Maize also provides us with mealie-rice and cornflour, and is found in canned pets' food and chicken feed. Salad oil is crushed from the germ or 'heart', and the stalks are chopped up and added to cattle feed. Maize is the country's most important crop as it is the staple food for thousands of South Africans.

Maize is grown in many parts of South Africa and its neighbouring states, mostly on huge, highly developed farms, but subsistence farmers grow just enough for their own families. South Africa's richest maize-producing region is called 'the summer crop area'. It used to he called the 'maize triangle', but its borders now look more like a quadrangle and include parts of the Free State, North West, Mpumalanga and KwaZulu-Natal. When farmers produce more maize than the country can use (when there is a surplus), it is exported to other countries.

A maize field ready for harvest

Sugar

Sugar is a very important crop. It has been cultivated in KwaZulu-Natal since 1847 when Edmund Morewood, an English settler, imported cane cuttings from the island of Reunion. The cane flourished and today the industry boasts an annual production of more than two million tons. The export industry is successful and creates jobs for many South Africans. Most sugar cane is taken by rail to the mills for crushing. The raw, sugar-rich juice is separated into a dark syrup and crystals. The molasses is used in cattle feed and the crystals are refined into brown and white sugar.

Fields of sugar cane

Wheat

The cereal that gives us our daily bread is wheat, the second largest of South Africa's grain crops, and one of the first to be grown here by European settlers. Since the mid-17th century, wheat has been grown in the winter-rainfall regions of the Western Cape, known as the **Swartland** and **Rûensveld**. Today, farmers using new scientific methods of cultivation are harvesting excellent wheat in parts of the summer-rainfall regions of the Highveld, particularly the Free State, which is now South Africa's top wheat-producer. Our wheat production has doubled over the past 40 years.

A combine harvester at work in a wheat field

Sorghum

Long before the first wheat seed was sown at the Cape, grain sorghum was being cultivated by people living along the Indian Ocean. Seeds of this cereal have been found embedded in fragments of pots almost 2000 years old. Today grain sorghum is produced in Mpumalanga, the north-eastern Free State and North West and Limpopo provinces. Rich in energy, it is ground to make porridge as well as beer.

Fruit

South African fruit is exported all over the world. **Deciduous** fruit grows on trees that lose their leaves during winter. Grabouw, in the Western Cape, is one of the best apple-growing regions in the world. **Citrus** needs lots of water and, if the rainfall is insufficient, the orchards must be irrigated. Oranges, lemons, grapefruit, naartjies and limes are grown in the Western and Eastern Cape, North West Province, Mpumalanga, Limpopo Province and KwaZulu-Natal. **Subtropical** fruit, like bananas, litchis, mangoes and avocados, are farmed in the warmer areas of KwaZulu-Natal, Limpopo Province and the Mpumalanga Lowveld. The Eastern Cape is famous for its pineapples.

Oranges grow well in warm, well-irrigated areas

Crops and Climate

Crop	Suitable climate
Maize	warm and wet in summer
Sugar	warm, subtropical areas
Wheat	winter-rainfall areas
Sorghum	summer-rainfall areas

PICKING YOUR OWN FRUIT

Some farms invite the public to pick their own fruit. From about late October, the strawberry plantations outside Stellenbosch have life-size **scarecrows** not only to frighten off greedy birds, but to encourage visitors to help themselves. Cherry-picking near Ceres in December can be quite an adventure. Table grapes may be picked on some farms from the end of January. Visitors pay for their fruit according to how much they have picked.

Grapes and Wine

The wines of the Western Cape are famous throughout the world. There are vineyards from the Olifants River valley in the west to the Aghulhas plain in the south. Wines matured on the famous estates of Constantia, Franschhoek, Paarl and Stellenbosch have won many international awards. South Africa produces the full range of wine styles: white, red, sparkling, dessert and fortified wines (port and sherry-style).

Red and white table grapes are cultivated in the Western Cape, notably the Hex River valley, and along the Orange River in the Northern Cape, where the sweet hanepoot grapes are turned into raisins and sultanas.

Other Crops

Peanuts (groundnuts) and sunflowers are mainly cultivated for their oil. Potatoes are grown in many parts of the country as both winter and summer crops so that there is a constant supply. Vegetables, such as tomatoes, onions and cabbages, are farmed in most parts of the country, especially close to the towns where they can be marketed easily.

Sunflowers are grown especially for their oil

ALL ABOARD THE APPLE EXPRESS

The Apple Express takes visitors from Port Elizabeth to Thornhill and back, along the narrow-gauge railway line built in 1906. It also puffs to Avontuur and at various times of the year makes trips to Loerie, Jeffreys Bay, Humansdorp and up the Gamtoos Valley to Patensie.

FLOWERS FOR ALL

South Africa has many beautiful indigenous flowers. **Protea** flowers, as well as other bulbs and cuttings, are exported worldwide. The value of flowers and bulbs amounts to several million rand annually. Plant nurseries grow indigenous and exotic flowers for export, and more than 70% of protea species are grown commercially. Proteas are also cultivated in the summer rainfall regions, where they do not occur naturally.

PLACES TO SEE

ℹ The North West Agricultural Museum, Lichtenburg

Money and Banking

STARTING EARLY

Most banks today offer special banking accounts for children to encourage them to start saving from an early age, and to teach them proper money management; they also have special accounts for pensioners, who pay lower fees for each transaction.

THE EXCHANGE RATE

When South Africans travel overseas or pay for foreign goods, they need to exchange their South African money for foreign currency, such as American **dollars**, **euros** or **pounds sterling** (British). The number of rands paid for a dollar, euro, pound or any other currency is called the exchange rate. This changes daily.

South Africa's earliest people did not use money, but obtained what they wanted from the environment or by barter from others. When foreign sailors visited our shores, they bartered with the Khoikhoi, offering them beads, copper and iron in exchange for cattle and sheep. In other countries, shells, tusks, cows, and even slaves, bird skulls and salt were used as money.

Coins at the Cape

After Van Riebeeck's arrival, gold and silver coins from Europe were accepted at the Cape. In the late 18th century, the Dutch East India Company minted special coins for their colonies. These coins included small copper coins called **doits**, and large silver **ducatoons**. Later the Company introduced its own **guilder** pieces.

The First Banknotes

The war between the Netherlands and Great Britain led to a shortage of coins at the Cape, so Governor Van Plettenberg issued paper banknotes worth almost 100 000 rijksdaalders. When the British took over the Cape in 1795, they introduced cartwheel pennies or **Koperen dubbeltjes**, but when the Batavian Republic took over in 1803, they melted down these clumsy, heavy coins and made smaller pieces.

The British returned to the Cape in 1806, so when a new system of gold sovereigns and silver coins was introduced in England in 1816, some reached the Cape. Other foreign currencies were abandoned in 1848 when England's **sterling** (pounds, shillings and pence) became South Africa's only legal money.

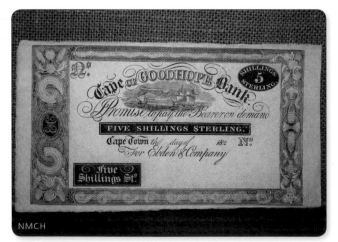

A five-shilling note from the Cape of Good Hope Bank

Gold from the Witwatersrand

In September 1874, gold from Mpumalanga mines was struck into coins in England, and became the official coins of the Zuid-Afrikaansche Republiek. The Pretoria Mint began striking coins for the ZAR in 1892, six years after the discovery of gold on the Witwatersrand. Near the end of the Second Anglo-Boer War, as money started to run out in the Transvaal, 986 coins known as **ZAR veldponde** were struck at an emergency mint at Pilgrim's Rest. These are now extremely valuable.

MONEY FOR ALL

The **tickey** was a small coin, worth three pennies in British sterling, but the term 'tickey' was only used in South Africa. Some people say the name is from a Malay word 'tiga' meaning three. Others believe that Bantu-speaking people called the coin 'i-tiki-peni' and that 'tickey' was a short version. Today, some people still refer to public telephones as 'tickey boxes'. The penny was worth so little that the people at the Cape called it the **ou-lap**, which means 'old rag'.

The **rix-dollar**, a silver coin issued in The Netherlands, was originally known as 'de rijks-daalder', meaning 'the kingdom's dollar'. It was also used as currency in other countries. In 1781, when paper notes were introduced to the Cape, a rix-dollar was worth 48 Dutch pennies or about four shillings British sterling. But by 1825, the rix-dollar was worth only one shilling five pence.

Pieces of eight were Spanish coins worth eight smaller coins. They were among the many coins used at the Cape. Other coins accepted by traders included Spanish **doubloons**, Dutch **guilders**, English **guineas**, and Portuguese **crusados**.

Decimalization

On 14 February 1961, the pound was replaced by the South African Rand, which was divided into 100 cents. The new coins bore South African emblems. Since then, several new series of coins have been introduced, smaller and lighter than the previous coins. Banknotes are issued for larger amounts (up to R200) .

The South African Reserve Bank

Banks were introduced to South Africa in 1793, when the Lombard Bank, the country's first bank, was established by the Dutch East India Company. In less than 50 years, almost every town in the Cape and Natal had its own bank. By 1920, there were three main banking groups: the National Bank of South Africa, the Standard Bank and the Netherlands Bank. They all issued their own notes, so the **South African Reserve Bank** was established. It is the only institution allowed to issue South African bank notes and coins. It buys and sells foreign exchange, controls the cash reserves of all banks, and stores stocks of gold and foreign currency. It is the Republic's most powerful financial institution and the centre of the country's money market.

The Reserve Bank building in Pretoria

Inflation

When we talk about inflation, we mean the general and steady increase in the price of services and goods. When inflation is high, you can buy less with the same amount of money than what you could have bought before. Over recent years, inflation has increased and the value of money has decreased. For example, a litre of Coca-Cola cost only 27 cents in 1976, but around R11.50 in 2012.

Modern Banking

Modern bank services include loans for hire purchase, study and travel; home and business loans; insurance and savings; foreign exchange and the administration of wills. People can make transactions through automatic teller machines (ATMs) and via computer at any time of the day. Most banks offer special savings accounts for children. Account holders are issued with bank cards to deposit and withdraw money.

ATMs provide 24-hour access to your bank account

WHAT DO THEY MEAN?

An **account** is an agreement with a bank that it will look after your money, and pay you **interest** (a percentage) for the use of your money. You can make a **deposit** (put money into your account) or a **withdrawal** (take money from your account). A **statement** tells you how much money is left. A **cheque** signed by you tells the bank to pay someone an amount from your account. **Credit** may mean the amount of money you have in the bank, or the amount the bank will allow you to spend, even though you may not have enough in your account. A **credit card** allows you to spend money you may not yet have, while an **overdraft** is an allowance for money you can borrow from the bank even though there is not enough money in your account.

GOLD, BRONZE AND PAPER

The South African Reserve Bank was created by law in 1921 and is the only organization in the country that is allowed to mint coins and print banknotes. The Reserve Bank also holds the country's reserve stocks of gold. Until the early 1930s, high-value coins were minted in gold, and banknotes could be exchanged for their printed value in gold. Some coins were minted in silver, copper and bronze, but now all coins are struck in lightweight alloys.

THE GLOBAL ECONOMY

In the past, each country's economy was separate, and banks and governments tended to act independently. Nowadays, people talk about the **global economy**, because the whole world is one system and events which occur on one side of the planet can often affect the other side. For example, in 2008, a 'sub-prime' mortgage crisis in the US banking system caused a worldwide recession. This is why finance ministers from different countries regularly meet to discuss matters of common concern.

PLACES TO SEE

ℹ First National Bank Museum, Johannesburg

Our Coasts and Oceans

A SHINING LIGHT
South Africa's first **lighthouse**, erected in 1824 in Green Point, Cape Town, is still in operation, although the old oil lamp and lens have been replaced with modern systems. When the foghorn sounds on dark nights, an old legend is recalled: Maqoma was a Xhosa chief who was imprisoned and died on Robben Island in 1873, and Xhosa dockworkers used to say 'Maqoma's cow is calling for him'.

The South African coastline varies from rugged cliffs and buttresses to smooth stretches of sandy beaches, but there are very few natural harbours or pronounced bays. There are two important sea currents which strongly influence both the country's climate and its coastal conditions.

The Cold Benguela Current

Moving northwards along the west coast is the slow, cool and narrow Benguela Current. It brings cold waters to the Cape Peninsula and continues up the west coast beyond the Angola-Namibia border. Off Cape Town, sea temperatures average 18°C in winter, and only 15°C in summer, when the strong south-easterly winds cause cold water to rise from the depths. The plankton-rich waters attract great numbers of fish, and much of the fishing industry is situated along the west coast.

The Warm Agulhas Current

The Agulhas Current is swift, warm and up to 160 kilometres wide. It streams south-westward from the tropical Indian Ocean, gradually cooling as it moves down the east coast. Sometimes it meets strong south-westerly winds that occasionally create huge waves, sometimes as high as a five-storey building. These terrifying freak waves have caused terrible damage to ships and may explain the mysterious disappearance of many ships off the south coast.

Making its way westward, the Agulhas Current reaches Cape Agulhas where it meets the eastern edge of the undersea shelf of land called the Agulhas Bank. The current then turns southward and eventually eastward towards the south Indian Ocean.

The Merging of the Currents

The Agulhas and Benguela Currents, as well as the Indian and Atlantic Oceans, mingle and merge along Africa's southernmost coast. These differing waters affect the climates of South Africa's coastal regions as well as the country's marine life.

The West Coast

South Africa's coast is occasionally lashed by gales that blow both on and offshore. On the west coast, the strong offshore summer winds drive the surface water of the Benguela northward, parallel to the coast. Or they would, except that the rotation of the Earth deflects the current out to sea. The water is replaced by an 'upwelling' of cold, nutrient-rich water from the bottom of the sea. These conditions are ideal for the nurturing of sea plants, known as **phytoplankton**. Sometimes, they multiply so rapidly that dense 'blooms' appear and actually colour the water. Tiny animals feed on these plants, making plankton the food for many sea fishes. Because there is so much of this food available for fish and seaweed (kelp), which shelters rock lobster (crayfish) and perlemoen, the waters off South Africa's west coast are some of the richest fishing grounds in the world. The abundance of fish also attracts thousands of seabirds and seals.

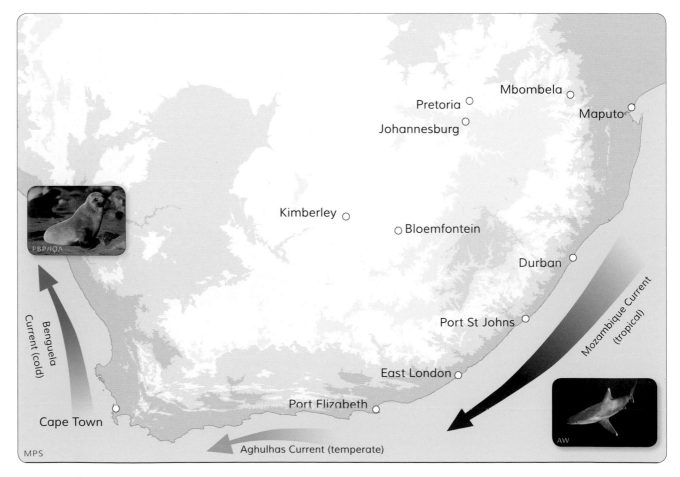

Mbombela

Pretoria

Maputo

Johannesburg

Kimberley

Bloemfontein

Durban

Benguela Current (cold)

Port St Johns

Mozambique Current (tropical)

East London

Port Elizabeth

Cape Town

Aghulhas Current (temperate)

RED TIDE

Red tide is a spreading, red-coloured stain on the surface of the sea, which is often seen along South Africa's west coast. It is caused by the very dense 'blooming' of phytoplankton in suitable conditions. If this bloom is near the shore, it can be very dangerous to mussels and other sea animals that feed on phytoplankton. When people eat seafood poisoned by red tide, they may develop a mild form of paralysis that lasts for a few days. But, sometimes eating only two or three mussels is enough to kill an adult. Rock lobster and perlemoen may be affected, and mussels can be poisonous for up to four months after a red tide. For this reason, the Sea Fisheries Institute regularly tests shellfish from the west coast. If it discovers poisoned mussels or seafood, it publishes 'red tide' warnings in newspapers and on radio.

GTY/GI

The Dry Plains of the West Coast

The Benguela Current is responsible for the dry climate of southern Africa's west coast. Moisture-laden winds blow from the Atlantic Ocean towards the shore. When these winds meet the cool waters of the Benguela Current, the moisture condenses, forming the mist that is so typical of the coastal desert plains, especially in Namibia. The mist which forms over the Atlantic Ocean is often the land's only source of moisture because it **seldom rains** in this area. Only in the southwest, where there are mountains fairly close to the coast, is there enough rain to enable farmers to cultivate the soil.

The Lush East Coast

As the warm Agulhas Current sweeps southward from the tropical Indian Ocean, it brings warm air. Carrying plenty of water, this air moves inland, giving coastal KwaZulu-Natal its hot, humid climate. When the air meets the Drakensberg and rises up its slopes, the temperature drops, moisture condenses and falls as rain. Because of these conditions, KwaZulu-Natal has the **highest rainfall** in South Africa. Lush vegetation flourishes in the moist warmth carried by the Agulhas Current. Dense evergreen bush and subtropical crops, like sugar cane and bananas, grow along the coast. As the current loses some of its warmth on its south-westward course, the humidity is reduced and the vegetation becomes less lush.

APT/IOA

Life In the Agulhas Current

Unlike the Benguela Current, the Agulhas carries no nutrient-rich water to nourish the tiny plants of the sea. Therefore there are few planktonic organisms to feed the surface fish. Although there are many kinds of seaweeds they are different from and not as big as the west coast kelps. Most of the sea life comes from tropical areas to the north-east. For example, larvae of the spiny lobster, which are common near Madagascar, drift on the current until they reach KwaZulu-Natal. Sharks and turtles may also use the current, and bluebottles and the bubbleraft shell float along on its surface.

RDLH/IOA

A turtle makes its way to the water

LIGHTHOUSES ALONG OUR COAST

Forty-six lighthouses flash warnings to ships passing South Africa's rugged coastline. Of these, 30 are automated, and the rest are controlled by a lighthouse-keeper. The automated lighthouses all have **custodians**, such as a local farmer who carefully watches the light in case of failure. Every **manned** lighthouse has a permanent lighthouse-keeper. Many of these lighthouses are situated in remote places, such as Dassen Island, off the Cape west coast. The original lighthouse at Cape Point was erected on one of the windiest places in South Africa but was built too high up, and the light could not be seen in foggy weather. In 1911, after the 'Lusitania' was wrecked on the rocks nearby, a new lighthouse was erected closer to the water. Its 19 million candle-power light is the most powerful along our coast. Other powerful lighthouses are at Cape Agulhas, Cape Columbine, Slangkop (Kommetjie), Cape St Francis, Danger Point, Cape Recife, Great Fish Point, East London and Durban. Each has its own system of flashes. These code flashes are described on navigational charts so that passing ships may locate their position from them.

TD/GI

THE SKELETON COAST

When winds from the Atlantic meet the cold Benguela Current, mists form. As the temperature rises during the day, the mist evaporates and no rain falls. The dunes of the Namib Desert, in Namibia, reach down to the sea. This stretch of coastline is sometimes known as the Skeleton Coast because so many ships have been wrecked there.

SA/IOA

THE CAPE OF STORMS

Our country's coastline is one of the most dangerous in the world. Mountainous seas and wind storms have wrecked many ships against rugged cliffs and huge boulders off our southern coast. Over 500 years ago, fearful Portuguese navigators called these waters the **Cape of Storms**.

PLACES TO SEE

ℹ️ L'Agulhas lighthouse and southernmost tip of Africa at Cape Agulhas

Seashore Life

A SWIMMING SWALLOW?
The beautiful sea slug, called a **sea swallow**, feeds on bluebottles. When its floating body is spread out, it has the shape of a swallow. The bluebottle's stings do not harm the sea swallow, but are put to good use. The stinging cells pass through the sea swallow's gut to the surface of its body, where they function as 'second-hand' defensive weapons.

LIVING SEASHELLS
Every one of the thousands of empty **shells** that are strewn along South Africa's shores was once part of a small, living, soft-bodied animal. The shell is left behind when the animal inside it dies.

Left to right: Reefs are home to colourful fish and corals; starfish and sea urchins are molluscs; crabs live in the intertidal zone. For the more adventurous, the beauty of corals and reef fish can be seen deeper down

Many fascinating forms of life can be seen on the seashore. Plants such as seaweeds and algae convert the sun's energy into food by photosynthesis. Plant-eaters, like shellfish, graze on seaweeds. Birds feed on limpets, and sand plovers gobble up the hoppers. Scavengers, like gulls, whelks and rock lobsters, eat dead fish or other animals. In the pools, fish prey on squid that prey on crabs, and the crabs prey on bluebottles. There are also poisonous creatures such as blaasops, and predators such as moray eels.

The Zones of a Rocky Shore

Between the high- and low-water levels, lies the **intertidal zone**. The plants and animals that live in this zone have to survive varying conditions. They are either covered by salt water or exposed to the air, wind and sunlight. Because of this, plants and animals live in distinct bands on rocky shores.

Thousands of small seashells called **periwinkles** are found in the area just above the high tide, called the **splash zone**. They feed on lichen covering the rocks. Below that, in the **upper intertidal zone**, there may be clusters of small turret-shaped **barnacles**, **oysters**, larger **winkles**, and a few **limpets**.

The **middle** and especially the **lower zones** of the intertidal area have an even greater abundance of plant and animal life. There are barnacles, **tubeworms**, limpets, **mussels** and **seaweed**. Pinkish-white seaweed crusts coat the lower parts of the rocks and reach into the **shallow-water zone**. Here, along the east coast, there are vast colonies of reddish **sea squirts** called 'red bait'. Along the KwaZulu-Natal coast, the middle and lower intertidal zones are often carpeted with greenish, slimy **zoanthids** that look rather like closed sea anemones.

The shallow-water zone is never exposed. **Urchins**, winkles and **perlemoen** live here, as well as **octopus**, fish and **sea slugs**. Fixed to the rock or sandy bottom are seaweeds and **sea anemones**. Anemones are flesh-eating animals. They wave their tentacles about, ready to grab and poison passing animals. **Corals** also eat flesh. Urchins nibble at drifting seaweeds. Like starfish, they have mouths in the middle of their underside and move about on tube feet.

Rock Pools

Pools of water in rocky hollows in the intertidal zone often contain plants and animals found nowhere else. You may find a small silvery-green **klipfish**, or even a **rock lobster** (also known as **crayfish**). The lobster's hard, jointed skeleton is on the outside and is shed when the animal gets too big. Sometimes a rock lobster may share its home with a **moray eel**. When an octopus gropes along the rocks searching for a lobster or something else to eat, the snakelike eel shoots out and gobbles up the octopus!

Goose barnacles grow on stalks that look like the necks of geese. They attach themselves to floating objects and collect food on their fringed tentacles.

Seaweed

Seaweeds are algae. Some types are used in agriculture, industry and medicine. They are divided into three groups according to their colour.

Green algae, such as sea lettuce, occur in the intertidal zone rock pools high on the shore, or near fresh water.

Brown algae occur in the deeper waters off the rocky west coast. These include **kelps** and **sea bamboos** that attach themselves to the sea-bottom so that currents cannot carry them away.

Red algae also occur in the intertidal zone, but are more common in deeper water. They dry out at low tide and absorb water at high tide.

Many sea creatures, such as perlemoen, **alikreukel** and **crabs**, make their homes and graze among the seaweed 'forests'.

BRITTLE STAR
The brittle star is aptly named as its arms break off very easily. It is the only starfish that does not have tube feet with suckers. It moves by writhing its arms or pushing against the rocks.

ENEMY ATTACK
Molluscs have many enemies; sea creatures in rock pools, such as the large pink starfish and even other molluscs, like **whelks**, feed on them. Seagulls snatch them up and drop them onto the rocks to break open their shells. Some fish swallow them whole in their shells, and crabs can break their shells with their strong nippers.

A STING IN THE TAIL

The stinging tentacles drifting beneath the float of the **bluebottle** (Portuguese man-o'-war) can be up to ten metres long. The stings are used for defence and to poison and kill fish and creatures on which the bluebottle feeds. The bluebottle is not a single animal, but a colony of animals living permanently attached to one another. One individual forms the float, another group catches the prey, another group digests it, and another group is concerned with reproduction. The float is filled with gas that contains 90 per cent nitrogen. Despite its sting, the bluebottle is eaten by sea slugs and snails.

Stars of the Sea

Starfish have no head, no eyes, no back and no front. They have few enemies. Most starfish have five limbs that have rows of tiny tube feet with suckers at their tips. If a starfish loses or damages a limb, it grows again. Starfish have no blood, but sea water enters through a sieve-plate and circulates through tubes in their bodies. When they find something to eat, starfish push their flimsy, bag-like stomachs out through the mouth on their underside. The stomach then covers the food, digests it and draws the bag back inside. Although most starfish feed on plant material, the large pink starfish eats red bait and molluscs.

Molluscs

The sea animals known as **shellfish** are molluscs. They have a 'head', a 'foot' and a hump containing the heart and other organs. Some have a rough, ribbon-like tongue, or radula, lined with rows of tiny teeth. A fleshy fold of skin, called the mantle, covers the animal and it uses sea salts to manufacture the shell. The gleaming mother-of-pearl inside it is made of a form of calcium carbonate called aragonite, while the horny outer layers of the shell consist of calcite.

There are various groups of molluscs. Some, such as the limpet, glide along on their broad, muscular stomach-walls. These molluscs are called gastropods. They breathe through fleshy plates called gills. But not all gastropods live in the sea – slugs and snails are also gastropods. Cone-shaped limpets cling to the rocks to prevent the waves from washing them away. A limpet may wander in search of fresh seaweed to eat, but it always returns to where its shell rim fits exactly to the rock's outline. The large shell of the perlemoen (or abalone) is rough, but the inside is lined with delicate mother-of-pearl.

Black mussels, which live on rocks, and white mussels, which live in the sand, feed by separating their shells slightly and sucking in water from which they filter tiny food particles.

Molluscs such as the octopus, cuttlefish and squid have no feet, but long, sucker-studded tentacles attached to their bag-like heads. Most have shells inside the body to support their flesh and help them float.

Live sea urchins are often covered with brilliantly coloured spines. These drop off when the animal dies and all that is left is the round, often green, shell known as a 'sea-egg' or a 'sea pumpkin'. Tube feet between the spines enable the sea urchin to climb rocks. The pansy shell (or sand-dollar), found occasionally along the coast from Knysna to Mozambique, is a flattened sea urchin. The pinholes on the pansy flower are for the animal's tube feet.

PLACES TO SEE

When next you are at the coast, study the many interesting sea creatures that make their home in rock pools on or near the beach and see how many species you can identify

Estuaries

FRESHWATER MULLET IN THE SEA?

The rare **freshwater mullet** is diadromous, which means that it migrates between freshwater systems and the sea. It prefers the deep pools of coastal rivers, and is usually found in estuaries that have a large amount of fresh water. It has been found up to 100 kilometres upstream in rivers such as the Great Fish River. The freshwater mullet returns to the sea to breed in areas close to estuaries, and the young then return to the coastal rivers. Here the males stay for up to four and the females for up to seven years before they return to the sea to breed once again.

Where the fresh waters of a river mouth meet the salty sea, an estuary is formed. Often the incoming tide carries sea water into a calm lagoon that is later emptied as the sea draws back. The mud flats left behind may seem uninteresting, but they are rich with unusual plant and animal life.

An estuary's water is always salty, even in the rainy season when the river floods. But, in the dry season, a sand bar can close off the river mouth and the water, which is left after evaporation, may be even saltier than the open sea. Because the water has so much salt, the plants and animals are different from those higher up in the river.

South Africa's Estuaries

Other than the estuaries at river mouths, estuarine systems are also formed by coastal lakes.

- **Verlorenvlei** at Elandsbaai on the West Coast sometimes runs into the sea through a narrow channel;
- The **Saldanha Bay** and **Langebaan** lagoons form a 20-kilometre-long arm of the sea
- The **Wilderness Lakes** are three coastal lakes linked to the Touw River estuary;
- The **Swartvlei mouth** and the **Knysna Lagoon**;
- **Durban Bay**, **Richards Bay** and South Africa's largest estuarine system, **Lake St Lucia**;
- The **Kosi lake system** in northern KwaZulu-Natal near the Mozambique border consists of four interconnected water bodies.

Life in the Estuaries

The only plants and animals that survive in this unique environment are those that have adapted to a constantly changing concentration of salt in the water.

Several grasses and grass-like **plants** grow in estuaries. The dried remains of the common eel grass have been found in the caves of coast-living Khoikhoi who used it as bedding. Reeds flourish in most estuaries, providing shelter for many small fish species.

Hundreds of **animal** species live in or on the mud. Pieces of decaying plants provide food for crabs and small shellfish, which in turn are food for larger creatures, such as fish or otters. In fact, more 'food' is produced in this way by the estuaries open to the sea in sub-tropical areas, such as KwaZulu-Natal, than in any other type of natural environment in South Africa.

At low tide, anglers dig in the mud for bait such as marine worms and mud-prawns. Mussels and hermit crabs also live in the mud, and you may even find the delightful pansy shell, a kind of sea urchin, in the sands of the Knysna Lagoon and the other eastern estuaries.

If the estuaries become severely damaged, some unique creatures, such as the Knysna seahorse, may be lost forever. Found only in the Knysna Lagoon and another nearby estuary at the Keurbooms River, this unusual fish with its horse-like head is only six centimetres long and swims upright.

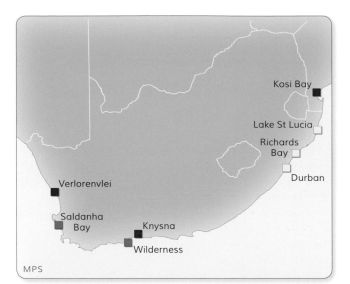

Pink ghost crab

White stork

Pansy shell

Hermit crab

Fish and Birds

Many kinds of fish visit estuaries. Leervis, known as garrick in KwaZulu-Natal, and penaeid prawns, that spawn at sea, use estuaries as nurseries where their young can shelter and develop. Every summer, huge shoals of young spotted grunters return to the estuaries and remain on the rich feeding-grounds for a year before returning to the open sea. The young flathead mullet may spend up to three years in an estuary. Large fish, such as elf and sharks, swim in with the tide to feed on smaller fish. Kob, stumpnose and steenbras feed on shellfish on the estuary's bottom.

Estuaries also provide food for several bird species. Waders that breed in the Arctic during the northern summer, migrate to our warmer shores as the northern winter approaches. Many birds, such as sanderlings and curlew sandpipers, may be found at Langebaan Lagoon reserve, and fish-eating birds, such as pelicans, are found all along the coast. Before swallowing their prey, pelicans store the fish in enormous pouches under their beaks. Flamingos wade through the mud to disturb the creatures below the surface, capturing their small prey by filtering water through their fringe-lined beaks.

Man and the Estuaries

Estuaries are popular among bathers, water-skiers and yachtsmen, but unfortunately these fragile ecosystems can be easily damaged by the activities of these people. Their waters are shallow, sheltered and close to land, and are often silted up by erosion and poisoned by pollution. Anglers may over-fish them and developers may crowd their banks with buildings. To preserve our estuaries, planners must work closely with conservationists.

LAKE ST LUCIA

The St Lucia estuarine system, a World Heritage Site, in the far north of KwaZulu-Natal, is South Africa's largest estuary; it is 60 kilometres long. Four rivers feed the estuary with fresh water, and sea water flows into it through an opening at its southern tip. The humid, subtropical climate, heavy annual rainfall, mangrove forests and swamps all influence the animal and plant life that flourishes in this unusual environment.

The shallow waters are enriched by decaying vegetable matter carried down by rivers. Hippos graze on the shore, fertilizing the estuary with their droppings. Plankton is plentiful and provides food for many water creatures. Fish prey on mud prawns and crabs while larger fish are food for pelicans, eagles and crocodiles.

Coastal dunes 120 metres high, the highest in the world, are found between the estuary and the sea. The forests that cover them are home to tropical plants and animals, including snakes such as the beautiful but venomous Gaboon adder.

There are four game and nature reserves on the estuary. Hippos are the main attraction, but there are also crocodiles, antelope and many bird species. On offer are also nature and game trails for hiking and tours to learn more about estuaries.

FORESTS IN THE WATER
Mangrove forests are well-known features of southern Africa's subtropical estuaries from the Eastern Cape to KwaZulu-Natal. With a canopy of green above and mud below, steamy mangrove swamps create a unique environment. Because mangroves cannot obtain oxygen from the waterlogged ground, they have developed strange 'breathing roots' to absorb it from the air. These grow from the trunks or jut out of the mud. Sometimes the fruits are also adapted to the swamps. The dagger-like seeds germinate on the tree and when they drop, impale themselves in the soft mud. Having anchored themselves firmly, they develop roots within a few hours. The seeds may also float on the water for long distances before the roots burst through the tough outer covering and grow, perhaps quite far from the parent tree.

Top to bottom: hippopotamus, crocodile, Curlew sandpiper

Eastern white pelican

PLACES TO SEE

- Wilderness National Park, Western Cape
- West Coast National Park, West Coast
- iSimangaliso Wetland Park (previously St Lucia Park), northern KwaZulu-Natal

Water for a Thirsty Land

THE FIRST DAM
Zacharias Wagenaer, who followed Jan van Riebeeck as commander of the Cape settlement, built South Africa's first proper dam on Table Mountain's Fresh River in 1663. Its stone and brick remains were dug up when foundations were excavated for Cape Town's Golden Acre building in 1975. Part of the dam wall is preserved in the lower concourse of the Golden Acre and is a national heritage site.

Although, by world standards, our rivers are not particularly impressive, water is very important in South Africa, a dry country that often experiences drought and very severe water shortages. The run-off from all our rivers together is equivalent to that of the Rhine River at Rotterdam, and only half of that of the Zambezi. It is therefore important to take care of all our natural water resources.

Low Supply and High Demand

Most of South Africa is hot and dry. Only the narrow belt of the southern and eastern coastal strip is fairly well watered. Inland, the rainfall is low. Each year, South Africa receives only about half the average of some countries. About 90 per cent of all the rain that falls never reaches the rivers, but is taken up into the atmosphere by evaporation or absorbed into the parched ground. Although water is often scarce, there is a constant demand for it because the country's population is increasing at an alarming rate. For some years, the government has organized special projects and schemes to supply more water for the population. Most of these supplies come from rivers, dams and storage schemes. But our resources are not limitless.

Our Rivers

The **Orange River** (Gariep) is South Africa's largest river and drains almost half the country. It rises in Lesotho's Maluti Mountains and after flowing west for some 2 250 kilometres, flows into the Atlantic Ocean. It passes mostly through dry country, but the land on its banks, which is irrigated by its waters, is lush with natural vegetation and planted crops. West of Upington, the Orange River passes through the Augrabies gorge and forms one of the world's largest waterfalls. Closer to the sea, it flows through sands rich in semi-precious stones. Diamonds are found both at the river mouth and in the sea immediately off the coast.

POLLUTING OUR RIVERS
Some experts believe that 30 per cent of our river water is polluted. Factories pour chemicals into rivers and the water is further polluted by sewage and waste such as plastic bags, tin cans and paper. Pollution kills fish and other creatures that live in the water, and thereby affects other creatures, such as birds, in the food chain.

The **Vaal River** is the Orange River's greatest tributary. It rises on the Drakensberg's western slopes and forms boundaries between Mpumalanga, Gauteng and the North West Province on one side and the Free State on the other. It joins the Orange River 1 000 kilometres from its source. Prior to reaching this point its waters generate electricity for industry and are also used to irrigate farms.

After the Vaal and the Orange, the **Tugela River** is South Africa's most important river. It rises on the eastern slopes of the Drakensberg at Mont-Aux-Sources and flows 560 kilometres into the Indian Ocean. Its waters are used for power and irrigation.

Other important rivers are the Limpopo, Olifants (Western Cape) and the Olifants (forming the boundary between Mpumalanga and Limpopo Province), Great Berg, Breede, Gourits, Gamtoos, Great Fish, Sundays, Mgeni, Komati and Phongolo. Towns and farmers have private irrigation schemes too.

BEATING THE DROUGHT
South Africa's irregular rainfall and frequent droughts cost farmers and the government millions of rands in crop and stock losses. Many farmers rely on irrigation, otherwise only one-tenth of the country's agricultural land could be cultivated. Some irrigation is carried out by farmers using windmills, pumps, boreholes and other water supplies. At present, more than one million hectares of agricultural land are under irrigation. The National Water Act of 1998 plans to manage all water sources so that all people who need it will have fair access to water. The act will also ensure that water is not polluted or wasted.

Government Water Projects

The **Orange River Development Project** is the largest water development project ever undertaken in South Africa. The project was started in 1962 to irrigate 184 000 hectares in the Orange River valley and, through its various tunnels and canals, to provide water for another 76 000 hectares in the valleys of the Sundays and Great Fish rivers. The project includes:

The Gariep Dam is the largest storage reservoir in South Africa

The **Gariep Dam**, which was completed in 1971 at a cost of R85 million. This is the country's largest storage dam and can hold almost 6 000 million cubic metres of water. It regulates the flow of the Orange River so that its water is available for farmlands and domestic use. A hydro-electric scheme provides power for Bloemfontein and Port Elizabeth. Water from the Gariep Dam is allowed to flow into the **Vanderkloof Dam**, 130 kilometres further down the Orange River, which stores water for irrigation and produces electricity for peak-hour needs. This dam also supplies water for the **Vanderkloof canals**.

The **Orange-Fish tunnel** was for many years the longest unbroken water tunnel in the world. It carries water, in a pipe 5.35 metres wide, over 82 kilometres from the Orange River to the Great Fish River.

The **Fish-Sundays River canal** project carries some of the Orange River water from the Great Fish River valley to the citrus orchards of the Sundays River valley and the city of Port Elizabeth. This project consists of 90 kilometres of canals and the Cookhouse Tunnel, which is five metres wide and 13 kilometres long.

Water from the **Welbedacht-Bloemfontein project** on the Caledon River provides Bloemfontein with water.

The Vaal Dam, the Vaal River barrage, the Bloemhof Dam and the Vaalharts Weir are also part of the **Vaal River schemes** that provide storage and irrigation. The Vaal and Tugela rivers are linked to the **Drakensberg project**, a combined pumped-storage and water supply scheme which also generates peak-hour electricity and provides water to the Vaal River basin.

The **Boland project** includes the Theewaterskloof Dam, in the Riviersonderend valley outside Villiersdorp. It is linked to the catchment areas of the Berg and Eerste rivers by tunnels 31 kilometres long. It provides irrigation for an important fruit-producing area and even water for ever-expanding Cape Town.

The **Palmiet river scheme**, started in the 1980s, is another important water storage and hydro-electric project in the Western Cape.

THE FIRST CANAL

The country's **first canal** ('gracht') was built in Cape Town in 1670 by miller and free burgher, Wouter Cornelisz Mostert. The stone-lined aqueduct carried water from the dam to the jetty in Table Bay. Mostert was paid 4 000 rix-dollars by the Dutch East India Company. He also built the Cape's first water mill and a tank to hold fresh water for passing sailors.

WATER FOR ALL

The **Lesotho Highlands Water Scheme** (LHWS) is one of the biggest engineering projects to be undertaken in southern Africa, and is even bigger than the Orange River scheme. Phase 1, which took 25 years, was completed in 2011, the same year that Phase 2 was inaugurated. The LHWS will eventually double the annual flow of water into the Vaal basin, and supply all Lesotho's electrical power.

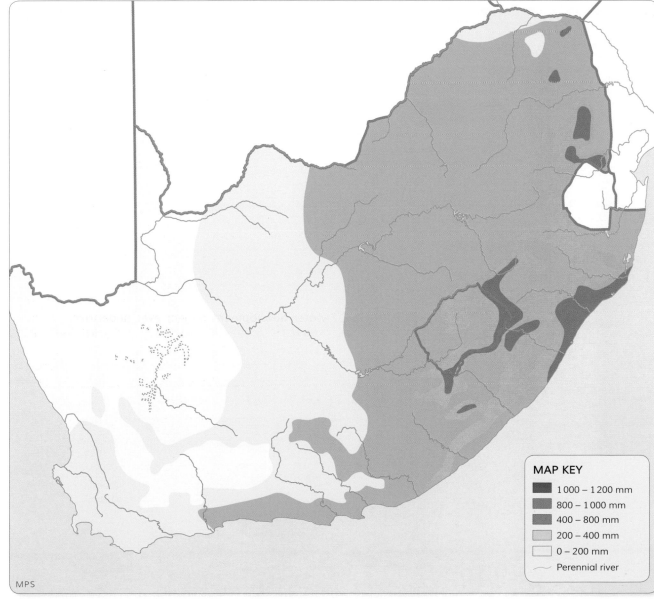

MAP KEY

■	1 000 – 1 200 mm
■	800 – 1 000 mm
■	400 – 800 mm
■	200 – 400 mm
☐	0 – 200 mm
〜	Perennial river

MPS

Average annual rainfall in South Africa

PLACES TO SEE

ⓘ Augrabies Falls in the Northern Cape

ⓘ The remains of the first canal, Golden Acre, Cape Town

Mountains and Caves

CATS THAT SWIM
The only known habitat of the endangered **cave catfish** is an underground lake in a cave near Otavi in Namibia. It is a pinkish-white, transparent fish with small eyes – or no eyes at all. It feeds mainly on bat guano, or on other small creatures that eat bat guano.

Mountains girdle South Africa almost all the way along its coast. The mountains in the Western and Eastern Cape are roughly parallel to the coast and form a natural border to the interior. Some inland mountains are extensions of the main ranges and others stand alone.

Making Mountains

Mountains are formed in various ways. Volcanic lava pushing through the Earth's crust may form mountains over thousands of centuries. Block mountains result when faults occur in the crust and a mass of rock may be pushed up between them, while dome mountains form when molten rock below the crust pushes the land upwards in a rounded, dome shape. Fold mountains are squeezed up from the crust from both sides. Land under pressure crumples and forms folds.

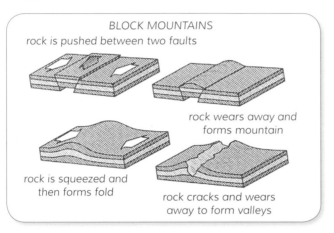

BLOCK MOUNTAINS
rock is pushed between two faults

rock wears away and forms mountain

rock is squeezed and then forms fold

rock cracks and wears away to form valleys

Mountain Ranges

The **Cederberg** mountains in the Clanwilliam district of the Western Cape are named after the Clanwilliam cedar trees that grow among its crags. The highest point is the 2026-metre Sneeuberg. The Cederberg is popular among mountaineers and famous for its rock formations and San cave paintings.

The **Hex River Mountains** in the Western Cape overlook the fertile Hex River Valley. Matroosberg, 2249 metres high, is the range's highest peak and is often snow-capped in winter.

Table Mountain, with its highest point at 1087 metres, and flanked by Lion's Head and Devil's Peak, is a landmark in South Africa. In 2011 it was voted one of the New Seven Wonders of the World.

The **Hottentots Holland Mountains**, forming the eastern boundary of the Cape Flats, were home to the Khoikhoi when Dutch colonists arrived and gave the mountains their name.

The **Drakenstein Mountains**, in the Stellenbosch-Franschhoek area, are crossed at their northern end by the Du Toit's Kloof Pass.

The **Langeberg, Outeniqua** and **Tsitsikamma mountains** form one chain, running roughly parallel to the southern coast of the Western and Eastern Cape. Part of the Cape fold mountains, they stretch from the Robertson district to the Humansdorp area. The Outeniqua and Tsitsikamma ranges are famous for their lush indigenous and man-made forests.

The **Swartberg**, which is 800 kilometres long, forms a barrier between the Little Karoo and the Great Karoo. Features include Seweweekspoort peak (2325 metres high), Towerberg overlooking Ladismith and the gorge of the Gamka River.

The **Winterberg** and **Amatole** mountain ranges in the Eastern Cape have rich rain-forest relics and extensive timber plantations. The Katberg and Hogsback areas are particularly beautiful.

THE DRAKENSBERG
The **uKhahlamba Drakensberg Park** was declared a World Heritage Site by the United Nations Educational, Scientific and Cultural Organisation (UNESCO) in 2000. It was selected because it is an area of outstanding scenic beauty, was home to the San people for more than 4000 years, and contains the largest and most concentrated group of rock paintings in Africa, south of the Sahara Desert.

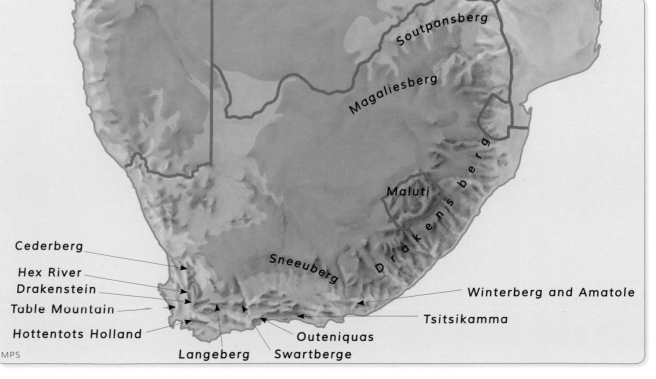

Soutpansberg

Magaliesberg

Drakensberg

Maluti

Cederberg

Hex River

Drakenstein

Table Mountain

Hottentots Holland

Sneeuberg

Langeberg

Swartberge

Outeniquas

Tsitsikamma

Winterberg and Amatole

MPS

The **Drakensberg**, South Africa's mightiest range, was formed about 150 million years ago. Volcanic action thrust up this dragon-like 'barrier of spears', which stretches 1046 kilometres from the Eastern Cape through KwaZulu-Natal to Limpopo Province. The highest peak in South Africa, Injasuti ('well-fed dog'), is 3459 metres high, but at 3482 metres, Thabana Ntlenyana ('beautiful little mountain') on the Lesotho border, is the highest mountain in Africa south of the equator. The 'Berg' is often snow-covered in winter. Centuries of rain, wind and snow have carved caves and shapes into the rocks. Features include Giant's Castle, Cathedral Peak, The Saddle, Cathkin Peak, Mont-aux-Sources and Champagne Castle. uKhahlamba-Drakensberg Park is a UNESCO World Heritage Site.

The **Maluti Mountains** form the border between the Free State and Lesotho. The streams that feed the Orange and Caledon rivers start in these mountains, which rise to a height of over 3000 metres.

The **Soutpansberg** is a 130 kilometre-long mountain range in the Limpopo Province and is named after the salt pan at its western base. The highest peak is Hanglip (1719 metres), five kilometres north of Makhado Town (Louis Trichardt).

The **Magaliesberg** is relatively low, averaging only 450 metres in height and stretching westwards from Pretoria. It is famous for its beautiful streams, varied wildlife and mountain climbs.

Other mountain ranges include the **Roggeberg** and **Nuweveld** mountains in the Karoo, and the **Sneeuberg** north of Graaff-Reinet. North-east of Graaff-Reinet, the **Bamboesberg** links with the **Stormberg** and the start of the Drakensberg range.

Caves

The **Cango Caves** in the Swartberg Mountains north of Oudtshoorn were created over millions of years through the formation of limestone deposits on the southern slopes. A maze of passages and halls was formed and the limestone was shaped into natural sculptures. Cango One includes Van Zyl's Hall, Botha's Hall, the Bridal Chamber, the Fairy Palace and the Banqueting Hall, all with fantastic rock formations. Cango Two, or the Wonder Cave, was discovered beyond the Banqueting Hall in 1972. Cango Three, twice the length of Cango One and Two, was opened three years later. Cango Four is still to be fully explored.

Between the 1930s and the 1970s many important archaeological discoveries were made in the dolomite **Sterkfontein Caves** north-west of Krugersdorp in Gauteng. The caves, now a World Heritage Site, have many rock formations (including dripstone formations), six cathedral chambers in one section of the complex, and a huge underground lake. Local villagers believe its waters have magical powers.

Eerie echoes can be heard when someone taps the dripstone formations in the **Echo Caves**. These dolomite caves north of Ohrigstad and Pilgrim's Rest in Mpumalanga have a maze of underground

WATERFALLS
The **Augrabies Falls**, 120 kilometres west of Upington, is one of the world's six greatest waterfalls. After flowing over flat, desolate land, the Orange River suddenly plunges over granite cliffs into a twisting gorge 149 metres below. The water cascades down 91 metres of falls and rapids before the main fall, 56 metres high.

The Mgeni River in KwaZulu-Natal plunges 111 metres over a narrow cliff near Howick. These are the **Howick Falls**. Local Zulus call them 'KwaNogqaza' meaning 'place of the tall one'. In the KwaZulu-Natal Midlands, 18 kilometres north of Pietermaritzburg, the Mgeni River cascades over a crescent-shaped cliff to form the **Albert Falls**. The area around the dam is a resort and a nature reserve.

Van Zyl's Hall at the Cango Caves

passages, and some are open to the public. The largest chamber is 100 metres long and 10 metres high. The Cannibal Chamber is home to millions of bats.

The **Sudwala Caves** are 35 kilometres north-west of Nelspruit in Mpumalanga. Over centuries, the water seeping through roof cracks in a network of limestone caverns created remarkable flowstone formations. A tongue-shaped stalactite named 'Somguba's Gong' produces weird echoes when struck. The P.R. Owen Hall, a natural 'theatre' 37 metres wide, is sometimes used for concerts.

The Makapan valley, north-east of Mokopane (Potgietersrus) in the Limpopo Province, is famous for its limestone caves. Many fossils and other remains from Stone Age to Voortrekker times have been found in the cavern known as the Cave of Hearths. **Makapansgat** was also the home of early man, *Australopithecus africanus*, whose skull was discovered by students from the University of the Witwatersrand in 1945.

SNOW ON THE MOUNTAINS
In winter, snow often caps the Drakensberg and the high peaks of the Western Cape. It has even been reported in the Soutpansberg. Clear, sunny weather usually follows, so the snow soon melts. Oxbow, in the Lesotho mountains, has an average of 14 snowfalls each year and Sutherland has at least four.

MOUNTAINS AND THE RAIN SHADOW
Mountains along the coast act as barriers to low-pressure storm systems. Moist air condenses on the seaward side causing rain on the coast, particularly in winter. Less rain falls inland of the mountains, causing a 'rain shadow'. The Karoo is much drier than George and Knysna on the coastal side of the Outeniqua Mountains.

PLACES TO SEE
- Cango Caves near Oudtshoorn
- Sterkfontein Caves near Krugersdorp

Land of Wonder

THE RICHTERSVELD

The Richtersveld area of north-western South Africa was declared a Cultural and Botanical Landscape World Heritage Site in 2007 because of its rich botanical diversity, shaped by the Nama people. This is one of the few areas in South Africa where transhumance – changing grazing lands from winter to summer – is still practised.

HILLS BY THE THOUSANDS

The Mgeni River and its tributaries have shaped the huge area north of the Durban-Pietermaritzburg road into many valleys and hills, known as the **Valley of a Thousand Hills**. Two notable features are the Nagle Dam, which provides Durban with much of its water, and KwaZulu-Natal's Table Mountain, rising to 960 metres, just south-west of the dam.

South Africa's landscape, from the KwaZulu-Natal Midlands to the Karoo, from the Western and Eastern Cape mountains to Free State plateaus, is spectacular and composed of many strange and unusual geographical features.

The Verneukpan Saltpan

Verneukpan is the most famous, and possibly the largest, of many saltpans found in the Kenhardt district of the Northern Cape. Like all saltpans, Verneukpan is absolutely flat and gets its name, which means 'deception pan' from the many mirages that shimmer over its surface. It covers nearly 30 000 hectares and, at its longest point, measures 36 kilometres.

Verneukpan became famous in February 1931 when Sir Malcolm Campbell flashed across it in his racing car, Blue Bird, at a speed of 246 miles per hour (396 km/h), breaking the world land-speed record, which was then 231 mph (373 km/h).

Sir Malcolm Campbell in 'Blue Bird' on Verneukpan

The Snake Pits

At **Danielskuil** ('Daniel's pit'), north-west of Kimberley, there is a deep sinkhole allegedly once inhabited by hundreds of snakes. Griquas living nearby used to lower people accused of evil deeds into the pit and leave them among the snakes overnight. If they survived, it showed that they were innocent and they were freed. However, it is very unlikely that poisonous snakes would congregate there. Trekkers chose the sinkhole's name because the tale reminded them of the Bible story of Daniel in the lion's den.

The Eye of Kuruman

Kuruman is about 84 kilometres north of Danielskuil. Its 'eye' is a spring of crystal-clear water that bubbles out of the barren dolomite rock and flows into a pool in the centre of a green and shady park. Even during the most severe drought, the spring provides about 20 million litres of water a day, enough for the town of Kuruman and to irrigate about 250 hectares of farmlands. The spring is also the source of the Kuruman River.

The 'Eye' of Kuruman is a natural fresh water spring

Sands that Roar

About 80 kilometres north-west of Griquatown, on the edge of the red sands of the **Kalahari**, there is a high outcrop of white sand dunes, some 12 kilometres long. If you walk through them, the sands will roar. Run your fingers through them and you will hear a snoring sound. Scooping up the sand in your hands makes a booming noise. When the night wind blows, a strange moaning sound can be heard. This may be the result of air escaping through the large gaps between the grains. Local tradition says that the dunes roar only during months that have an 'r' in their spelling.

The roaring white sand dunes of the Kalahari

Sinkholes

Sinkholes are naturally formed holes in the ground, usually in limestone or dolomite areas, where water has dissolved the rock over thousands of years. Sometimes the hole may be widened when the ground around it suddenly collapses. The sunken lake of **Otjikoto**, north of Tsumeb in Namibia, is a natural sinkhole in dolomite rock, 180 metres deep, and filled with clear water. In the Wonderfontein valley on the Far West Rand there is an enormous ancient sinkhole known as Doornfontein. Sinkholes can appear without warning; roads and houses in nearby Carletonville have suddenly disappeared into sinkholes. In 1962, 29 people were killed as the reduction works of the West Driefontein gold mine suddenly vanished into the ground.

The crystal-clear waters of Lake Otjikoto in Namibia

A Shaped Landscape

Steep cliffs, strange rock formations and huge caves form a fantastic landscape in the upper valley of the Little Caledon River on the Free State-Lesotho border. Water, which has sculpted weird and interesting shapes over many years, reacts with iron in the sandstone rocks to produce vivid oranges, reds and yellows, particularly at sunrise and sunset. Spectacular rock formations in the 11 600-hectare **Golden Gate Highlands National Park** include the Sentinel and Gladstone's Nose.

An impressive rock cliff in the Golden Gate Highlands National Park

AS THE RIVER RUNS

About 25 kilometres north of Pilgrim's Rest in Mpumalanga, the Blyde River tumbles headlong into a gorge hundreds of metres below. Over millions of years, the rushing waters have carved their way between towering dolomite cliffs to create the **Motlatse River Canyon** (previously Blyde River Canyon), the third largest canyon in the world. The area has some of the most spectacular views in South Africa, and fantastic rock formations. In the river bed above the canyon, are huge holes known as Bourke's Luck Potholes, named after Tom Bourke who once owned a nearby gold mine.

Healing Waters

Many people believe that springs rich in minerals have healing powers, particularly for ailments like arthritis and rheumatism. About 90 hot **mineral springs** are found throughout South Africa. Some of them are popular health resorts, including the mineral baths at Goudini and Montagu in the Western Cape and Aliwal North in the Eastern Cape. The Natal Spa at Paulpietersburg is popular, while the resort at Warmbaths provides visitors with healing mud-and-hot-water baths. People almost certainly bathed in the warm waters of Caledon, Malmesbury and other springs long before the Dutch occupation of the Cape.

Eruptions Below the Earth

The **Vredefort Dome**, an area of 48 by 16 kilometres, is the oldest meteorite impact structure (or astrobleme) found on Earth. Dating back 2 023 million years, it is the site of the greatest known single energy-release event and is thought to have caused devastating global changes, including affecting the evolution of most of the plants and animals on the planet. The outlines of the Dome, which was declared a World Heritage Site in 2005, can clearly be seen from the air.

The **Pilanesberg volcanic crater**, in the North West Province, about 56 kilometres north of Rustenburg, consists of six rings of hills, one within the other, 28 kilometres in total diameter. At the centre, there is a volcanic mountain rising 600 metres above the surrounding countryside.

SPRINGS OF LIFE

Remains of Stone Age tools and a skull buried in the mud at **Florisbad** mineral springs in the Free State show that hot springs were known to South Africa's earliest inhabitants.
The mineral spring at Brandvlei, near Worcester in the Western Cape, is the hottest and strongest in South Africa.

THE VALLEY OF DESOLATION

In the parched wilderness of the Karoo west of Graaff-Reinet, lies a vast valley of weirdly shaped dolerite rock formations, crumbling cliffs and unusual stone peaks. This desolate place was created over thousands of centuries of erosion working on the relatively soft sandstone of the area. Today, it is known as the **Valley of Desolation**.

PLACES TO SEE →

ℹ️ When next you travel on holiday through South Africa, try to visit some of the curious geographical formations featured on this page

Erosion

THE ROCKS OF THE CEDERBERG

Much of the 100 kilometre-long Cederberg mountain range has been eroded into a variety of weirdly shaped rocks and peaks. Examples of these formations include the large cave known as the **Stadsaal**, or 'town hall', and a huge stone structure called the **Maltese Cross**.

It would be difficult for us to exist without soil. Soil covers the Earth's surface in a layer that is very thin in some places, but several metres deep in others. All the wild plants and cultivated crops that feed both animals and people grow in soil. We should all be taking care of the soil, but neglect, ignorance and natural disasters have led to serious erosion in our country. Experts believe that 25 per cent of the fertile soil of South Africa has already been destroyed by erosion.

What is Soil Erosion?

The wearing away of soil, which leaves the land infertile and bare, is called soil erosion. Very often, it is the result of vegetation being removed without any steps taken to replace it or to protect the exposed soil. Plant cover holds the Earth together with a network of roots and provides a shield against the driving power of rain. As plant cover dies and decays, it becomes humus that enriches the top layer of the soil (or **topsoil**) and improves its texture. When the ground is stripped of its vegetation, the rich topsoil can be swept away by wind or water and is then wasted.

Natural Erosion

Natural forces, such as wind and water, floods and drought, have always caused some soil erosion. **Floods** can sometimes be sudden and very destructive. Rain pelting down at a speed of up to 50 kilometres an hour, may uproot plants or even whole trees. Swollen rivers gather up the vegetation along their banks and swirl the topsoil into the sea. When the floods subside, wide areas of land are left eroded and bare.

FIGHTING SOIL EROSION

Parliament has passed many Acts to protect the land and punish people responsible for damage. Soil erosion has been reduced, but the problem is far from solved. Farmers need to be educated to apply the most scientific methods and make the best use of their animals and land. Important steps to fight soil erosion include **contour ploughing**, **crop** and **pasture rotation** and **reforestation** (planting trees to bind the soil). About 80% of South Africa's total land area is farmed, but overgrazing and erosion have led to the loss of 250000 hectares. In 1995, South Africa signed the international Convention to Combat Desertification.

CROP ROTATION

Wheat growing in healthy soil

Fallow ground

Legumes to enrich the soil

THE MARCHING DESERT

Since the beginning of the 20th century, the semi-desert **Karoo** has spread north and east into once fertile grasslands. In some places, the Karoo has even expanded by as much as 250 to 300 kilometres. The reason may be that farmers had overstocked with sheep and goats, which stripped the ground of much of its natural vegetation.

The effect of soil erosion

Less spectacular, but equally damaging, is **sheet** or **surface erosion** – the gradual removal of thin layers of topsoil by wind or rain. Surface erosion is slow but steady. It may not even be noticed until serious damage has been done, by which time it has turned into **gully erosion**. When the topsoil has been washed away, ruts begin to appear and, over time, these deepen into gullies or dongas, sometimes many metres deep.

Drought is as damaging to the soil as are floods. Without water, plants die. Their roots shrivel in the dry ground and can no longer hold the soil together. The dry soil becomes dust and is blown away or, when rain eventually comes, it washes away into rivers.

Erosion Caused by Man

Far more serious than natural erosion, is the destruction of the soil brought about by man. It has been estimated that for every ton of maize, sugar, wheat or other crops produced annually, we lose 20 tons of soil to erosion. This soil cannot be replaced as the rate at which new soil is formed is far lower than the rate at which nutrient-rich topsoil is lost through erosion.

Incorrect farming methods are extremely destructive to the soil. Until recently, one of the main causes of soil erosion in South Africa was the traditional custom of ploughing straight up and down a hill. When rain fell, the water rushed down the slope, scouring the furrow and carrying away the topsoil. Most farmers have now learnt that this type of soil erosion can be prevented or reduced by ploughing along the contours – at right angles to the slope so that each furrow acts as a barrier to hold back the rainwater.

Well-nourished soil results in healthy plants, while plants grown in **neglected soil** often die. Unless a farmer fertilizes his fields, the plants will not develop strong root systems or have the strength to hold the soil, which will then wash or blow away. Crop rotation – planting different crops in the same ground at different times – is essential to maintain or increase soil fertility.

If a farmer **overstocks the land** by allowing too many animals to graze on a pasture, the animals eat the grass and herbs down to the ground and the plants' root systems become weak. The soil surface is exposed to wind and rain and the stunted roots are unable to hold the soil, making erosion inevitable. The answer to this problem is either to reduce the numbers of animals or to practise pasture rotation – herds are grazed on different fields in succession, allowing enough time for the vegetation to recover.

Paths trampled by animals between the cattle kraal and their pasture easily become ruts in rainy weather, and ruts soon become **dongas**.

Thoughtless veld-burning may also cause erosion. Sometimes farmers burn the veld to encourage the growth of fresh, young grass for grazing. As long as this is done in the correct season, it may not necessarily damage the ground. But strong winds following veld-burning may blow away the nutrient-rich ash and the surface layer of the topsoil, or heavy rain may even wash the scorched plants out of the ground and leave it both bare and barren.

Uncontrolled fires can seriously damage the veld

CAUSES OF NATURAL EROSION

1981	Laingsburg floods; drought
1984	Cyclone Demoina floods in KwaZulu-Natal
1986	KwaZulu-Natal floods
1988	Floods in the Northern Cape and Free State; drought
1989	Veld fires in the Western Cape
1991	Floods in the Free State
1992	Drought
1994	Widespread floods
1996	Severe floods in Pretoria and Ladysmith
1999	Tornado in the Eastern Cape
2007	Storm damage at Ballito/Durban on the East Coast
2012	Floods in Mpumalanga and KwaZulu-Natal

EROSION – THE ARTIST
When sand is carried by fierce winds, even the hardest rocks can be eroded, resulting in peculiar rock formations. In the **Valley of Desolation** near Graaff-Reinet, wind has gouged solid rocks to form strange peaks and sheer cliffs. Sudden floods and wind erosion have also created unusual rock structures around **Vryheid** in KwaZulu-Natal.

STOP THAT SOIL!
In the 1960s it was calculated that about 400 million tons of fertile silt were lost through soil erosion annually. If that soil was spread 30 centimetres deep, it would cover nearly 70 000 rugby fields! Engineers later reported that up to 400 million tons of silt were deposited annually in the **Gariep Dam**. This excludes soil washed out to sea!

PLACES TO SEE

ⓘ Valley of Desolation near Graaff-Reinet
ⓘ The Maltese Cross and Stadsaal in the Cederberg

Incorrect ploughing

Correct ploughing

Overgrazing

Erosion

113

The Weather and the Climate

GLOBAL WARMING

The term 'global warming' refers to an average increase in the Earth's temperature, caused by human activities such as burning fossil fuels, and deforestation. Scientists estimate that the Earth has warmed by about 0.5°C over the last 100 years, mainly because of an increased concentration of so-called **greenhouse gases**, such as carbon dioxide, which 'trap' heat in the lower atmosphere. There is evidence that global warming is already having an impact on the world's climate and is causing unpredictable changes in the Earth's weather patterns. These changes are expected to have wide-ranging effects on plants, wildlife and humans. Many experts fear that Africa's poor countries are more vulnerable to the impacts of global warming than the rich countries of the world.

The sun, the atmosphere, water vapour and wind – these four elements work together to create weather. Through their interaction, weather conditions, such as cloud, rain, hail and snow, are formed in a certain place at a certain time. In some places, like the Karoo, the weather can remain unchanged for weeks. In areas close to mountains or the sea, it can change several times in a day.

Temperature

By 'fine weather' we understand that the sun is shining, the sky is clear, there is little wind and the air is warm. This warmth comes partly from heat rising into the atmosphere from the Earth's surface and partly from the sun. The heat that reaches the Earth from the sun varies with the height of the ground above sea level (the altitude), the latitude (distance from the equator), the season and the time of day. Air temperature depends on the movement of air, and the amount of water vapour, clouds, dust and carbon dioxide in it.

Atmospheric Pressure

Good or bad weather also depends on the atmosphere that surrounds the Earth. Each square metre of the Earth's surface has about ten tons of air above it – twice as much as the mass of an adult elephant. The force this mass exerts is known as atmospheric pressure. It changes constantly, and the weather changes with it. Air always moves from a place of high pressure to a place of low pressure. Air movements, or winds, are caused by differences in atmospheric pressure. They are named according to the direction from which they blow and, naturally, affect the weather.

Humidity

Weather is also affected by humidity – the amount of water vapour in the air. When humidity is high, the weather can make you feel uncomfortably hot and sticky, because warm air holds more water vapour than cold air. Visitors to KwaZulu-Natal, with its humid, subtropical conditions, are often aware of this combination of humidity and heat. Moisture such as rain, snow, fog and mist that falls to the Earth from the atmosphere is called **precipitation**.

This tree indicates the direction of the prevailing wind

A DOCTOR FOR THE CAPE

In the early days of Cape Town, the sight of the 'tablecloth' cloud over Table Mountain was always welcome. It heralded the arrival of the south-easterly wind that swept out to sea all the rubbish that had been left to rot in the canal running the length of the Heerengracht – today's Adderley Street.

Capetonians, who believe that the Southeaster blows away the town's germs, and has a generally healthy effect, call it the **Cape Doctor**. This often gale-force wind is said to blow away the smog and other stagnant air pollution that sometimes forms over the city.

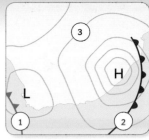

1. Cold front
2. Warm front
3. Isobars

Climate

Weather and climate are closely related, but are not the same. Climate is the general pattern of weather recorded in an area over a long time. We might say that the **climate** of KwaZulu-Natal's coastal region brings a high annual rainfall and warm temperatures, while the **weather** on a particular day may be cloudy and cold.

South Africa is situated between two oceans which, with the subtropical conditions on either side of latitude 30°S, largely determine its climate. Surging southwards from the Mozambique Channel and along the east coast as far as South Africa's southernmost tip, is the warm Agulhas Current. The high temperature of the air above its waters is mainly responsible for Durban's hot, humid climate. The Benguela Current rises in the icy South Atlantic Ocean, flows slowly northwards towards the Cape Peninsula and Cape Agulhas and then up the west coast of South Africa, Namibia and Angola. On-shore winds blowing over its chilly surface cause the cool and dry conditions of the west coast.

Climatic Regions

Only the southwestern Cape, an area stretching from Garies in the Northern Cape to Mossel Bay in the Western Cape, has the rainy winters and dry summers of a typical **Mediterranean** climate. The southern Cape has a **temperate** climate; summers are hot, winters can be cool and it rains throughout the year. From the Kei River to northern KwaZulu-Natal, the climate is **subtropical**. Summers are hot and humid and winters are quite dry. Along the south and east coast, the interior tends to be cooler than the coast.

The coast from Namaqualand in the Northern Cape through Namibia to Angola is largely **desert**. Rain seldom falls but fog regularly sweeps from the sea to the land and across the shifting sand dunes.

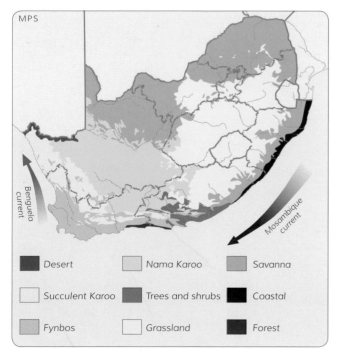

Desert	Nama Karoo	Savanna
Succulent Karoo	Trees and shrubs	Coastal
Fynbos	Grassland	Forest

South Africa's natural vegetation

The Karoo covers a vast area of South Africa. In this **semi-arid plateau**, cool, dry winters are followed by hot summers. Rain seldom falls, but when it does, the dusty brown land is covered with brilliant flowers.

Bloemfontein, Johannesburg and Pretoria lie within the **temperate eastern plateau** of the Highveld where crisp, dry sunny winters contrast dramatically with drenching summer thunderstorms. Along the eastern edge of the Highveld, the plateau of the escarpment drops southwards towards the rolling hills of the Eastern Cape and north to the Limpopo Valley, where summers are warm and wet and winters cool and dry.

In the **subtropical Lowveld**, rain falls in the hot, humid summer and the winters are warm and dry. This region stretches into Mozambique from northern KwaZulu-Natal and Swaziland.

Wet and Dry Facts

Average of rainy days per year

Durban	130
Cape Town	103
Johannesburg	99
Bloemfontein	84
Alexander Bay	23 (in a good year)

Wettest year on record

Durban	1917	1903 mm
Cape Town	1941	2771 mm
Johannesburg	1917	1394 mm
Bloemfontein	1988	1119 mm

Driest year on record

Durban	1992	50 mm
Cape Town	1973	348 mm
Johannesburg	1984	490 mm
Bloemfontein	1992	212 mm

Rainfall

South Africa is considered to be a dry country. It receives an average annual **rainfall** of 492 millimetres, compared with the world average of 857 millimetres. About 65 per cent of the country has an annual rainfall of less than 500 millimetres, which is regarded as the minimum for successful dry-land farming (farming that does not require any irrigation). Some regions are much wetter than others. For instance, KwaZulu-Natal, the Drakensberg and the Mpumalanga lowveld usually receive more than 1000 millimetres of rain a year, whereas in parts of the west coast, less than 50 millimetres of rain may fall in a year.

BERG WINDS

Berg winds occur in some coastal areas of our country. They are formed in winter when air from high pressure areas on the interior plateau flows down the escarpment towards low pressure cells at the sea. As the air descends, its temperature rises – sometimes by as much as 20°C – and it reaches the coast as an unpleasantly hot, dry wind.

THE BUSTER

The Buster is a strong southwesterly wind that blows in KwaZulu-Natal, often springing up without warning on a calm, hazy day. It blows at speeds of up to 30 knots and can be dangerous for ships and aircraft. The Buster is caused by high pressure off the KwaZulu-Natal coast ridging in behind a weak cell of low pressure.

PLACES TO SEE

ℹ Look out for weather vanes on church steeples next time you travel through our cities and towns

Forecasting the Weather

JDP/IOA

**THE COLOURS OF
THE SUN**
Rainbows arch across the
sky when the sun's rays
break up as they strike
falling rain, mist or spray.
You can see a rainbow only
if you have your back to the
sun. The colours of sunlight
appear in order from the
outside of the bow to the
inside: red, orange, yellow,
green, blue, indigo and
violet. (Use the mnemonic
Richard **O**f **Y**ork **G**ave **B**attle
In **V**ain to memorize the
order of the colours!)

IS/BC

HOW MUCH SUNSHINE?
Weathermen use a
Campbell Stokes recorder
to measure sunshine. It
consists of a glass ball that
concentrates sunshine onto
a thick piece of card. The
sun burns a mark on the
card, and this indicates the
hours of sunshine in a day.

Early farmers and sailors used to forecast the
weather by watching the clouds and the direction
of the wind. Today we can consult a barometer (for
air pressure) and a thermometer (for temperature).
Meteorologists use sophisticated scientific instruments to forecast the weather.

Synoptic Charts

To interpret synoptic charts accurately, we need to
understand the signs and symbols shown on them, as
well as the meanings of the terms used.

Isobars are lines on a map that join all places of
equal atmospheric pressure. High-numbered isobars
show areas of high pressure. Sometimes the lines may
form closed circles called **pressure cells**. These may
be high-pressure cells, with the highest pressure at the
centre, or low-pressure cells, with the lowest pressure
at the centre. The letters **H** and **L** on the chart indicate
whether the cell is a high- or low-pressure cell. Low-
pressure systems usually bring cold and rain while high-
pressure systems indicate sunny, dry weather.

Cold and **warm fronts** are boundaries between air
masses that can be warm, cold, dry or moist depending
on the type of land or sea they pass over. Cold fronts

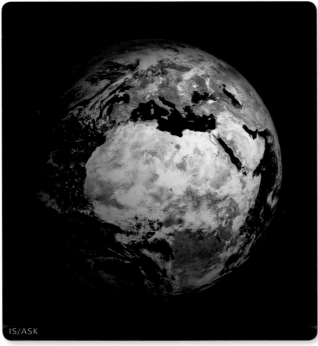

IS/ASK

A satellite photograph of the African continent

Measuring Instruments
Anemometer –   measures wind speed in
    kilometres per hour (km/h)
Barometer – atmospheric pressure in millibars
Thermometer – temperature in degrees Celsius
    or Fahrenheit
Wet-and-dry-bulb thermometer – humidity
Wind vane – wind direction
Campbell Stokes recorder – sunshine in hours
Rain gauge – rainfall in millimetres

---

move faster than warm fronts and may catch up with
them. When this happens, an **occluded front** will
develop. Clouds and rain may result.

Arrows on a synoptic chart indicate **wind**. They
always point in the direction towards which the wind is
blowing, although the wind is named according to the
direction from which it comes. 'Feathers' on the arrows
show the **speed** of the wind. A full feather indicates a
speed of ten knots, while a half feather shows one of
five knots. A wind of 50 knots (about 100 kilometres an
hour) is indicated by a triangular flag.

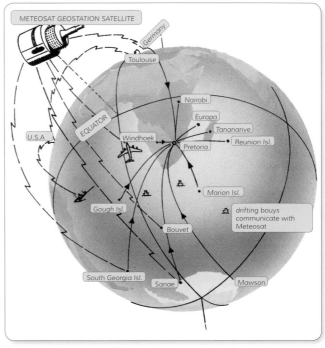

METEOSAT GEOSTATION SATELLITE

Germany

Toulouse

Nairobi

Europa

Tananarive

EQUATOR

U.S.A

Windhoek

Reunion Isl.

Pretoria

Marion Isl.

Gough Isl.

drifting bouys
communicate with
Meteosat

Bouvet

South Georgia Isl.

Sanae

Mawson

A geostationary satellite provides weather information

Satellite Images

Satellite images of weather conditions are taken from
two satellites – a polar satellite orbiting the Earth from
west to east, and a geostationary satellite fixed at an
altitude of about 36 000 kilometres above the equator.
This satellite transmits cloud images to Earth.

The weather images we see on TV come from this
geostationary satellite and are received at the Remote
Sensing Centre of the Council for Scientific and Industrial
Research (CSIR) at Hartebeesthoek. Information from
the satellites is fed into computers at the South African
Weather Bureau's telecommunications centre. Cloud
cover and cold fronts approaching from the southwest
can be seen on satellite images several days before
they reach us.

Clouds

Clouds also indicate weather conditions. In 1803 an
English meteorologist, Luke Howard, divided clouds
into three different families and gave them Latin
names. He called them **cirrus** ('curl of hair'), **cumulus**
('heap') and **stratus** ('layer'). These can combine in
several ways to form ten main cloud-types.

CLOUD TYPES

Cirrocumulus – ripples of cloud warn of unsettled weather.

Altocumulus – larger than cirrocumulus, they are fluffy rolls of cloud that bring showers.

Altostratus – thin, flat clouds that cover most of the sky and can develop into rain clouds.

Cumulus – white puffs of 'cauliflower'-topped clouds in sunny summer skies.

Stratus – a grey layer of heavy cloud close to the ground that often brings drizzle.

Cirrus – high, ice-crystal clouds with a streaky appearance. Usually followed by a cold front.

Cirrostratus – thin sheets of high cloud that often bring rain.

Stratocumulus – uneven, dark grey rolls or patches of cloud. They seldom bring rain.

Cumulonimbus – towering clouds with dark grey undersides. Often seen in the Highveld on summer afternoons, they bring heavy thunderstorms with high winds and hail.

Nimbostratus – heavy, dark cloud masses that bring rain or even snow.

DAMAGED BY HAIL

Hail often damages crops in South Africa. Some **hailstones** are so big that they knock dents in cars. Ice crystals formed in cumulonimbus clouds are tossed up and down and become bigger and bigger as water freezes onto them. When they are heavy enough, they fall to the Earth as hailstones.

WEATHER SYMBOLS

Weather symbols tell us about our likely weather conditions. Some newspapers and TV channels may not use standard international symbols.

sunny

partly cloudy

cloudy

rain

thunderstorm

sunny, becoming cloudy with rain

wind speed

PLACES TO SEE

ℹ Look for anemometers and wind vanes near airports

Natural Disasters

DBR/M24/GI

LAINGSBURG IS FLOODED
One of South Africa's most devastating natural disasters occurred in the sleepy Karoo town of Laingsburg. On Sunday 25 January 1981, there was a cloudburst in the mountains of the southern Karoo. Water rushed down, washing away large parts of the town and sweeping 103 people to their death.

TL/GTY/GI

PR/GTY/GI

CHANGING THE LAND
After the 1933 drought, many Transvaal and Free State farmers gave up keeping sheep. They used their relief money and equipment provided by the government of the time to plant crops. Areas that had once been grazing land were ploughed so that wheat and maize could be cultivated. The drought drastically changed the land's appearance.

Natural disasters include fire, drought, floods, tornadoes, earthquakes, storms, plagues and pests. Disasters have occurred all over the world throughout history and South Africa has also experienced many of them.

Fire

When Vasco da Gama first sailed round the Cape in 1497, it is said that he saw so many fires along the coast that he named the land **Terra da Fuma**, or 'land of smoke'. During thunderstorms, lightning can strike a tree and set it alight. Wind fans the flames and the surrounding area is often destroyed. Sparks from rocks tumbling down mountains can set dry grass alight.

Fires that start in this manner often occur in places that are difficult to reach, even by helicopter. A fire on the Cape Peninsula in January 2000 destroyed 8000 hectares of vegetation, as well as damaging property. Occasional fires, however, are sometimes good for the health of fire-adapted vegetation such as the Western Cape's fynbos.

Drought

Rainfall in most of South Africa is low and unreliable. Water in rivers and vleis evaporates rapidly under a scorching sun. Drought follows and grazing lands turn to dust. When this happened in the past, stock farmers had to trek with their goats, sheep or cattle to find new grazing and a fresh supply of water. But, as the population has grown, farms have become smaller and it is no longer possible for stock farmers to undertake long treks with their animals. A farmer who loses his animals or crops in a drought may be able to claim compensation through insurance, or he might have to sell up what is left of his farm and move to the city.

Because South Africa's climate is dry, many parts of the country are often devastated by drought

HURRICANES AND TORNADOES

Hurricanes, more correctly known as **tropical cyclones** in South Africa, are gigantic swirling storms of wind, clouds and rain that spin at speeds of between 120 and 200 kilometres per hour. They rise over warm, tropical seas and whirl clockwise towards the west, dying down when they reach land. Sometimes, in the late summer, a hurricane sweeps down the Mozambique Channel, creating huge sea swells and very high tides along the KwaZulu-Natal coast and bringing with it torrential rainstorms.

A **tornado** is a twisting, funnel-shaped column of air that leaps across the land causing havoc when it touches ground. It may be up to 800 metres across and its winds can rotate at 300 kilometres per hour. Tornadoes can suck up objects in their path and drop them some distance away.

IS/IDP

Floods

South Africa's weather is sometimes affected by climatic changes as far away as the Pacific Ocean. Abnormally high sea temperatures cause the condition called El Niño, when KwaZulu-Natal experiences drought instead of the usual rainy season. While some parts of the country experience drought, others parts may have floods that destroy bridges, buildings and vehicles, and wash tons of valuable topsoil out to sea.

In 1856, 868 millimetres of rain fell in Durban in four days and the swollen Mgeni River gathered up terrified elephants and swept them out to sea. A storm that broke over Cape Town in May 1865 stranded 45 ships in Table Bay. Two vessels were wrecked on the rocks (the remains of one, the *Athens*, may still be seen at Mouille Point) and many lives were lost. A cyclone over Mozambique in February 2000 damaged the harbour town of Beira and caused flood damage estimated at almost R2 billion. Over 500 000 people were left homeless and unknown numbers were drowned.

An example of devastation caused by floods

Wind and Hail

Destructive strong gales (called hurricanes in the USA and Europe; typhoons in Asia) are caused in southern Africa by tropical cyclones. Another disastrous form of strong winds is the tornado, which can cause death and terrible destruction. A tornado tore through Roodepoort on the West Rand in November 1948. In little over an hour it ripped across the town, leaving a path of devastation 66 kilometres long and 300 metres wide. Whole streets were reduced to ruins and three people were killed. A heavy thunderstorm broke at the same time and torrential rain fell, accompanied by hailstones as big as hens' eggs.

WHEN LIGHTNING STRIKES

In South Africa, people are killed by lightning every year. The worst incident occurred in 1934, when a group of huts in Tembuland in the Eastern Cape was struck and 56 people were killed. Stay indoors during a thunderstorm, but if you are caught unaware:

- do not find shelter under a tree or near a metal fence
- do not hide in a hole in the ground or even under a hedge
- get out of a swimming-pool, river or dam as soon as possible.

Shocking

The power of **earthquakes** is measured on the **Richter Scale**. Beginning with 1, each number on the scale is ten times more powerful than the one below it. An earthquake measuring 7 is as mighty as a one megaton nuclear bomb. The most powerful recorded earthquake struck Chile, in South America, in 1960. It measured 9.5 on the Richter Scale. Major earthquakes rarely occur in southern Africa.

Pests and Plagues

Plagues of insects and other pests can destroy South Africa's crops and natural vegetation. Occasionally, swarms of **locusts** sweep in their millions across the countryside, stripping bare all the plants in their path. The brown locust destroys grazing, wheat and maize, whereas the red locust is a menace in the sugar plantations of KwaZulu-Natal. Millions of rands are spent every year in destroying them. Light aircraft are used to spray swarms with poison, but this method of control may also harm or kill the locust's natural enemies and many other creatures.

A tiny red-billed bird called the **quelea** does almost as much damage as the locust. Enormous flocks feed on the seed of ripening crops. Like locusts, queleas move from place to place in huge numbers, covering great distances and roosting in over-crowded thorn trees. Scientists have still not succeeded in ridding South Africa of this plague.

Locust swarms can destroy entire crops

THE EARTH MOVES

Disaster struck on the evening of 29 September 1969, when the Western Cape shuddered under the most powerful **earthquake** in the country's recorded history. The Tulbagh-Ceres-Wolseley area was the worst hit. Several historic buildings collapsed and nine people died. The earthquake measured 6.5 on the Richter Scale.

LADIES WITH A TEMPER

Tropical cyclones were formerly given women's names in alphabetical order, although now they receive men's names as well. The system was invented by an Australian, Clement Wragge, who called the most violent hurricanes after people he didn't like. When tropical cyclone Demoina struck the coast of KwaZulu-Natal in January 1984, about 597 millimetres of rain fell in one day at Lake St Lucia.

PLACES TO SEE →

ℹ Visit the Geology Education Museum at the University of KwaZulu-Natal's Westville Campus

Preserving Our Country

LOST AND FOUND
In 1989 a pair of mounted **bloubok** horns found among some old sporting trophies in Cape Town, was identified and examined by experts. Four mounted specimens of this long-lost animal are exhibited in European museums but these horns are the only bloubok relics in South Africa.

South Africa has the world's biggest land mammal (African elephant), the tallest mammal (giraffe), the fastest mammal (cheetah), the smallest mammal (dwarf shrew), the largest bird (ostrich), and the largest flying bird (kori bustard). But this rich wildlife heritage may be in danger of being lost forever if we do not make a special effort to take care of our beautiful country.

Our Big Mammals
National and international laws on wildlife preservation have helped to make South Africa's more than 10 000 **elephants** safe. Today there are so many elephants in the Kruger National Park that culling is necessary because, unless their numbers are kept under control, there will not be enough water and food for them all and they will starve.

The **hippopotamus**, once found in lakes and rivers from Zeekoeivlei to the Limpopo River, is now found only in KwaZulu-Natal and Mpumalanga. However, hippo have been successfully reintroduced to the Cape Peninsula's Rondevlei Bird Sanctuary, and to the Great Fish River in the Eastern Cape.

Mammals Lost Forever
By the end of the 18th century the **blue antelope**, or *bloubok*, had vanished from the Overberg area of the southern Cape. It may have disappeared because sheep deprived it of its natural food, but hunting also took its toll. The **quagga** was the southernmost sub-species of the plains zebra, with colour variations, and not, as people used to think, a separate species. It had a brown coat and creamy white legs. Its black stripes were only on its head, neck and foreparts. Large herds of quagga once roamed the Cape and southern Free State, but the last quagga, held in captivity, died in the Amsterdam Zoo in 1883. Hunting and farming north of the Vaal led to the disappearance from South Africa of **Lichtenstein's hartebeest**, although it still exists in countries further north. In 1985, SA National Parks obtained several specimens from Malawi and settled them in the Kruger National Park.

THE RETURN OF THE QUAGGA
In 1987 a quagga rebreeding programme was started at the Vrolijkheid Nature Reserve near Robertson. Zebra from KwaZulu-Natal and Namibia are being used to breed the 'new' quaggas. The **newly bred quaggas** have been moved and can be seen below the famous Rhodes Memorial in Cape Town.

Saved!
Bontebok have increased in number since a few survivors were protected in the Bontebok National Park, near Swellendam, in 1931. About 20 years later, plans were made to protect the remaining 100 **Cape mountain zebra** in the Mountain Zebra National Park outside Cradock, and now there are over 200 zebra in the park. The southern subspecies of the **white rhino** was saved from extinction when the KwaZulu-Natal Nature Conservation Service protected the few survivors in reserves. There are now more than 1 500 in Hluhluwe-Mfolozi alone (see box on page 121).

The numbers of the **southern right whale** were drastically reduced by whaling during the 19th century, but conservation programmes have today restored this giant mammal to our waters.

SUPPORT OUR LIVING WORLD
WWF-South Africa, part of the World Wide Fund for Nature, aims to conserve the biodiversity assets (endangered species, habitats and ecosystems) of our country, ensure natural ecosystems are valued and integrated into sustainable development, and make people aware of climate change. WWF-South Africa needs donations to finance projects to save species like the blue crane, marine turtle and rhino.

WESSA, the Wildlife and Environment Society of South Africa, is a non-governmental conservation organization that works in areas such as energy, biodiversity, waste and water. It publishes *Environment* and *EnviroKids* magazines.

Plains zebra with feint hindleg stripes used in quagga re-breeding

Blue antelope (now extinct)

GETTING INVOLVED
How you can help conserve our environment:
• **Join a society** or a bird club.
• **Organize a 'hack'** to destroy invading plants.
• **Plan a clean up** of a local area or river.
• **Support conservation schemes** such as the 'Save the Rhino' campaign.
• **Find out more** about the environment.

Black wattle   Weeping willow

Jacaranda trees line many streets in Pretoria

Plant Invaders

Invasive plants damage the natural vegetation and use up scarce water resources, and may not be planted. Several species of Acacia (wattle) were introduced to South Africa from Australia in the 19th century. Both the **Port Jackson willow** and **rooikrans** (red wattle) were introduced to bind the shifting sands of the Cape Flats, but have since spread rapidly inland. Rooikrans has twisted pods containing red-edged, black seeds. **Black wattle** was introduced to KwaZulu-Natal as a windbreak and for firewood, and its bark was used to tan leather. Black wattles choke river beds and are a serious threat to indigenous forests and fynbos.

Hakea, another Australian invader, is particularly bad for Cape fynbos. When an area is swept by fire, the fruits of this bushy shrub or small tree burst open and release black, winged seeds that grow into dense thickets and smother and kill fynbos.

The **cluster pine** was probably introduced by the French Huguenots. It is a tall tree with clusters of large cones. It is indigenous to the Mediterranean, so the Western Cape's winter climate is ideal. Pine needles fall and cover the forests' floors, preventing the growth of indigenous plants. The seed germinates quickly after fires and dense thickets of trees develop. But the cluster pine is also a valuable plantation tree; it is only when it gets out of control that it is considered a threat.

The blue-flowered **jacaranda** is common in Pretoria, but it also grows in other parts of South Africa. Originally from Argentina, it has an aggressive growth habit. Only a sterile cultivar, 'Alba' may be planted.

The **weeping willow**, orginally from China, has spread from city gardens to river banks in the northern provinces and KwaZulu-Natal.

The **water hyacinth** was brought to South Africa in the 1880s from South America and planted in ponds and pools. The hyacinth, with its mauve flowers, floats in dams or rivers, or roots itself in mud. It reproduces very quickly by forming side shoots that form separate plants. It clogs up rivers, dams and irrigation canals and is considered to be the world's worst waterweed.

Oleander was introduced from the Mediterranean region, and has spread eastward from the Cape, where it forms hedges and wind breaks. It now clogs up river beds and the leaves are also very poisonous.

The **blackjack** weed, originally from South America, grows wild in the veld and gardens. Its dry, barbed seeds cling to animals, clothes or other objects that brush past.

The Role of Government

The Departments of **Water, Environmental Affairs** and **Tourism** all play a role in conservation. **SA National Parks (SANParks)** maintains our national parks, such as the Kruger National Park and Kgalagadi Transfrontier Park. The **Forestry Division** of the **Department of Agriculture, Forestry & Fisheries** maintains our forests and marine environment. The **Chief Directorate of Sea Fisheries** controls the quantities of fish harvested, and has established protected marine conservation areas along our coast. Research to prevent over-fishing is carried out by the **Sea Fisheries Research Institute**.

The **South African National Biodiversity Institute (SANBI)** leads and coordinates research, and monitors the state of biodiversity in South Africa. It also manages the nine national Botanical Gardens, including Walter Sisulu in Johannesburg, Hantam in the Northern Cape and the Karoo Desert Garden at Worcester.

Special Days

On **International Museum Day**, 18 May, museums all over the world present special functions and displays concerning cultural historical conservation.

World Environment Day, 5 June, helps us remember our responsibility towards the environment.

National Arbor Week is celebrated in September and reminds us of the importance of trees. Many schools and organizations plant trees, especially those that have been chosen as the Tree of the Year.

National Marine Day, second Friday in December, is the day on which attention is given to caring for the sea and all forms of marine life.

PRETTY DEADLY

Lantana, which originated in South America, is one of the world's 10 worst weeds. It was brought to the Cape in the 19th century, and spread rapidly. It forms dense thickets, and the berry-like fruits can be toxic to people and cattle. Because its flowers are so pretty, people used to plant this invading shrub in their gardens.

South African
NATIONAL PARKS

environmental affairs
Department:
Environmental Affairs
REPUBLIC OF SOUTH AFRICA

agriculture,
forestry & fisheries
Department:
Agriculture, Forestry and Fisheries
REPUBLIC OF SOUTH AFRICA

SANBI
Biodiversity for Life

PLACES TO SEE

Whether you are visiting a reserve, the beach, or the park, remember not to litter, and not to kill or feed any wild animals, pick wild flowers, or cause veld fires

Endangered Wildlife

THE BLUSHING BRIDE

First discovered in the Franschhoek mountains in 1773, the blushing bride, (*Serruria florida*) was not seen by botanists for over a century, when its home was rediscovered. By 1930, its numbers had fallen drastically because foresters had taken care to prevent fires. It was only when new plants sprang up after an accidental fire in the 1960s, that scientists realized that, like all proteas, the blushing bride needs occasional fire for its seeds to germinate.

CITES

The **United Nations Convention on International Trade in Endangered Species** was formed in 1975 to prevent the extinction of animals and plants through trade or the destruction of their natural habitat.

PLANT INVADERS

Many foreign (**alien**) plants in our gardens were deliberately introduced from other countries. Others arrived by mistake and have spread rapidly. Although some invaders are beautiful, they destroy indigenous flora. These 'invaders' usually grow out of control because their natural enemies stayed behind in their countries of origin. They should be pulled out by the roots and destroyed.

When Europeans arrived in southern Africa, they initially shot wild animals for their meat and leather. However, over time, big-game hunters shot elephants for their valuable ivory, while birds, antelope and other game were hunted for sport. Herds became smaller and some species came close to extinction. Fortunately, most South Africans realize the importance of wildlife conservation.

Species to Protect

Some animals are **endangered** (they will disappear if steps are not taken immediately), or **vulnerable** (they will become 'endangered' unless steps are taken to protect them).

Riverine rabbit

The critically endangered **riverine rabbit** is found in the vegetation beside dry river beds in the Karoo. It was first bred in captivity in 1989 and five young rabbits were born at the De Wildt Cheetah Reserve outside Pretoria.

The **wild dog**, with its large, rounded ears, bushy, white-tipped tail and blotched coat of white, black and yellow, used to occur all over South Africa, but is now found in the north-west of Mpumalanga as far south as Swaziland, and in Botswana.

The **roan antelope**, the second largest antelope in Africa after the eland, is endangered because it cannot compete with farm stock for grazing, and its habitat has been severely altered by overgrazing. Antelope species classed as 'endangered' include the oribi, the glossy-black sable antelope, the shy suni and the tsessebe.

The **honey badger** (or 'ratel') sometimes raids fowl-runs and bee-hives and many are killed by farmers. The scales of the **pangolin**, or scaly anteater, are used by sangomas and herbalists to make medicines. Some people regard the flesh of **aardvarks**, or antbears, as a delicacy. Aardvarks sometimes burrow under jackal-proof fences and allow jackals into stock enclosures. Sangomas use their snouts and claws in medicines.

Other vulnerable animals include the giant and rough-haired golden moles, the white-tailed rat, African wild cat and Hartmann's mountain zebra.

Birds At Risk

Many birds are now rare because man disturbed their natural habitats by building cities and roads, ploughing farmlands, draining vleis and swamps, and introducing pesticides. Some birds were hunted or trapped and eggs and nests destroyed. The yellow-billed oxpecker did not breed in South Africa for many decades, and the African skimmer last nested at St Lucia in 1944. Fortunately, both birds are found further north in Africa and the yellow-billed oxpecker has been successfully reintroduced to KwaZulu-Natal's Mfolozi Game Reserve. Five South African bird species are 'critically endangered', eleven are 'endangered' and 43 are 'vulnerable'. A further 64 species are flagged as 'near threatened' meaning they need to be protected.

Birds of Prey

The **bateleur** eagle streaks across the sky at more than 50 kilometres per hour, scanning the ground for carrion or live prey such as birds, hares, small antelope or leguaans. When there is too much human activity, the bateleur leaves the area. Its numbers and range have decreased in South Africa and it is now classed as 'vulnerable' in this country.

THE IMPORTANCE OF PLANT RESEARCH

World-famous **Kirstenbosch**, on the eastern slopes of Table Mountain, is one of the great botanic gardens of the world. It lies in the heart of the **Cape Floral Kingdom**. More than 2 500 of South Africa's 24 000 flowering plants are threatened. Some are being successfully grown in research laboratories. Thin slivers of plant tissue are taken from a surviving plant and, by using new techniques, hundreds of new specimens can be grown from it.

Many plants contain chemical compounds and research is constantly carried out on their functions and uses. Some are used to make medicinal drugs, while others are utilized by traditional sangomas and herbalists. Scientists must try to prevent any single plant species from becoming extinct; its disappearance could mean the loss of a future cure for diseases such as cancer or AIDS.

Golden mole

A CRANE IN DANGER
Cranes are large birds, rather like storks. Fewer than 100 breeding pairs of **wattled cranes** remain in South Africa today. Dam building and the draining of swamps drove wattled cranes away from their marshy breeding grounds.

The **martial eagle** is also classed as vulnerable. Some farmers believe it preys on sheep and goats and therefore often kill it. Its natural food includes game birds and, not knowing the difference, it may swoop down on chickens. Young martial eagles are known to eat lambs, but conservationists believe that most of these are either dead or dying when the eagle takes them. It is a powerful bird and may even kill small buck as large as the common duiker and the impala.

The **Egyptian vulture**, a whitish bird with a bare, yellow face and black-tipped wings, was once found all

over South Africa, then for some years was only seen in the Eastern Cape. But recent searches in the Eastern Cape have been fruitless and it is sadly already extinct as a breeding species in South Africa. With decreasing numbers of large wild animals, there are fewer carcasses for vultures to feed on. Some vultures died after eating carcasses poisoned by farmers who were trying to kill black-backed jackals, which preyed on their stock. Others were shot after carrying off ostrich chicks and breaking open the eggs by dropping stones onto them. The Egyptian vulture has also been known to eat the contents of flamingo and pelican eggs.

Martial eagle

Egyptian vulture

Other Threatened Birds
Terns are sea birds usually with long forked tails, and pointed wings. The population of **roseate terns** has decreased in recent years, particularly in South Africa. If a tern's nest is disturbed, it flies off and takes some time to return. Gulls then rob its nest, and frightened nestlings may wander into the territories of neighbouring roseate terns and be killed by them. The roseate tern is protected on the breeding grounds of St Croix Island and Bird Island, east of Port Elizabeth.

The turkey-like **ground hornbill** uses its big, tough bill to catch lizards, frogs, rats and mice and even large snakes and tortoises. It is sometimes shot because it occasionally smashes windowpanes after mistaking its reflection for an intruding rival. Many ground hornbills have been accidentally killed by eating poisoned bait left for raiding jackals and other pests.

Other birds that are classed as vulnerable include the African penguin, Cape vulture, lappetfaced vulture, Natal nightjar, spotted thrush, African broadbill, Cape parrot, yellow-breasted pipit and Rudd's lark.

Ground hornbill

Plants to Protect
Some plants have already disappeared and botanists and conservationists are doing their best to protect those that remain. When a plant becomes rare, it is declared 'endangered', 'vulnerable' or 'rare'. Anyone who damages or illegally digs up these plants may have to pay a considerable fine.

The **renosterveld**, which once covered the Western Cape was once home to beautiful flowering plants, many of which aren't found anywhere else in the world. Then came the builders and roadmakers, and much of the natural vegetation was uprooted and destroyed. Only two small groups of *Protea odorata*, the rarest protea, still survive and must be protected. The **golden gladiolus** was rescued from its last home near Kommetjie and

then successfully replanted in the Cape of Good Hope Nature Reserve at Cape Point where it is now surviving. The **halfmens** grows in mountainous regions of Namaqualand near the banks of the Orange River. The Khoikhoi called it 'halfmens' because they thought it was half human. These strange-looking plants are very rare and people found stealing them have been fined.

Halfmens

SAVE THE RHINO
In 1970 there were 65 000 **black rhino** in Africa, but there are fewer than 2 000 left in South Africa. Due to poaching, black rhinos are 'critically endangered' and threatened with extinction in the wild. The year 2008 saw the start of a poaching epidemic and since 2010, South Africa has lost over 1 600 rhinos; this figure increases daily. The more numerous **white rhino**, of which there are about 18 000, is also 'threatened'.

PLACES TO SEE

- Kirstenbosch National Botanical Garden in Cape Town
- National parks and game reserves throughout the country

Discovering Our Mammals

THE DASSIE AND THE ELEPHANT

The sturdy little **rock dassie** may be related to the elephant! Its front teeth are tiny tusks that curve from the skull. Of course, the dassie and the elephant have adapted to very different life styles. To help it climb rocks and crags, the dassie has moist pads under its feet that act as suction cups.

Mammals are warm-blooded animals that feed their young with their own milk. There are about 4 200 mammal species, of which nearly half are rodents and almost a quarter are bats. Let us take a look at some of the more common mammals in South Africa's many national parks and reserves.

The African Elephant

Elephants once lived throughout southern Africa. They were once plentiful in the Knysna forests, but hunting and old age eventually killed them all. The slaughter of elephants in the Port Elizabeth area left only seven survivors, which were settled in Addo Elephant National Park in 1931. Today this is one of South Africa's best-known reserves and the home of about 200 descendants of the original seven elephants.

The African elephant is the world's largest land mammal

Baboons

Baboons are clever animals, but they can be very aggressive, and can inflict serious bites with their long, powerful canine teeth, so never tease baboons or offer them food. They occur all over South Africa and are particularly common in hilly regions. They are

very good climbers, and forage for their food, which consists of a wide variety of plants, as well as small animals. They turn over stones in search of insects, scorpions and slugs, and if there is a plague of locusts or termites, baboons will eat them too. They may kill a small hare or antelope if they come upon it by chance. Leopards prey upon baboons.

Baboons live in troops. In small troops, a single, powerful male is usually the leader, but larger troops may have several dominant males. Females are treated as inferiors by the males, although the leaders will protect those with offspring. A new-born spends its first few weeks clinging to its mother's belly. After that the young baboon rides on its mother's back.

Vervet monkeys are found throughout South Africa. They have black and white, yellow-flecked fur with white around their black faces and on their underparts. They scamper about in loud, noisy troops, chattering from the tree tops. They forage on open ground for insects, fruit and birds' eggs. Vervet monkeys are unpopular among farmers as they raid fields and orchards for grain and fruit.

Vervet monkey

SWEATING BLOOD?

Hippos have no sweat glands, but a sticky, pinkish fluid is secreted from pores on their skin. This protects their skin by forming a waterproof film. Because of the colour of the discharge it looks as though the hippo is actually sweating blood!

The Hippopotamus

A hippopotamus has a huge body, short legs, and an enormous mouth. The eyes, ears and nostrils are on top of the head so they can remain above the water when the hippo's body is submerged. A male hippo can weigh up to two tons and eats about 130 kilograms of grass every day. The hippo has tough, thick skin, but it is very sensitive to sun, and cannot stay out of the water for too long. Hippos can be aggressive if annoyed, and may attack people and even overturn boats. In spite of its weight, the hippo is an excellent swimmer and can remain underwater, sometimes walking along the bottom, for up to six minutes. New-born hippos can swim before they can walk. They suckle from their mothers in the water, but come up to breathe.

Hippopotamus

Hyaenas

The **spotted hyaena** is yellowish with brown spots and rounded ears. It used to be found all over South Africa, but is now restricted to game reserves. It is a scavenger, but will often catch its own prey. Although adult males are known to eat cubs, females are dominant and are larger than males.

The rare **brown hyaena** has pointed ears and is dark brown with lighter, yellowish hair on its neck and shoulders. Its legs are striped. Once common all over South Africa, it is now found in parts of Namibia and Botswana, the North West Province and the Free State. Occasionally it makes excursions into the Karoo and is resident in the Richtersveld and the Kalahari. In KwaZulu-Natal, it was re-introduced at Lake St Lucia and Itala Game Reserve. It is a scavenger and eats the remains of dead animals, but may kill a hare or antelope with its jaws. The hyaena 'laughs' as it tears at the flesh of a victim and the loud 'whoop' is its long-distance communication call.

Brown hyena

Black-backed jackal

Side-striped jackal

FULL CYCLE

The **spotted hyaena** has the most powerful jaws of any mammal, and crushes the bones of its prey with its molars. It plays an important role in nature, by ridding the veld of rotting carcasses. Once it has splintered, chewed and swallowed the bones, they are dissolved in strong acid juices in its stomach. The droppings are white and contain large amounts of calcium from the bones the hyaena has swallowed. Other animals, such as tortoises, eat these calcium-rich droppings.

Meerkats (suricates)

Meerkats

The **suricate** is often seen sitting upright at the entrance of its burrow, surveying the veld with large, alert eyes. This interesting meerkat (a member of the mongoose family) is a social animal. It lives in colonies of up to 30 members, and may share a burrow with ground squirrels and yellow mongooses. Meerkats scratch in the soil, using their sharp sense of smell to sniff out insects, spiders, scorpions and lizards to eat.

Jackals

Jackals eat a variety of food, both hunted and scavenged. The **black-backed jackal** lives in the veld. Although farmers destroy jackals because they attack sheep and poultry, they play a role by catching pests. The larger **side-striped jackal** occurs in Mpumalanga, northern KwaZulu-Natal, Botswana, northern Namibia, and northern and eastern Zimbabwe.

OLD 'BIG EARS'

The large ears of the **bat-eared fox** have two functions: they give off body heat to control its body temperature, and are very sensitive to faint underground sounds when it hunts. This helps it locate larvae and other insects – and even mice and small reptiles. It may have up to 50 teeth, more than any other land mammal.

A PROBLEM FOR FARMERS

Yellow mongooses live in colonies in underground burrows. Like suricates, they are largely insect-eaters but will also feed on small mice, lizards and frogs. They can be a problem for farmers because they occasionally take hens' eggs and kill free-ranging chickens.

PLACES TO SEE

- The Addo Elephant National Park in the Eastern Cape
- The Kruger National Park in Mpumalanga and Limpopo Province

125

The Cat Family

TAMING THE AFRICAN WILD CAT

The house cat is descended from the African wild cat that the Egyptians began to tame nearly 4 000 years ago. Today, the pure wild cat has bred so freely with house cats that it is becoming threatened. African wild cats weigh between four and five kilograms and are slightly larger than domestic cats.

Members of the cat family are found in almost every part of the world. They vary in size from the majestic tiger to the tame house cat. Cats are predators, which means that they hunt animals for food. The cat's muscular body, powerful claws and sharp teeth are suited to killing its prey.

Lion

The lion is known as the King of the Beasts, but is really quite lazy. The male spends his days eating, sleeping and playing with his cubs. But he can break a zebra's neck or bring down a giraffe with one swipe of his huge paw. A male lion can weigh up to 250 kilograms yet he can sprint 100 metres in just six seconds.

The adult male has a golden-yellow mane that usually darkens with age. Its tawny-brown hide blends perfectly with the bush and dry grass. Cubs are born with spots, but these fade in time. The rare 'white' lions found in and around the Kruger National Park is not a separate species, but just a colour variation.

The male lion roars more often and more loudly than the lioness. His roars proclaim his pride's territory and warn other lions not to trespass. Lions live in prides of up to 30 members and usually hunt together. Often the male lion strolls up to a herd of antelope or zebra while the lionesses circle them and lie in wait on the far side. The male stalks the prey and drives them toward the hidden lionesses, which jump out of the bush and leap at the victim's head or throat. They do the killing, but the male eats first.

Lions used to be common in most of southern Africa, but today are found only in the larger reserves. There are about 1 800 lions in the Kruger National Park.

Cubs Feed the Hard Way

Lions follow a strict eating order. Although the lionesses usually do all the hard work, they wait until the dominant male has eaten before they feed. Although the males sometimes allow the cubs to share their meal, cubs usually eat last – if there is anything left. If a hungry cub tries to grab a bite before its turn, an adult might hit it away with a vicious blow, sometimes even strong enough to kill it. When food is scarce, some cubs may die of starvation.

Poster for Beauty Without Cruelty

THAT SPOTTED COAT

The same spotted coat that camouflages a leopard from its enemies has made it man's prey. Within a few decades after it became fashionable to wear coats made of leopard skin, the leopard was threatened with extinction in many countries. Fortunately, coats made from **animal furs** are no longer popular and world conservation societies work hard to protect the leopard and other animals hunted for their fur.

A lioness takes her very young cubs for a drink

LEOPARD

The leopard is solitary by nature. Its movements are swift, its body is supple. By day the leopard rests in caves or in thick bush. By night, it prowls silently, preying on antelope, baboons or smaller animals. A hunting leopard stalks its prey, creeping up and then pouncing swiftly. It often seizes the carcass in its powerful jaws and stores it in trees, out of reach of lions and hyaenas. Leopards have been known to hoist heavy antelope, and even young giraffe, that weigh far more than them, into trees.

Leopards have survived in many areas from which other big cats have disappeared. The dark rosettes that spot the leopard's white to golden-yellow hide enable it to blend perfectly with the shadowy bush. A male leopard may be twice as heavy as a female, but size seems to depend on area. Leopards from the mountains of the Western Cape may be half the size of those from the northern bushveld. Farmers dislike leopards because they sometimes prey on lambs or chickens.

Cheetah

The cheetah is the fastest land animal, and is capable of reaching almost 100 kilometres an hour in short spurts. The cheetah's yellowish-brown body is spotted with black. It has small, rounded ears and two dark 'tear marks' running from the eyes to the mouth. Because it has been hunted and shot by farmers, it is found mainly in reserves today. In KwaZulu-Natal it has been reintroduced into the local game reserves. Cheetahs occur sporadically in the Kgalagadi Transfrontier Park and in the Kruger National Park.

Cheetahs move in small groups usually consisting of a mother and her cubs, or a bachelor group of males. Unlike leopards and lions, they hunt by day, most often at dawn or at sunset. The prey is usually small antelope such as springbok or impala, and sometimes the young of larger antelopes.

Although cheetahs can easily be tamed, they have been bred in captivity only recently, after pioneering work at the De Wildt Cheetah Research Centre in Gauteng. De Wildt's greatest achievement has been the successful breeding of the so-called king cheetah, which has larger and darker markings than the more common cheetah.

THE SPOTS OR THE TIPS?
Although the marks on the **large-spotted genet** are generally bigger and darker than those on the small-spotted genet, the difference in their tails is far more noticeable. The tail of the large-spotted genet has a black tip, whereas the small-spotted genet's tail ends in a broad white band.

THE SPEED OF THE CHEETAH
The cheetah's slim body, long and powerful legs and small, streamlined head are built for speed but, although the cheetah is the fastest mammal, it has little stamina. Unless it catches its prey within 400 metres or so, it has to give up and catch its breath before it can charge again.

Cheetah

Caracal or rooikat

Caracal

Known as **rooikat** in Afrikaans, the caracal is a fierce reddish-black animal with tufted, pointed ears. It preys at night on dassies, hares, birds, some reptiles and other small animals, although it has been known to kill medium-sized antelope too. It is an expert climber and will hide among tree branches when hunting. In some areas sheep-farmers find the caracal an even more serious threat to their flocks than the jackal.

Serval

The serval is a long-legged cat with a golden, black-spotted coat. It stands about 60 centimetres high at the shoulder, has quite a short tail, and a smallish head with large ears. Serval prefer to live in grassy areas inhabited by its favourite prey, the vlei rat, although it also eats other small animals. Unlike most cats, it hunts in swampy areas. In spite of its long legs, the serval is an expert climber.

Serval

PLACES TO SEE

Visit the Kruger National Park in Mpumalanga and Limpopo Province, and the many other game reserves and national parks throughout South Africa

127

Antelopes and Buffalo

AGILE ANTELOPE

The **springbok** has a dark band along its flanks and white underparts. Its face and rump are white. When it is alarmed, the springbok leaps straight-legged into the air. Because it is fast and dodges as it runs, it is used as the emblem of the South African rugby team.

THE WAY THEY EAT

If an antelope eats grass, we call it a **grazer**. If it eats leaves from trees, we call it a **browser**. Because antelopes eat only plant material they are called **herbivores** (plant-eaters).

Antelopes and buffalo belong to the same family of even-toed, hoofed animals as cattle, sheep and goats. They are all plant-eaters that chew the cud and have stomachs divided into four separate chambers. All male antelopes have horns, but the females of many species are hornless.

Species in Southern Africa

In southern Africa, there are 33 species of **antelope**. They range from the tiny dik-dik, hardly bigger than a hare, to the majestic eland, with a shoulder-height of 1.7 metres. Many antelopes live in herds, but some smaller species are shy and solitary. They adapt well to their environment. Gemsbok, for example, live in semi-desert regions and can do without water for long periods.

Buffalo are very large and powerful animals related to domestic cattle. They have heavy, upward-curving horns that rise from a bulky mass at the top of the head. Buffalo are good swimmers and often wallow in muddy pools, especially on hot and humid days.

Eland, which can weigh over 700 kilograms, have a slight shoulder hump and a large flap of skin, called a dewlap, hanging from the throat. Both males and females have long, backward-sloping, spiral horns.

Kudu are timid animals. The males, which can stand well over a metre and a half tall at the shoulder, have splendid spiral horns.

Bushbuck are quite small and have almost straight, sharp horns and a crest of long, whitish hair along their backs. The males can be fierce and, during the mating season, may fight each other to the death.

Nyala males have long horns and grey, shaggy coats with whitish, vertical stripes and spots. The females are hornless and orange-brown in colour.

Red and **blue duikers** live in forests while the **grey duiker** prefers open woodland or scrub country. All duikers, except female grey duikers, have short, straight horns. The rare blue duiker dives into thick cover when disturbed and is rarely seen. The red duiker is found in KwaZulu-Natal and Mpumalanga and the grey duiker is found all over South Africa.

Reedbuck are grey-brown antelopes that run with a 'rocking-horse' motion. They live among tall grass and reed-beds near water. Males have forward-pointing horns. **Mountain reedbuck** are similar-looking, but live in mountainous, rocky areas. **Waterbuck** are usually found near water. They have shaggy, brownish-grey coats, their eyes and nose are patched with white and there is a clear white ring on the hindquarters. The males have long horns that curve forward. **Lechwe** are yellowish in colour. Herds live in swampy areas where they wade in the water and feed on flood-plain grasses. Males have long, ringed horns. They are found in the Okavango Swamps and along the banks of the Chobe River, also in the Caprivi Strip.

Duiker

Dik-dik

Bushbuck

Buffalo

Eland

Steenbok

Waterbuck

Nyala

Reedbuck

128

Gemsbok are mainly grey with black and white markings on the face and legs. Males and females have long sharp horns that are capable of killing lions. They live in semi-desert areas of southern Africa.

Roan antelopes are the second-largest antelope species in Africa after the eland. Their faces are black and white and they have greyish-brown coats. Both males and females have heavily ringed, backward-curving horns. In South Africa, the roan antelope is classed as endangered. **Sable antelopes** are relatives of the roan. Males have glossy jet-black coats, white underparts and white-patched faces; females are reddish-brown. Males have long, backward-curving horns and a black mane.

Great herds of **blue wildebeest**, or gnu, are found in the Kruger National Park and on the plains of the Kalahari in Botswana. The blue wildebeest has a silver-grey body, a long black mane and tail, and a black beard hanging from the throat. Both males and females have curving, buffalo-like horns. The smaller **black wildebeest** has a long white tail.

Red hartebeest have long, horse-like faces. Males and females have ringed horns that curve backwards at the tip. Herds of these swift-moving antelopes live in the north-western semi-desert areas.

Tsessebe look rather like hartebeest, but their faces are less horse-like. They are said to be the fastest of all our antelopes. They are inquisitive animals, and hunters have recorded that they will often remain in the open, trying to see what is happening, even after several members of the herd have been shot.

The graceful **impala** is reddish in colour and is usually found in savanna woodlands. Impala eat short grasses and the leaves of bushes and trees.

Klipspringer, oribi, steenbok, grysbok, suni and dik-dik are small, agile antelopes, and only the males have horns. The hoofs of the **klipspringer** are specially suited to its home on rocky hills. **Oribi** live in open grassland and are classed as vulnerable. **Steenbok** are common and live in open grassland with scrub cover. **Grysbok** are solitary little antelopes which, when threatened, lie flat on the ground trying to hide. They live in thick bush and are usually active at night. The tiny, shy **suni** may emerge from thick bush to feed at dawn and dusk, but tends to be active at night. The spindly-legged **dik-dik** of the semi-desert bush scrub of northwestern Namibia, has a long snout with a constantly twitching, hairy tip.

Grey rhebok are medium-sized antelopes with soft, woolly coats. The males have short straight horns. They are found mainly in the hilly areas of South Africa, Lesotho and Swaziland.

WHEN DANGER LURKS
Many antelopes use signals to warn each other of danger. The **impala** snorts loudly to let the herd know that a predator is on the prowl, and when it runs off, the rest of the herd can follow the clear stripes on its rump. The **kudu** also has a signal. To warn other kudu of danger, it lifts its tail so that the white underside can be seen.

Clockwise from top left: gemsbok, grysbok, sable antelope, kudu, blue wildebeest and roan antelope

Tsessebe

Bontebok

FROM THE BRINK OF EXTINCTION
Bontebok and **blesbok** are medium-sized antelopes and are, in fact, subspecies of the same species. The bontebok occurs in the Western Cape and the blesbok in the Eastern Cape and Free State. Both have a clear white blaze on the face and around the rump, and curved, ringed horns. Bontebok were once quite plentiful but were later threatened with extinction. Fortunately, today these antelopes are successfully multiplying in many reserves and game parks in southern Africa.

WORKING TOGETHER
Oxpeckers sit on the backs and heads of some antelopes and buffalo and pick off ticks and other parasites. **Cattle egrets** eat insects, which jump out of the grass as antelopes graze, and nyala often follow baboons so that they can eat the leaves and fruit that fall from trees when baboons feed.

PLACES TO SEE
- The Kruger National Park in Mpumalanga and Limpopo Province
- The Bontebok National Park near Swellendam

Curious Creatures

South Africa has a rich variety of animal life, not the least of which are the many different mammal species we already know so much about. But our country is also home to many unusual mammals with curious habits and even stranger features.

Aardvark

COLOURS THAT TELL A STORY

Have you ever seen a **baboon** with a bright red patch under its tail? Although this may look rather strange, it is quite natural. These swollen patches are seen underneath the tail of a female baboon and tell the male baboon that she is ready to mate.

Aardvark

The aardvark, or antbear, eats ants and termites. It forces open their mounds or underground nests with its powerful claws, pokes in its long snout and catches the ants on its long, sticky tongue. The aardvark digs very well and lives in burrows, which can be over two metres deep and 15 metres long. It scrapes soil out of the tunnels, banking some of it up to form an encircling mound that prevents water from flooding in during the rainy season. Unoccupied aardvark burrows are home to many other animals such as porcupines, warthogs, pangolins, jackals and even birds and snakes.

FOOD FOR ALL

There are different **feeding levels** among plant-eating animals (herbivores). The tall giraffe feeds on the topmost branches of trees, where no other browsers can reach. The warthog digs below ground for bulbs and tubers. Grazers feed on grass, and small antelope, such as the klipspringer, browse at the bottom of trees. Larger antelope, such as eland, browse on the middle branches.

Warthogs

Warthog

The warthog has short legs and a long body. Its almost naked skin is scattered with bristles and it has a coarse, untidy mane. The male has two large, wart-like lumps on either side of his snout, but the female has only one pair. Warthogs eat mainly grass and other plant matter. To feed, especially when rooting for underground tubers, it kneels on its front legs and uses its hard snout to dig, sometimes 15 centimetres deep. When alarmed, it trots off with its tufted tail held high in the air. The warthog often shelters in burrows dug by other animals. It enters the burrow backwards so that it faces the entrance and can use its sharp upward-curving tusks to defend itself against enemies.

Honey badger

The honey-badger, or ratel, is about as big as a medium-sized dog. It is powerfully built, with very strong claws. Honey-badgers are quite fearless when attacked and have been known to put up a fight against lion, wildebeest and python. A broad, greyish-white streak covering the top of its head and back contrasts with the black hair of its body. The honey-badger eats small creatures including lizards, snakes, tortoises, frogs and rodents. It also eats fruit and likes honey and bee larvae, using its strong claws to rip open hives or nests. Although angry bees attack it ferociously, its thick hide protects it from their stings. The little bird known as the greater honey guide may lead a honey-badger to a hive and then eat what honey is left.

Clockwise from top left:bushbuck, giraffe, warthog

Honey badger

A LONG, LONG TONGUE
Did you know that the **pangolin**'s tongue may be 25 centimetres long, while its body is only 40 centimetres long? It has no teeth to chew its food, but has a strong muscular stomach where the food is ground and digested.

WD/IOA

A SPINY COAT
The **porcupine** is almost completely covered in long quills. Much of the time, the quills lie flat but, when it senses danger, the porcupine raises and rattles its hollow quills and stamps its feet. If the predator is not frightened, the spiny creature will turn its back on the attacker and scurry backwards so that the sharp points stick into the predator's face (see the picture of the lioness's face on page 126).

Shrews

Shrews are small, mouse-like mammals with long, tapering snouts. They have thin tails and velvety fur. Although they give off a strong, unpleasant smell when attacked, cats, dogs and owls will hunt and kill them, but only owls actually eat them. Shrews can eat two-thirds their own weight in insects, worms or other small creatures every day. They hunt at night.

LH/IOA

Shrew

Bushbaby (galago)

Galagos are called bushbabies because they make a noise like a crying baby. In Afrikaans, they are known as a nagapie ('night monkey'). There are two species of bushbaby in southern Africa. The thick-tailed bushbaby is about the size of a small monkey, has large ears, enormous eyes, long soft fur and a thick bushy tail. It is active at night. Because its big eyes help it to see in the dark, it can leap about safely among the trees. During the day, family groups sleep in trees in nests of leaves and grass. They are gentle creatures but, although their food consists mainly of insects, berries, fruit, seeds and gum, they also catch birds and small animals if they can. Lesser bushbabies are much smaller than thick-tailed bushbabies and eat mostly insects.

MHY

Bushbaby

THE BIGGEST HEART
Because the **giraffe** has such a long neck, its heart has to pump blood a long way to the brain, so the giraffe has one of the biggest hearts in the animal kingdom. Other adaptations include a special valve in the jugular vein between the heart and the brain that prevents blood flooding back to the heart and lungs and starving the brain of oxygen. When the giraffe stoops to drink, these valves also stop the blood from rushing to the brain.

Pangolin

The pangolin, or scaly anteater, looks quite alarming but is rather timid. The upper side of its body, from its small cone-shaped head to the tip of its long tail, is covered with an armour of large, hard scales with very sharp edges. The pangolin's face is naked, showing its small, heavy-lidded eyes and weak, toothless jaws.

Pangolins live in burrows or under piles of plant debris. They come out at night and walk slowly on their hind legs, and may use their tail for balance or support. Pangolins use their strong, five-clawed forefeet to break open anthills, and catch ants, and sometimes termites, with their long, sticky tongues. When frightened, it rolls itself into a tight ball, which is almost impossible to force open. The mother pangolin protects her young from danger by curling her body around it. When travelling, she carries her young on her back.

DSR/IOA

Giraffe

Giraffe

A full-grown male giraffe is the world's tallest creature. It can grow to almost six metres (to the top of its head) and weigh 1.5 tons. The giraffe's dusty-brown markings, shadowy spots, long neck and spindly legs enable it to blend perfectly with the acacia thorn-bush in which it lives. When it browses, the giraffe curls its tongue around twigs and thorns to get to the leaves. Thorns do not hurt it as the roof of its mouth is covered with horny skin and thick saliva covers the spikes. Although a long neck helps it to reach tree tops, the giraffe must splay out its legs to reach the water when drinking, an awkward position that makes it an easy prey for lions, its only natural enemy. A mother giraffe becomes quite aggressive if her young is threatened.

PLACES TO SEE

ℹ️ You will be able to see almost all these curious creatures in South Africa's many game reserves and wildlife sanctuaries

Speckled padloper

THE BIG AND THE SMALL
The smallest tortoise in the world is the **speckled padloper**, which only reaches a length of 75–85 millimetres and is found in southern Africa. In contrast, the leopard tortoise, the biggest tortoise in southern Africa, can weigh up to 40 kilograms.

Leopard tortoise

TURTLE, TORTOISE OR TERRAPIN?
To South Africans and Britons, a tortoise is a land animal; a turtle has flippers and lives in the sea; and a terrapin lives in fresh water and has clawed, webbed feet. In the USA, freshwater species are called either turtles or terrapins. In Australia, where there are no tortoises on land, they are called water tortoises, whether they are found in the sea or in fresh water.

Reptiles

Reptiles are cold-blooded animals with backbones. They have lungs for breathing air and are protected by a scaly or horny skin. They probably developed from the amphibians about 300 million years ago. Over 400 of the world's 6 000 reptile species are found in southern Africa.

Crocodiles

Crocodiles may be the last living relatives of the dinosaurs. Southern Africa's only species is the **Nile crocodile**, which lives in rivers and lakes of warmer, tropical parts. It has tough, horny scales and can be longer than six metres. In its long, strong jaws, it has about 60 sharp teeth that are constantly replaced. The Nile crocodile swims very fast, propelling itself with its powerful tail. It basks on banks or lies almost undetected in the water with only its eyes and nostrils showing. The crocodile can kill large animals, and even people, by pulling them under the water and drowning them. Crocodiles lay clutches of up to 80 eggs and bury them in the sand above water level. The mother guards them for three months and when they hatch, she gently carries the young to the water in her mouth.

Tortoises, Terrapins and Turtles

When they are threatened, most species are able to withdraw their heads and legs into their hard, bony shells for protection. Their eggs are laid in holes in the soil. All South African tortoises are protected by law. Land tortoises are mainly herbivores or plant-eaters. The small and rare **geometric tortoise** (pictured top right) has a yellow pattern on its knobby upper shell. It can live only in the renosterveld of the Western Cape, a type of vegetation almost completely taken over by farmlands.

The shell of the **angulate** or **rooipens tortoise** is black and yellow, and the underside is often reddish. It is common on the western and southern Cape coast. Males are very aggressive and will turn rivals on their backs by ramming them with a special 'beak' that protrudes from their undershell.

The **marsh terrapin**, or **African water tortoise**, and several species of the **hinged terrapin** are mostly carnivorous (flesh-eating) and use their paddle-like feet for swimming in rivers and dams. The marsh terrapin's four stink-glands give off a disgusting smell to discourage predators from eating it.

The **leatherback turtle**, which may weigh over 600 kilograms and reach a length of two metres, is the world's largest and fastest-swimming turtle. It breeds along the beaches of northern Zululand, where a female may lay over 1 000 eggs in a season. The smaller **loggerhead turtle** also breeds in this area.

Lizards

Nearly all lizards are insect-eaters, and are useful because they destroy pests. When threatened, many lizards, such as geckos, shed their tails, which continue to wriggle about and distract the attacker. The tail-less lizard then escapes and grows another, but less attractive, tail. Lizards live in or on the ground, in trees or rocks and in areas ranging from tropical forests to desert. Many lay eggs, but some give birth to live young.

Crocodiles

Water leguaan

The **giant girdled lizard**, also known as the sungazer, is a large, rare lizard with big, spiky scales.

The **gecko** is a tiny lizard. It is often found clinging onto wall surfaces with the sticky pads under its feet. **Ground geckos**, found in dry parts of the Western and Northern Cape and Namibia, are quite aggressive. They eat beetles, moths, scorpions and spiders.

The **water leguaan**, or Nile monitor, is South Africa's biggest lizard. It is a powerful swimmer and feeds on small fish and other water creatures. It makes a hissing sound when cornered. People trap the **rock leguaan** for its patterned skin or use its flesh for medicine.

Snakes

Snakes have scaly bodies and are legless. Their long forked tongues flicker from between their closed lips and are used to smell. They have no eyelids and no outside ears. A snake's lower jaw is divided into two parts that move separately, enabling it to swallow large prey. In some cases their curved, pointed teeth are used as poison fangs. Some snakes lay eggs, but others produce live, fully formed young.

Southern Africa has about 130 snake species, of which about a tenth are deadly to humans. One of the more useful snakes is the common **mole snake**, which eats moles and other rodent pests. The timid **aurora house snake** and **brown house snake** both live near houses and rid them of mice and rats. These snakes suffocate their prey by squeezing them with their coiled bodies.

Mole snake

LIZARDS OF A DIFFERENT COLOUR

Did you know that **chameleons** belong to the lizard family? When searching for insects, their bulging eyes swivel in different directions. They catch insects by darting out a long, sucker-tipped tongue. Chameleons change colour according to temperature or mood, and merge well with their surroundings. They cling to branches with their toes and curly tails. Chameleons in southern Africa are usually small. In tropical regions they can be up to 35 centimetres long, but are all quite harmless.

The non-poisonous **egg-eater** (above) stretches its mouth to swallow birds' eggs, breaks them with bony 'teeth' in its gullet, digests the inside and regurgitates the shell. The **African rock python**, (below) one of the world's largest snakes, can be up to six metres long. It coils its body around its prey, which may be as large as an antelope, and suffocates it by tightening its coils every time the victim breathes out. Pythons often lie in water with just their nostrils and eyes above the surface.

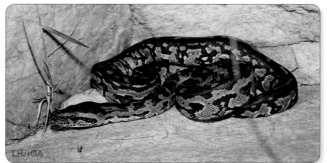

NO SNAILS IN THE GARDEN!

The common **slug-eater** is a small snake with a reddish-brown band down its back. It pulls the snail from its shell before swallowing. Unfortunately, these snakes are often killed by snail bait. Its Afrikaans name is *tabak-rolletjie* because, when it is frightened, it rolls up like a spring much like the rolls of tobacco used by pipe smokers in days gone by.

A NEW COAT

Except for crocodiles and tortoises, all reptiles shed their outer layer of skin as they grow. This process is known as **ecdysis** or **sloughing**. Some snakes shed their skin hours after birth, while others do so only after a few weeks. They hook the old skin onto a rough object in the grass and then slide out of it, rather as one would slide a hand from a glove.

PLACES TO SEE ➤

ⓘ Many snake and crocodile parks in South Africa are open to the public. They keep the most common reptiles, and sometimes even rare species

Amphibians

ACROSS THE LAND
Platannas (African clawed frogs) spend most of their time in water and are strong swimmers. Occasionally, a group will migrate overland in search of a new habitat. The **Cape platanna** is now an endangered species. They were quite common in the vleis of the south-western Cape but, because of the growth of the Cape Flats, many vleis have been drained or polluted.

IN THE TREES
Foam-nest frogs are tree frogs found in northern KwaZulu-Natal and the Lowveld. Their fingers and toes end in rounded discs, which help them to stick onto leaves and grass stems. The female lays her eggs in a slimy liquid, which she deposits on a branch hanging over the water. When the tadpoles hatch about five days later, they drop into the water below.

Amphibians are animals that spend part of their lives in the water and part on land. They belong to the most primitive group of animals with backbones. Millions of years ago, they were the first creatures to leave the water to live on the land. The best-known groups of amphibians are frogs, toads, newts and salamanders. Only frogs and toads are found in southern Africa.

Frogs and Toads

Most frogs and toads lay their eggs in or near water where they hatch into **tadpoles**. The tadpoles swim about, propelling themselves by their tails, and breathe oxygen from the water through their gills. As they grow, their tails and gills gradually disappear and lungs and legs develop. The tiny amphibian then hops out of the water onto the land.

Some amphibians, such as toads, produce poisonous or unpleasant-tasting substances in glands that look like warts. These substances are irritating to an animal's nose, mouth and stomach, and some frogs and all toads use it as a defence against their enemies. Poisonous amphibians are usually brightly coloured.

Tadpoles slowly lose their tails as they grow older.

ADZ/RHS

Some South African Frog Species

The **micro frog** is one of our most endangered species. It grows just 16–18 millimetres long and is South Africa's smallest frog. Its call sounds like a series of harsh, low-pitched scratches.

Micro frog

Reed frogs, **water-lily frogs** and **arum frogs** are all related and their common names tell us where they may be found. These frogs are usually brilliant green, but some change their colour to a paler shade or even to pale yellow. Eggs are usually laid under water on submerged water plants, but two local species lay them just above the surface of the water. The eggs are attached to the stem of a reed or even to a leaf, and when the tadpoles hatch they drop down into the water below. The **painted reed frog**, which lives in east coast vleis, has attractive striped or marbled colouring. It may be found basking in the sun on a reed or even a tree some distance from the water. As the day becomes hotter, the frog's skin turns white to reflect the heat, but later returns to its normal colouring. Its piercing whistle can be heard in the early evening.

Painted reed frog

Eleven species of **rain frog** occur in South Africa. These strange amphibians have a blunt snout, stocky body and short legs. When a rain frog is alarmed, it inflates like a balloon. Unlike most other frogs, it never enters the water, but lives permanently on land, using its back legs to dig burrows in which it lives during the day, and in which the female lays her eggs. The eggs are very large, and when the tadpoles hatch, they stay within the egg capsule while they develop further. They are unable to swim.

Rain frogs emerge only at night, but heavy rain can flood their burrows and force them to the surface in great numbers. On rainy summer nights, when flying ants shed their wings and crawl about on the ground, rain frogs come out of their burrows to eat.

Rain frogs inflate their body when alarmed

The **bull frog** gets its common name from its loud, whooping call, which sounds like the bellowing of a calf. It is very big and can measure nearly 20 centimetres in length. Unlike other species, the male is bigger than the female. Bull frogs are found over much of southern Africa, from the Eastern Cape northwards.

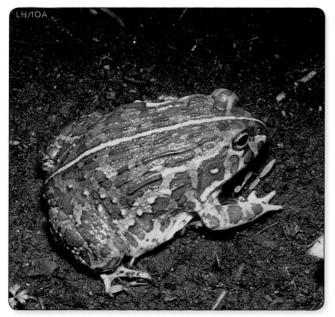

Bull frog

DISAPPEARING GHOSTS

Ghost frogs are most often found in damp areas of mountain fynbos. **Hewitt's ghost frog** is found only at Elandsberg Mountain in the Eastern Cape. It is brown with large, dark spots and has a loud call. The **Table Mountain ghost frog** occurs in moist, forested gorges and ravines on Table Mountain. The adults and tadpoles are adapted for living in fast-flowing mountain streams. Ghost frog tadpoles have large suction discs around their mouths that help them to cling to rocks as they feed on tiny algae. The adults have strong, clubbed fingertips, which help them to grip slippery rocks. Table Mountain ghost frogs are well camouflaged. They are active at night and have a clear ringing call.

Western leopard toads get their name from their yellow-and-black colouring. They have a loud, snoring call and are found in the Eastern Cape. They help farmers by eating insects.

Guttural toads are quite common in city gardens, where they prefer to live near the water – often in holes close to a dripping tap. They hunt at night for moths and flying ants attracted to garden lights.

Guttural toad

DANGER AHEAD!

The bright red-and-black coloration of the **banded rubber frog** warns predators that it is poisonous. Its glands produce a special substance that can kill other frogs and small animals, which eat it. The substance is also very irritating to human skin.

WET AND DRY

Frogs breathe through their lungs and also through their thin, moist skin. As their skin can easily dry out, it is kept moist with a slimy substance produced by special skin glands. Toads have a dry, warty skin. Although their tadpoles develop in water and adults return to the water to breed, toads usually live on land.

PLACES TO SEE

ⓘ Visit a vlei or swampy area near you; see how many different species of frog you can identify

Freshwater Fish

Although South Africa has a variety of sea fish, only about 100 indigenous freshwater fish live in our lakes and rivers. In the 1890s, brown trout were brought to South Africa from Britain. About 20 other foreign species have been introduced to our inland waters, and most have harmed our native stocks.

Indigenous South African Fish
Catfish (barbel) are scaleless, freshwater fish of which several species are found in dams and rivers all over South Africa. Barbel are omnivorous, meaning they eat both plants and small water creatures. They are among the biggest of southern African freshwater fish, some weighing as much as 30 kilograms. A catfish has special breathing organs, so it can live in shallow, muddy pools and even flop or 'walk' over short distances. It has a long, eel-like body and eight thick, fleshy bristles (or barbels) around its mouth. These look like whiskers, giving the barbel its common name of 'catfish'.

IL/RHS   Catfish

The odd-looking **bulldog** is a member of a group known as 'snout fishes'. It is a tropical fish, but can be found as far south as the waters of the Lowveld and in the coastal lakes of KwaZulu-Natal. It can grow as long as 30 centimetres.

IL/RHS   Bulldog

Four species of **eel** are found in those South African rivers that flow to the Indian Ocean. The largest, the African mottled eel, may be as long as 1.6 metres and weigh as much as 20 kilograms.

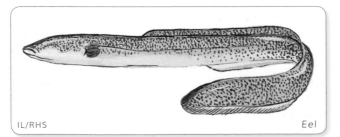

IL/RHS   Eel

The strange **labeo** (mudfish) has a sucker-like mouth that it uses to dredge decaying plant matter off river-bottoms. It lives in most of South Africa's larger rivers and sometimes leaps over rocks and rapids as it swims upstream to spawn.

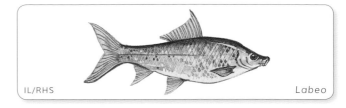

IL/RHS   Labeo

Tropical **lung-fish** are found as far south as the pans of the Kruger National Park where they were discovered only recently. They can survive droughts by burrowing into mud and lining a secure chamber or underground 'cocoon' with dried mucus. There they wait for the waters to return, using their specially developed lungs to breathe air through a tube in the mud. They are regarded as a link between fish and land animals. Lung-fish breed in swamps, pans and river floodplains and feed on crabs, small fish and insects.

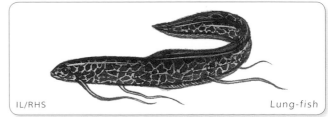

IL/RHS   Lung-fish

Squeakers got their name because they grunt when removed from water. They are scaleless, tropical fish found as far south as the Limpopo and Phongolo rivers. Squeakers have three pairs of barbels (sometimes branched) around their mouths, and the strong, sharp spines inside their fins can inflict painful wounds.

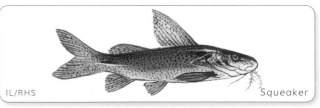

IL/RHS   Squeaker

The famous **tiger-fish** is no longer as plentiful as it was, but is still found as far south as the Limpopo and Phongolo rivers. It can weigh up to 15 kilograms, has sharp teeth, a silvery-white body with tiger-like black stripes and orange fins. It is distantly related to the South American piranha, but has very different habits.

IL/RHS   Tiger-fish

GB

THE SPAWNING EEL
Every January, currents carry millions of tiny, leaf-like eel larvae from beyond Madagascar to South African shores. The young eels, known as elvers, enter the rivers and swim upstream. They are so small that they can wriggle up waterfalls and mossy banks. After eight to 18 years, when they are old enough to breed, their backs become dark and their undersides become silver. In summer, the eels move downstream with flood waters. They reach the sea and swim to their breeding-grounds where they spawn.

PROTECTING THE FISH
Freshwater angling is a popular sport, so regulations protect fish in our lakes and rivers. But some fish are eaten by crocodiles, otters or crabs, and birds such as fish eagles, kingfishers and cormorants. Sometimes fish die from fungus diseases, parasites or drought. Tropical species die in cold weather. But pollution is still the most serious threat.

Tilapia, **bream**, and **kurper** are all common names of related species of freshwater fish with long, spiny fins on their backs. Some females brood their eggs in their mouth and, after the 'fry' hatch, they return to the female's mouth when danger threatens.

IL/RHS   *Tilapia*

Six species of **yellowfish** occur in South Africa, from the Limpopo River to the southwestern Cape. They weigh between one and 14 kilograms, and their streamlined bodies are yellow, silvery-olive or silver.

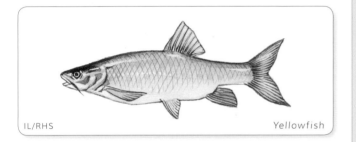

IL/RHS   *Yellowfish*

Imported Fish in South African Waters

The **mosquito fish** (gambusia), introduced to South Africa from the Americas, can eat as much as its own mass of mosquito larvae every day.

IL/RHS   *Mosquito fish*

Both the large-mouth and small-mouth species of **black bass** were introduced to South Africa from North America. Both species are light olive-green with darker back and side markings. The large-mouth bass can weigh up to 3.5 kilograms, but the small-mouth bass reaches only two kilograms. The male builds a nest that he guards, fanning the eggs with his fins to keep them clear of mud, and defends the fry when they hatch. Freshwater crabs sometimes destroy the nests.

IL/RHS   *Black bass*

FINE FOOD

Trout, considered to be a delicacy, is probably the best-known freshwater fish, and trout fishing is a popular sport. In about 1890, the rivers of KwaZulu-Natal were stocked with brown trout fry (baby fish) imported from Britain. In 1893, a trout hatchery and research station was opened at Jonkershoek in the Eerste River Valley outside Stellenbosch. Brown and rainbow trout were successfully bred and moved to cold mountain streams and dams all over South Africa. The hatchery now breeds only indigenous fish, and private hatcheries and fish farms are responsible for trout breeding.

Brown trout

IL/RHS   *Rainbow trout*

Since the **carp** was first introduced to South Africa and bred at Jonkershoek Hatchery near Stellenbosch in 1896, it has spread to rivers and dams throughout South Africa. It is a fairly large fish, greenish-brown in colour and with a pair of large barbels on its upper jaw. It prefers weedy, mud-bottomed pools that it stirs up in search for plants and small fish to eat.

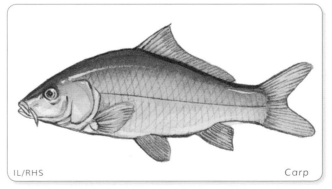

IL/RHS   *Carp*

The brown trout was the first **trout** to be introduced to South Africa, but the rainbow trout is more common today because it is easier to breed and fares better in our warmer waters. Both have spots, but those on the flanks of the brown trout are reddish, surrounded by a pale ring, like a halo. The head and sides of brown trout are brownish-gold and the rainbow trout is marked with a pinky-mauve flush. The rainbow may weigh up to five kilograms and the brown is slightly smaller.

FLY-FISHING

The trout's natural food is small and brightly coloured **flies**. Trout fishermen attract the fish to their lines by using skilfully made artificial bait, which looks identical to real flies. Silk, tinsel, feathers or scraps of fur are used to imitate the small creatures on which trout feed.

KEEPING AN AQUARIUM

Have you ever thought of keeping your own aquarium? Most pet shops sell a variety of small colourful fish suitable for tanks. Watch your own fish breed, feed and grow, but remember that it is illegal to take fish from rivers and dams – and also to release tank fish into a natural habitat.

► PLACES TO SEE

ℹ The Jonkershoek Fish Hatchery at Stellenbosch, and other freshwater hatcheries all over South Africa

Sea Fish

IL/RHS

WHAT IS A 'GALJOEN'?

Galjoen are medium-sized fish found close to rocky shores all along our coast. They may only be caught by recreational anglers, with a permit, and may not be bought or sold.

Galjoen is the Dutch word for a 16th century sailing and warship, the galleon, and refers to the galjoen's strength and fighting ability when hooked.

IL/RHS

EYES THAT MOVE

Soles are flat fish with extremely delicate flesh. The eyes of a young sole are on either side of the head, but as it matures, the left eye moves over to the right side. They live on the sea-bottom and lie with the blind side against the sand and eyes facing up.

Pelagic fish live in the upper layers of the sea in waters rich in plankton. Many of those caught off South Africa's coast are either canned or turned into fishmeal or oil. Most pelagic fish are caught in purse seine nets, but larger ones, such as maasbanker, are taken in trawls.

Look Out for Birds!

Flocks of sea birds dipping and screeching over the sea usually indicate that there is a shoal of fish just below the surface. But wherever there are shoals, there are also larger fish from deeper waters – snoek, yellowtail and tuna. Seals, dolphins and certain whales feed on pelagic fish. But when man intervened, the numbers of certain fish, such as pilchards, dropped to dangerously low levels. Today, strict laws ensure that fishing companies catch no more than their permitted quota.

Pilchards

The pilchard is a dark, silvery fish about 25 cm long. It has a row of spots on each side of its body. Pilchards were once plentiful off the coast of Namibia and the west coast of South Africa, but so many were caught in the 1950s and 1960s that laws have been passed to prevent over-fishing. Pilchards are still found along the South African coast from Durban to Walvis Bay.

IL/RHS   *Pilchard*

Anchovy

The anchovy is barely five centimetres long and rich in oil. It was not well known in South Africa until the 1960s when shoals appeared off the west coast. It is possible that the anchovy population may have increased to replace the disappearing pilchard. Fishermen replaced their pilchard nets with finer-meshed purse seines and recorded catches of between 138 000 tons and 600 000 tons per year between the 1960s and the mid-1990s. Most anchovy spawn (lay and fertilize their eggs) in the seas around Cape Agulhas between October and January. A female fish lays thousands of eggs.

IL/RHS   *Anchovy*

THE KWAZULU-NATAL SARDINE RUN

Every June and July, huge shoals of pilchards (sardines) swim close to KwaZulu-Natal's beaches. People gather the fish in baskets and anglers crowd the rocks to catch the elf and other predatory fish that follow the pilchards inshore. Sharks lurk beyond the breakers and seabirds hover overhead. The pilchards come from South Africa's west coast. During the summer they avoid the warm seas of the Eastern Cape and KwaZulu-Natal, but when the water becomes cooler they move closer to the shore following the plankton eastward and northward.

RH

Maasbankers

Maasbankers (also known as horse-mackerel) can be up to 70 centimetres long. They are found along the Namibian and South African coasts, but are particularly plentiful in the cold waters of the west coast. Small maasbankers are caught in purse seine nets and large adults are taken in trawls. The larger fish are caught mainly during the night as they swim close together well off the sea-bottom.

IL/RHS   *Maasbanker*

Red Eye Round-herring

The red eye, which looks rather like a large anchovy, spends the first year of its life swimming in mixed shoals of pilchards, anchovies and other pelagic fish. The adults move to deeper water, rising to the surface in the evening and returning closer to the seabed at dawn. They are found in southern African waters from Namibia to KwaZulu-Natal.

IL/RHS   *Red eye*

FISH ON THE MENU

SASSI

WH/RHS

ET/IOA

FISH ON A STRING

Bokkems are usually harders (mullet) or maasbankers, salted and dried in the sun. The whole fish is pickled in salty brine. The air is squeezed out, a string is threaded through the eyes and the fish, hung in bunches, are traditionally smoked. Some fishermen believe that if water drips from the tail of a fish hung in the open, it will rain within 24 hours.

A NURSERY FOR FISH

Our main anchovy and pilchard nursery (where many young fish are found) stretches from St Helena Bay to the mouth of the Orange River. Young fish grow quickly and build up oil in their bodies. When they are big enough, they move southwards along the shore. Shoals of young 'recruits', as they are called, arrive off the Western Cape in about May when they are caught and processed.

Fish suitable for eating abound in the waters off South Africa's shores. However, our marine resources are seriously threatened by overfishing and, as a result, it has been necessary to declare certain fish species 'unsustainable'. The South African Sustainable Seafood Initiative (SASSI), a project of the Worldwide Fund for Nature (WWF), seeks to educate consumers so that we can all continue to enjoy fresh fish in the future. SASSI has three lists: fish on the Green list can be eaten freely; fish on the Orange list are vulnerable or threatened and should be eaten only occasionally; while Red list species are overexploited or endangered and have restrictions on their catch and/or sale.

Hake is South Africa's most popular table fish. It occurs on the east and west coasts, and is caught by both deep- and shallow-water trawlers as well as by longline. Depending on where and how it is caught, hake's status varies from Red to Green. Most hake is sold as frozen, prepackaged portions. Look for the logo of the international Marine Stewardship Council (MSC), which certifies that the hake comes from a sustainable and approved source.

Elf (shad) are very popular with skiboat and surf anglers in KwaZulu-Natal, but overfishing means they are now on the Red list. While elf can still be caught (subject to size and seasonal conditions), it is illegal to sell them in KwaZulu-Natal.

Snoek, a member of the mackerel family, are caught off the Cape west and southern coasts in autumn and winter. These large, bony fish may be eaten fresh or smoked; whole snoek are good on the braai, especially when butterflied or 'vlekked'.

Kingklip, a staple on restaurant menus around the country, is a slow-growing, bottom-dwelling species found mainly in deep water. It is on the SASSI Orange list. If you like eating firm white-fleshed fish, good 'Green' alternatives are gurnard or kob (**kabeljou**), which is farmed on land in large tanks. (Sea-farmed kob is also on the Orange list.)

Tuna is used for sushi and sashimi, as well as canned. There are many different kinds of tuna, some of which, like bluefin tuna, are very vulnerable. 'Green listed' yellowfin tuna is an open ocean fish that is caught mainly by hand lines or poles. Tuna (tunny) is popular with sport anglers.

Yellowtail (Yellowtail amberjack) are found in warm temperate waters. This firm-fleshed fish is the second most commonly caught linefish, after snoek. In the Western Cape it is caught by recreational ski- and deckboats, linefishers and traditional treknetters. It is also farmed in sea cages, although this practice is considered less sustainable than wild-caught fish.

PLACES TO SEE

- ℹ Visit Saldanha Bay or Kalk Bay harbour
- ℹ Watch the sardine run on the KwaZulu-Natal coast

Whales, Dolphins and Sharks

SAVING THE WHALES

In 1977, Nan Rice started the **Dolphin Action and Protection Group**, which later extended its work to include whales. Through it, laws were passed to protect South African cetaceans. Another campaign was to rid our seas of plastic and other pollutants that trap marine creatures.

GI/GTY/BBG

HUNTING AT SEA

Whaling was once a very important industry. In the days when petroleum fuels were almost unknown, whale blubber was made into oil and commanded high prices. Every part of the whale was used. The flesh provided meat; soap, margarine, candles and even medicines were manufactured from the oil; while whalebone was sewn into ladies' corsets.

Man has always been fascinated by the intelligence of whales and dolphins, and by the fear and mystery surrounding sharks. These magnificent creatures have ruled the oceans for millions of years, but man has hunted them for centuries, some species almost to extinction.

The Cetaceans

Dolphins, whales and porpoises are called **cetaceans**. Dolphins are small whales, and porpoises (not found in southern African waters) are small and dolphin-like. About 38 species of cetacean are found in our waters. They range in size from Heaviside's dolphin (just over a metre long), to the biggest mammal ever to exist, the blue whale (about 30 metres long).

Cetaceans are not fish, but mammals – warm-blooded animals with backbones, which feed their young with their own milk. Their distant ancestors once lived on land but, over millions of years, adapted to the sea. Their torpedo-shaped bodies are propelled by the broad tail fin, and what were once forelegs are now flippers. To store food during long migrations and to keep the body warm in icy seas, many whale species have a thick layer of blubber, or fat, under the skin. Cetaceans rise to the sea's surface to **breathe** air through their nostrils, or blowholes, on the top of the head. When warm breath is forced out of the lungs through the blowholes, the moisture condenses as it meets the cool atmosphere and a 'spout' of what looks like a spray rises into the air.

Sometimes large groups of whales or dolphins swim onto a beach. This has happened at various beaches along our coast. The animals suffocate because their lungs cannot expand when their heavy bodies collapse, and they die. Sometimes people on the beach try to rescue them by returning them to sea, but they seem determined to return to the shore and die. No one is certain why this happens. Scientists have ruled out suicide and believe that these whales and dolphins have really made a navigational mistake.

Schools of dolphins often leap and dive through the waves. Whales also enjoy these acrobatics. Even a humpback whale 15 metres long and weighing about 40 tons, will often leap clear of the surface before twisting and crash-diving into the water.

Dolphins often join the famous sardine run off the coast of KwaZulu-Natal to feast on pilchards moving towards the shore. While in cold polar regions, blue and southern right whales feed on huge quantities of krill. Some whales dive deep down in search of bigger prey, such as octopus. The great sperm whale may plunge deeper than 2 000 metres.

WHALE WATCHING

Once there were whaling stations along our coast, and boats, known as whale-chasers, which armed with harpoon guns used to hunt the whales that visited the shallow coastal waters every year. But whales and some dolphins became endangered species, and most whaling countries decided to reduce hunting. The last South African whaling station closed in 1975. Now whale watching has become an international attraction that attracts tourists, especially to the southern Cape resort of Hermanus, where **southern right whales** come close inshore to calve and raise their young.

BP/AL

Southern right whale

RH

Humpback whale

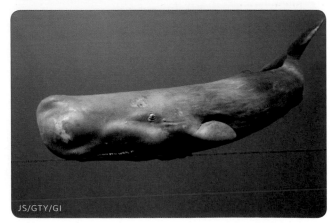

JS/GTY/GI

Sperm whale

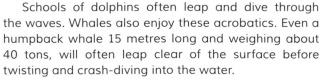

AW

Whales in South African Waters

Instead of teeth, **baleen whales**, such as the southern right whale, have rows of horny combs, called baleen plates, which hang from their huge upper jaws. They gulp in water and then squirt it out again, trapping the krill against the baleen. Baleen whales include the blue whales and humpback whales, but our most commonly seen species is the southern right whale. It was once seriously threatened by whalers and the southern African population was reduced to a hundred animals. But ever since it became protected in 1935, its numbers have risen. Today it is estimated that the numbers of southern right whales off our coast are roughly between 1600 and 2000 whales, although only a quarter of this number is present at any given time.

Toothed whales and **dolphins** (which are small 'toothed whales') use their teeth to catch fish or squid, which they swallow whole. The largest toothed whale seen in our waters is the 20-metre long, deep-diving sperm whale.

The **killer whale** is the largest member of the dolphin family and the only one to prey on other mammals. They can reach about eight metres long, and prey on sea birds, seals and fish and even attack huge whales. Killer whales, porpoises and dolphins can swim at speeds of up to 48 kilometres per hour.

AW

Dolphin

Taking Care of the Young

Unlike most mammals, the young whale is born tail-first so that it does not drown. The mother whale gently lifts it to the surface to take its first breath of air. She lies on her side while the baby feeds from the two teats under her belly. This way, the young whale's blowhole is above the water's surface and it will not drown. Mother whales care for their calves for a long time – up to 15 years in the case of pilot whales. If the mother should die the calf is cared for by another female in the pod.

THE SHARKS BOARD

The Natal Anti-Sharks Measures Board was founded in 1964. Now known as the KZN Sharks Board, it controls shark nets set up on beaches, which act as shark traps and are laid in two overlapping rows about 500 metres offshore. They keep most sharks from the bathing areas, but every day members of the Board remove captured sharks from the nets.

Shark!

Unlike whales and dolphins, sharks are not mammals, but fish. Of the more than 370 species worldwide, about 100 occur in southern African waters. Only 20 are considered potentially dangerous to man.

Instead of a bony skeleton, sharks have a skeleton of tough, flexible cartilage. They have an excellent sense of smell and a special organ, the 'lateral line', which they use for detecting vibrations in water. Most species prefer warmer seas, but several cold-water species are found along the south-west coast.

AW

BP

Top: Whale shark; above: bullshark

The **Zambezi (bull) shark** is found worldwide, including off South Africa's east coast. It can reach three metres and has a grey and white body with two big triangular fins. Its jaw is large and its snout is blunt. It sometimes swims into river mouths and is probably responsible for attacks off the KwaZulu-Natal coast.

The most active sharks swim continuously. This keeps water flowing over their gills and out of the body through five gill slits on each side of the 'neck' and ensures a constant supply of oxygen. Most sharks cruise at about one to three kilometres per hour, but some may make short bursts of up to 40 kilometres per hour. Sharks are most active at twilight and at night, but most attacks on humans take place in muddy water after storms or floods. The shark's jaws are at the underside of its head. Crab-eating and shell-eating sharks have blunt crushing teeth, but sharks that feed on fish, squid and seals may have several rows of sharp, jagged teeth that are constantly shed and are replaced from behind. Many sharks produce live young, but some lay tough egg pouches.

THE GREAT WHITE

The **great white shark** can be between six and seven metres long, and has small, black eyes, a crescent-shaped tail and large, triangular saw-edged teeth. The great white is found all along the South African coast and sometimes comes into the shallow waters. It occasionally attacks swimmers and surfers, who it might mistake for seals.

ECHOES IN THE SEA

Most cetaceans hunt by means of their sharp sense of hearing, even though their ears are merely tiny holes on either side of the head just behind the eye. They whistle and make clicking sounds that reflect as echoes from the objects around them. From the echoes, they can tell the shape, size and texture of objects, and whether they are food or not. This is called **echolocation**.

PLACES TO SEE

- *The Oceanarium, Port Elizabeth*
- *uShaka Marine World, Durban*
- *The Whale Well, Iziko South African Museum, Cape Town*

Venomous Creatures

GREEN FOR DANGER?
The **green mamba** is smaller, and not as dangerous, as its close relative, the black mamba. It lives in trees in the bush along the coast of KwaZulu-Natal where it is well camouflaged. The inside of its mouth is almost white.

DANGER AT SEA
Although a **sea snake** seldom attacks, it is poisonous and dangerous, especially when stranded on a beach. It is black above and yellow below, and often has a mottled tail. It has a flat body and uses its tail as an 'oar' when swimming.

Venomous animals produce poison and inject it into victims by a sting, bite or jab. They should be handled only by people who have been trained to deal with them. But they should not be killed or harmed unnecessarily as they all have an important part to play in nature.

Snakes

Only about a quarter of the 115 snake species found in southern Africa have poisonous bites that kill or subdue victims. Poisonous snakes produce poison (or venom) in special glands at the base of grooved or hollow fangs (teeth that carry poison). Front-fanged snakes are usually more deadly than back-fanged snakes, mainly because it is difficult to grip the prey with the back of the mouth. Examples of front-fanged snakes are cobras, mambas, sea snakes and adders. The boomslang and the skaapsteker are back-fanged. Some snake venoms destroy blood cells, others destroy tissue, and still others attack the nervous system and cause paralysis. Nearly two-thirds of the poisonous snakes in South Africa do not have enough poison, or strong enough poison, to kill adults, although children may be at risk.

The shy **boomslang** lives in trees, well camouflaged by its green or brownish colouring. It has large, shimmering green eyes. It is about 1.5 metres long and feeds on small tree lizards, such as chameleons, and birds and eggs. The back-fanged boomslang usually bites only when cornered or frightened. When alarmed, it puffs out its throat and strikes repeatedly.

The **rinkhals** is a close relative of the cobra. It also rears up and spreads its hood when alarmed and its bite is just as poisonous. The rinkhals may be black with a white belly, or brownish-yellow with white bands on the underside. It feeds mainly on toads, but it will also eat other snakes, lizards, mice and birds. Beware of what might seem to be a 'dead' rinkhals. It may be pretending. It can also 'spit' venom at an attacker's eyes through its two fangs.

The front-fanged **black mamba** is Africa's largest (up to four metres long) poisonous snake. It is olive-grey to brownish black with dark flecks. The inside of its mouth is black. Black mambas live in old burrows or among rocks. They eat dassies and rodents such as rats and mice. It may strike several times and paralyses its victims with its poison.

Adders, or vipers, are all poisonous, some dangerously so. The **puff-adder** is one of South Africa's most common and dangerous snakes. This slow-moving snake is usually about one metre long and has black or yellow zigzag markings on a brown or brownish-yellow body. When alarmed, it puffs up and hisses before striking. Its poison destroys cell tissue and causes painful sores and swellings. If not treated immediately, the victim usually dies.

Puff-adder

Boomslang

Rinkhals

Black mamba

The yellow, brown or black (sometimes spotted) **cobra** raises the front of its body and spreads out its hood when alarmed. The forest cobra, the largest species found in southern Africa, can be 2.7 metres long. The venom of the front-fanged Cape cobra is probably more dangerous than that of any other cobra in Africa. It stops the victim's breathing by paralysing the nervous system and, unless treated immediately, the victim will die. Five species of cobra occur in southern Africa. Two of these 'spit' venom at an attacker – usually at the eyes. If this happens, the victim should not rub his eyes, but wash them immediately.

Cape cobra

The patterned and beautifully camouflaged **Gaboon adder** can be up to 1.8 metres long and 360 millimetres around its middle. Its fangs, up to four centimetres long, are the longest of any snake in the world and look terrifying when the Gaboon opens its mouth to strike. Gaboon vipers are found in forests along the coast and are cleverly hidden amongst the leaves in the forest. They eat frogs and birds.

The small **horned adders** and **desert adders** live in the dry and arid areas in the western half of southern Africa. Like the puff-adder, they puff up and hiss when danger threatens. They are very easily angered and will strike repeatedly when disturbed, but their venom is not as poisonous as that of either the Gaboon adder or the puff-adder.

Gaboon adder *Horned adder*

Spiders

South Africa's big spiders are not as dangerous as they look. Some smaller species are more venomous. The **black button spider**, or **black widow**, one of South Africa's most venomous, is usually found under rocks, the base of grass and bushes. The female has a round, black body (abdomen), ten millimetres across, often with one or more red stripes on the upper surface of the abdomen. It has no markings under the abdomen. The much smaller male, which is not dangerous, is black. It has been said that the female eats the male after mating, which explains the name, black widow. When threatened, a button spider rolls itself into a ball and pretends to be dead. It will only bite if squashed or hurt in some way. The round, white egg cases are suspended in the untidy web and are quite smooth.

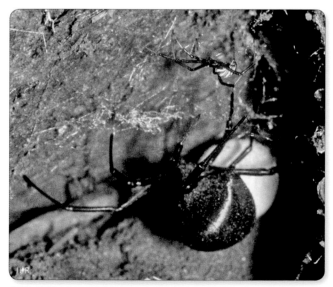

A black button spider female with an egg sac dwarfs the male

SCORPIONS

Scorpions are found all over southern Africa, but are more common in hot dry areas. They are often found under stones. They eat insects caught in their strong pincers. The long tail curls forward over the scorpion's back and jabs the paralysing poison into the victim. Thick-tailed scorpions with thin pincers are the most dangerous. The sting is very painful and people can die if not treated. Some species spray their venom for up to a metre.

The **brown button spider** or **brown widow** is less venomous than the black button spider, and seldom bites. Females are often black and may be confused with the black widow, but always have orange 'hourglass' markings on the underside of the abdomen. Brown widow spiders often spin their untidy webs under window sills or in crevices.

Sea Creatures

The prickles of some colourful **sea urchins** contain poison. The pointed spines break off under the skin and are difficult to remove as they have tiny hooks.

Several fish are poisonous. If disturbed, the flat, disc-shaped **stingray** lashes out with its tail and digs its poisonous spine deep into the victim's skin. The rather ugly **stonefish** is the most dangerous and carries deadly poison in spines along its back. Because it is well camouflaged, it is difficult to see the stonefish, which makes it even more dangerous. It is found along the north coast of KwaZulu-Natal. The stab can kill, but if the wound is soaked in very hot water for at least 30 minutes, the poison may be destroyed.

ONCE BITTEN OR STUNG ...

- Keep the person calm. Movement may spread the venom through the body more quickly.
- Bandage the wound as high up the limb as possible, but not too tightly.
- Call for help or take the victim to hospital as quickly as possible.
- Venom in the eyes must be washed out with water or any other bland liquid. Get to a doctor as quickly as possible.

SIX-EYED SAND SPIDER

The body of this medium-sized spider is 8–15 mm, and its legs span up to 50 mm. Found in deserts and other sandy places in southern Africa, it is a member of the Sicariidae family. Close relatives are found in Africa and South America, while near cousins, the recluses, are found worldwide. Due to its flattened stance, it is sometimes known as the six-eyed crab spider.

A DAY IN THE VELD

When you go **hiking**, be sure to take a first aid kit and a field-guide to identify spiders, scorpions and snakes that may be poisonous. Prevent bites by wearing boots and thick socks, and do not turn over rocks and stones, which may possibly be home to a venomous creature.

Sea urchin

Stingray

PLACES TO SEE

Visit one of the many parks In South Africa and see how trained handlers work with snakes

Incredible Insects

THE LADYBIRD
Ladybirds may be useful, as they, and their larvae, feed on aphids or plant lice, but they can be pests to crop farmers. Their bright colours warn birds and other predators that they taste rather unpleasant.

THE AMAZING FIREFLY
Glow-worms and fireflies are beetles. Their light-producing organ is situated at the tip of the underside of the abdomen, and contains a substance that reacts with an enzyme in the insect's blood, producing light. The light enables males and females to find each other for mating.

Insects are the most plentiful creatures in the world. There are at least a million species of insects on Earth, and over 100 000 are found in southern Africa. Insects are found in almost every habitat and some live in organized colonies. Many are useful to man, but some are pests.

What is an Insect?

Typical insect bodies are divided into three parts: the head, thorax and abdomen. Attached to the **thorax**, are three pairs of legs and one or two pairs of wings. But there are also many species of wingless insects. The circulatory, digestive and sex organs of insects are all found in the **abdomen**.

On the **head** there is a pair of antennae, or feelers. There is usually a pair of compound eyes and often two or three simple eyes. The compound eyes are like diamonds with many small lenses, called facets, which produce an image like a mosaic. Each simple eye has one lens. The insect cannot see outlines clearly but notices the tiniest movements.

Many small creatures are not insects at all. Spiders, scorpions, ticks and mites have eight legs and no wings, and the wood louse and the centipede, which have many legs, are not insects.

Head

Antennae

Wings

Thorax

Abdomen

Legs

ADZ

Butterflies and Moths

All butterflies and moths have four wings with patterns made by thousands of tiny scales. Butterflies are usually active by day, while most moths come out at night. Butterflies have club-shaped feelers, but moths do not. Moths rest with their wings folded flat over the body, while most butterflies hold their wings upright and closed against each other. In southern Africa, there are over 830 butterfly and more than 10 000 moth species.

The **emperor swallowtail**, which can have a wingspan of up to twelve centimetres, is southern Africa's biggest butterfly. Some butterflies, like the **mocker swallowtail**, imitate the colours and markings of poisonous butterflies to ward off enemies.

Butterflies and moths can be useful to man. While collecting nectar, they pollinate the blossoms of fruit trees and other crops. The Chinese silk moth spins silk, and a Mexican moth helped kill South Africa's unwanted prickly pears. Unfortunately, caterpillars are often destructive. The caterpillar of the beautiful **citrus swallowtail**, or Christmas butterfly, strips citrus trees of their leaves. Codling moths destroy deciduous fruit. Cabbage moths infest cabbage plants.

SA/IOA

Citrus swallowtail

PROTECTED PEST
Aphids are tiny pests that cause problems in our gardens. They develop so rapidly that unborn females within the mother already produce young within themselves. They are protected by **ants** that harvest their 'honey-dew', so you will often find ants and aphids on the same plants.

BP/AL

ROLL UP FOR DINNER
Dung beetles feed on animal dung. Using its strong front legs, a dung beetle shapes animal droppings into a large ball. Then, with its back legs, it rolls the ball and buries it as food for itself or its larvae.

Termites

Termites are sometimes known as white ants, although they are more closely related to cockroaches. They live in colonies, which, in some species, may include a million individuals. After shedding their wings, a male and female termite burrow into soil or wood and make a nest. The pair then becomes the king and queen of a colony. Soldiers and workers hatch from the eggs and spend their lives foraging for food for the royal pair and keeping the nest tidy. The queen may grow to an enormous size and lays thousands of eggs every day of her lifespan, which may be over twelve years. The king remains the same size. The colony will produce a swarm of winged young that fly off to start new colonies. When the queen of the original colony dies, the workers replace her with some of her fertile offspring who start laying eggs. Termites live on dead wood, bark, living plants or humus. But they can do serious damage by eating wood in our houses or fences and by destroying trees, crops or garden plants.

THE LIFE CYCLE OF THE BUTTERFLY

Young insects change several times before they become adults, in a process called **metamorphosis**. The butterfly's metamorphosis is one of the most spectacular. The female usually lays eggs on a plant. The eggs hatch into tiny **larvae** called caterpillars that feed on leaves. Because the caterpillar grows very quickly, it sheds its skin and eventually becomes a **pupa** or **chrysalis**. Sometimes the caterpillar forms a pupa inside a protective cocoon. Inside the pupa, the caterpillar changes gradually into a **butterfly**, and eventually forces its way out, spreads its wings, allows them to dry and flies away. A female and male mate, the female lays eggs and the cycle begins again. The life cycle of some insects may take as little as a week. Others may take a year.

KNOCK! KNOCK!
Toktokkies knock their abdomens loudly on the ground to attract mates. These shiny, black beetles have no wings and scurry across the veld in dry areas.

Termite colony

Grasshopper

Familiar Insects

Only female **mosquitoes** 'bite'. They pierce the skin with a long, slender proboscis (snout) and then suck the victim's blood. Eggs are laid in water where the larvae swim and feed, breathing at the surface of the water through a 'snorkel' or breathing tube. The female drinks blood so that her eggs can develop, but the normal food of adult mosquitoes is plant juices. Malaria is carried by one mosquito sub-group only.

There are over 350 species of **grasshopper** in South Africa, some beautifully coloured and others very well camouflaged. Only four of these are locusts, which is the name given to those grasshoppers that sometimes form swarms and destroy farmers' crops.

The **locust** lays its eggs in dry soil in early summer, to hatch a month later, usually after the first summer rains. If they become too many, they change their appearance and behaviour and become very active, eventually forming huge swarms. Swarms of the South African brown locust often cause serious damage to the wheatlands in the Free State, while the red locust invades southern Africa from central Africa and can destroy the lush cane-fields of KwaZulu-Natal.

Praying mantis

The **praying mantis** captures its prey with its long front legs, and holds them up as if in prayer. This strange-looking creature has two large compound eyes and three simple ones in its triangular head, which can swivel in all directions. Mantises are usually excellently camouflaged and the common green species could easily be mistaken for a leaf. After mating, the female eats the male and lays her eggs in a foamy substance that soon hardens. The praying mantis eats insect pests in the garden.

PLACES TO SEE
ℹ When travelling, look out for both big and small termite mounds, which are quite common throughout the country

Birds of Prey

A POWERFUL KICK!
The **secretary bird** feeds on insects, rats and mice or the young of ground-nesting birds. When it finds something larger or more dangerous, such as a snake, it will kick its prey to death with its powerful feet. Although it flies very well, the secretary bird, with its broad wings, seldom takes to the air.

FLIGHT ACROBATICS
The **African marsh harrier** hunts over marshes. It holds its head down and its wings in a shallow 'V' when looking for prey. During courtship, the talons of the male and female sometimes touch in flight.

Birds of prey, otherwise known as 'raptors', are flesh-eaters that hunt other animals. They range in size from the enormous Cape vulture, weighing up to 8 kilograms, to the tiny, pearlspotted owl (80 grams). Raptors have very sharp eyesight, and their eyes are set well in the front of the head to help them judge distances when swooping down on their unsuspecting victims. Their strong beaks are hooked for tearing flesh, and their claws are ideal for catching and crushing victims.

Rulers of the Sky

In flight, the jet-black feathers of the **black eagle** contrast with the clear white 'V' on its back and the 'windows' on its wings. Its face and feet are vivid yellow. It feeds mainly on dassies and occasionally on small buck and game birds. It swoops down to snatch its prey, but sometimes it kills its victim by knocking it off a precipice. It may also dive on baboons and even young leopards, which it regards as enemies. The black eagle builds its nest of sticks on the ledge of a cliff and then lays two eggs that hatch three or four days apart. As soon as the younger chick appears, the older one, to increase its own chance of survival, pecks the younger chick until it dies of its injuries and starvation.

The **African fish eagle** is a magnificent bird with brown, white and black plumage and a yellow face and legs. It soars and then dives to snatch a fish near the surface of the water below. It has sharp little spikes on the pads of its feet to help grip its slippery prey. The fish eagle occurs in many parts of southern Africa where there is open water. Its haunting cry is familiar to many South Africans.

The **osprey** is another fish-eater. Its feathers are brown and white and it has a 'mask' of dark brown across its owl-like eyes. Like the fish eagle, the osprey's feet have short spikes for gripping its wriggling and slippery prey. Sometimes it catches two fish at a time, one in each foot!

The **peregrine falcon** nests on cliffs far out of reach and high above river gorges. With wings folded against its sides, it dives down on its prey (usually a dove or pigeon) and, with its powerful claws, can cut the bird's head off in one swift movement.

The **lammergeier** or **bearded vulture** is a massive vulture-like eagle, which is found mainly high in the Drakensberg where it shelters at night in cold caves, tucking its feet under its feathers for warmth. By day, these birds can often be seen sunbathing on a rock with their wings spread wide. The lammergeyer feeds on dead animals, but also catches small prey such as dassies and small buck. It shatters bone by dropping it from a height onto rocks. It then pecks at the marrow and eats the bone fragments. The bearded vulture is reddish-brown with black wings and a whitish head. It has a black mask of feathers across its eyes, which meets under its chin in a tufted 'beard', from which it gets its name.

Clockwise from top: black eagle, bearded vulture, African marsh harrier, african fish eagle, osprey, Falcon wearing hood

FALCONRY

Falconry is a sport in which a falcon is taught to hunt under a trainer's direction and return to him. The falcon is blindfolded with a hood that is slipped over its head. It then becomes calmer. The sport may be one of the reasons for the declining raptor population worldwide, as large sums of money are offered for falcons and hawks, which are often trapped or taken from their nests. In South Africa, falconry is permitted in all provinces, but permits must be obtained to keep and hunt falcons.

Vultures

Vultures eat carrion (the flesh of dead animals). With their huge beaks and powerful claws, a flock of vultures can strip a carcass within a few hours. When the meal is over, the vultures wash themselves and dry their enormous wings in the sun.

The **Cape vulture** can reach over a metre in height. It has a pale appearance and two patches of blue skin at the base of the neck. It is found throughout South Africa. The **lappetfaced vulture** is sometimes known as the 'king of the vultures'. It is mainly black with white feathers on its legs and black, spear-shaped feathers on its white chest and a frill of feathers around its neck. Its yellowish bill is huge and on its bare neck there are folds of red skin, or lappets, which flush deep red when the bird is excited. A lappetfaced vulture may often loaf around a scavenging flock, but when this powerful bird decides to feed, the other vultures will scatter.

Owls

Owls usually hunt at night. Flying noiselessly, with their brown or greyish feathers blending into their shadowy surroundings, they swoop down on their prey and carry it off in their powerful claws. Owls help farmers by destroying rats, mice, caterpillars and other pests.

Pel's fishing owl is a rare bird with tawny feathers. It perches on a branch overhanging a river or lake and drops down to catch fish that rise to the surface of the water below. It closes its eyes as it touches the water. It even eats young crocodiles.

The white spots on the body of the tiny **pearlspotted owl** form neat rows on its tail. On the back of its head there are two eye-like patches of dark feathers surrounded by white. The pearlspotted owl may hunt both by day and by night. It sometimes 'showers' in the rain with wings and tail spread wide. Although it feeds on insects, frogs and lizards, its big claws help it to catch bigger prey. It usually nests in tree-holes that were once occupied by other birds.

FRIEND OR FOE?

Many eagles are accidentally poisoned through eating animals that have been killed by chemicals. The **black eagle** is sometimes shot by farmers who wrongly believe that it kills their lambs. But many farmers do not realize that these eagles prey on dassies and other pests, which compete with their sheep for grazing.

RARE SPEED

The rare **peregrine falcon** is the fastest bird in the world, and can dive at a speed of 280 kilometres per hour when chasing another bird. When it pursues its prey, the peregrine falcon dives with its wings partially folded. This is known as 'stooping'. It catches its prey in mid-air and slashes it with its powerful talons as it dives.

THE RAPTOR CONSERVATION GROUP

The Raptor Conservation Group (RCG) is committed to the conservation of the natural populations of raptors in southern Africa. Some of the RCG's successes include the return of the bateleur eagle to the Kalahari and the breeding of raptors in the Platberg Karoo district. Education has also given thousands of South Africans an insight into the life of raptors.

Clockwise from top: whitebacked vultures feeding on carcass, lappetfaced vulture, Pel's fishing owl, pearlspotted owl

PLACES TO SEE

ⓘ *The World of Birds* in Hout Bay, Cape Town

Our Coastal Birds

OYSTERCATCHERS
Surprisingly, **African black oystercatchers** do not eat oysters. These jet-black birds prise limpets and other shellfish off the rocks with their long, sharp beaks, or probe wet sands for mussels. The brilliant red of the oystercatcher's eye-rims and legs matches the colour of its beak.

South Africa's coast is home to many different types of birds. Some remain in the same area throughout the year, often nesting in large colonies. Others visit our country from across the world during the summer season. Thousands of birds are attracted to the teeming fish-life off the west coast. Further east, where the sea is warmer and not as rich in food, fewer birds are found.

The African Penguin

All 16 species of penguin are found in the southern hemisphere, but the African penguin is the only species that lives and breeds along our coasts. Penguins can't fly but they swim fast, using flippers and webbed feet. On land they stand upright and waddle along. Huge colonies of these penguins once nested along our coasts, but today it is a threatened species. Penguin eggs were considered a delicacy and, over the years, thousands have been eaten by man. To protect its eggs and chicks from the sun and thieving gulls, it usually nests in burrows in the sand or under rocks. Recently, nests have been damaged and birds driven from their breeding grounds by the growing population of Cape fur seals. Penguins are also vulnerable to oil-spills from large tankers and shipwrecks. Fortunately African penguins are now protected in reserves on offshore islands as well as on the shore. Penguins spend the day fishing at sea. When the birds come ashore at night, their call keeps them in touch with one another. The African penguin has been known as the 'jackass penguin', from its call, which sounds like the bray of a donkey ('jackass' is an old name for a male donkey).

Cormorants

Cormorants are black birds with short legs, webbed toes and stiff tail-feathers. They bob about on the waves or stand on the rocks drying their widespread wings in the sun. They breed in colonies, building their nests of seaweed and sticks on islands off the west coast.

Huge flocks of cormorants skim over the sea in 'V' formation to search for fish. The flock rises and falls in wavelike motions, different birds taking turns as leader. As soon as they locate a shoal of fish, they land on the surface of the water and dive down, chasing the fish under water and catching them in their hooked beaks. There are four species of cormorant to be found along our coastline, while a fifth, the **reed cormorant**, is found near fresh water inland where it feeds on frogs and fish.

Cape cormorant

Gulls

Gulls are noisy scavengers that scrounge around harbours, rubbish dumps and canning factories, as well as vleis and estuaries. They pick up refuse from ships, eat dead fish or steal eggs from other birds' nests.

Hartlaub's gull occurs along the coast from Namibia through to the Eastern Cape. Colonies of these noisy, sociable birds usually crowd on offshore islands to breed, and this gull has even been known to nest on the roofs of beachfront buildings.

Hartlaub's gull

African penguin

'TREASURE' ISLAND
Guano is actually formed from the dried droppings of fish-eating sea birds. It is usually found on rocky beaches, especially on the nesting grounds of offshore islands. Because guano is rich in phosphates and calcium, it is a valuable fertilizer. Unfortunately, people collecting guano often disturb or damage birds' nests and drive the birds away.

The big black and white **kelp gull** (below) is found all along the South African and Namibian coasts. It eats almost any creature it can find, from fish and insects to birds' eggs and nestlings. Sand mussels and limpets are a favourite food. With a mussel in its powerful yellow beak, it sometimes flies about 15 metres into the air, and drops the shell to smash it on the rocks. Then the gull swoops down to devour the tasty flesh.

Gannets

Cape gannets (below) are large birds with yellow heads, white bodies and black-edged wings and tails. Colonies of thousands jostle about on offshore islands, every bird looking and sounding just like its neighbours. Somehow, a returning Cape gannet will hear the call of its mate and chicks above all the racket, and drop directly onto its own nest of guano, seaweed and sticks.

As the Cape gannet steps between its neighbours' nests, it points to the sky with its long beak. This shows that its intentions are peaceful. Once free of the crowd, it runs to gain speed and then takes off.

Terns

Terns look rather like gulls with short legs. Huge flocks wheel and hover above the waves, following shoals of small fish, which they snatch up during shallow dives.

Some species of tern come from thousands of kilometres away. **Arctic tern** breed in the Arctic Circle and the **common tern** comes from Europe. Species of tern that do breed here nest on the ground close to the beach, but people, and particularly beach-buggies, have driven away many brooding birds from such colonies. The **roseate tern** has become an endangered species and several others are rare.

LONG-DISTANCE FLIER

The **Arctic tern** holds the record among birds for long-distance flying. It breeds along the northern coasts of America, Europe and Asia and flies south to avoid the northern winter, travelling across the Atlantic ocean to the Antarctic where it spends the southern summer, before returning to the Arctic. Recent research reveals that each bird flies up to 70 000 kilometres on a round trip – making this the longest animal migration in the world. As Arctic terns can live for up to 30 years, the birds cover an enormous distance in their lifetime; the equivalent of three trips to the moon and back.

The Albatross

The magnificent albatross is a huge sea bird found mainly in the southern hemisphere. Various species visit the South African coast but the birds breed on the cold, wind-swept islands of the sub-Antarctic. Mysteriously, they find their way across the oceans to lay their eggs on the same small island where they were hatched.

The albatross soars in the air and sweeps to and fro over the sea carried by the air currents. Sailors were once bewildered by the great birds that often followed their ships and hung aloft for days with long, narrow wings outstretched. They believed that the albatross brought good luck to a ship, but that disaster would strike any person foolish enough to kill one.

Yellow-nosed albatross

PLOVERS

White-fronted plovers are busy little birds that scurry about on beaches, darting first in one direction and then in another. They eat the sandhoppers that inhabit washed-up seaweed, as well as other small creatures on our sandy shores.

SANCCOB
saves seabirds

The South African National foundation for the Conservation of Coastal Birds (**SANCCOB**) is a volunteer organization based at Table View in Cape Town. SANCCOB cares for sea birds that have been injured by oil spills. It removes the oil, restores the birds to health and releases the recovered birds into the sea. Among many potential shore disasters in which it played a part was the loss of the *MV Treasure* near Cape Town in 2000 when many beaches and birds were badly affected.

PLACES TO SEE

ⓘ The *World of Birds* in Hout Bay, Cape Town

ⓘ The penguin colony at Boulders Beach, Simon's Town

Birds Around You

A SECURE HOME
The **spectacled weaver** is a bright yellow bird with a greenish back and a black eye-stripe or 'spectacle'. Its nest, which often hangs from a tree over water, is woven from plant fibres, but sometimes from nylon thread or fishing line! The long, spout-like entrance helps prevent snakes from getting inside and taking its young.

There are more than 800 bird species in South Africa. A keen bird-watcher may see, or hear the call of, as many as 100 different species in a suburban garden or during a weekend visit to the country. To identify a bird, there are many clues to look out for.

Telltale Features
The shape of a bird's **beak** will help you to recognize it. Seed-eaters have short, stubby beaks for cracking husks. Insect-eaters need longer beaks to help them catch their food. Sugarbirds have long, curved beaks for delving deep into flowers. Birds of prey have powerful, hooked beaks for tearing flesh.

Some birds have broad, rounded **wings** to give them speed when escaping predators or pursuing prey. Others have long, straight wings to keep them in the air for a long time. As in some of the terns, **tails** can be long and forked. Gulls have short, rounded tails. Woodpeckers' tails are rather stiff, as they use them for support when climbing trees.

BIRDS OF A FEATHER
Feathers keep birds cool in summer and warm in winter, and streamline their bodies for swift movement in the air, on the ground or in the water. Birds preen their feathers with their bills and most species add oil from a special preen-gland under the tail. Feathers fall out at least once a year, during moulting, and are replaced with new ones.

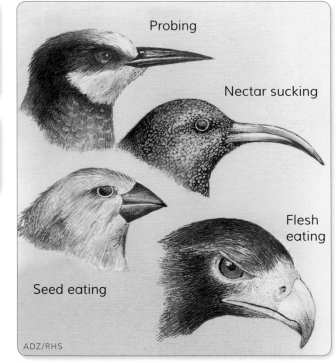

Beak shapes

Yellow-billed stork

Nests For All
Members of a family or group of birds may build similar nests. Most woodpeckers make holes in trees. Doves build a simple platform of twigs. Some birds weave a nest from grass or other material. Others, like the crowned plover, lay their eggs in a shallow hole in the ground. Birds such as the Cape sparrow, which often nests near houses, use string or wool, paper, plastic and scraps of cloth. Robins and wagtails sometimes nest in old flower pots or watering-cans. Indian mynas and European starlings seem to prefer a hole under a roof. Some swallows burrow into sand banks, while others build tunnels of mud under bridges or the eaves of houses. Hundreds of queleas may cram their nests into one thorn tree. Eagles balance platforms of branches and twigs on narrow mountain ledges.

Nest styles (clockwise from top): ground, hanging, tree

Patterns in the Air
The **flight-patterns** of various species differ. Some birds fly in straight lines, while others, such as cattle egrets and white pelicans, fly in a V-shaped formation called a skein. Some birds are so heavy that they have to run along the ground, flapping their wings to gather speed before take-off. Some large birds are excellent gliders, spreading their wings and using air currents to do the work for them as they search for food. Small birds flap their wings very fast.

Across the Seas
Some birds **migrate**, which means that they live in one place in the breeding season and fly to another for the rest of the year, usually in winter when food is scarce. These two places may be thousands of kilometres apart. Birds of a species may gather in the autumn before flying away. Some birds have distinctive markings so that members of the flock can recognize them while flying. They also keep together by calling to one another. Some birds leave South Africa to breed in other parts of Africa. Others migrate to Europe or to the Arctic. Mountains and other landmarks may guide them, or they may rely on instinct to lead them to roughly the same place each year. Many birds, including most garden birds, do not migrate at all.

OUR COMMON GARDEN BIRDS

The **rock pigeon** has a bare red face and white-spotted, brown and grey-blue feathers. It once lived among craggy mountains, but many have adapted to cities, nesting in nooks and on high ledges. The **little swift** has also taken to living in towns where it nests in gutters and under eaves. It is brownish in colour with· a large white patch on its rump and a white throat. Unlike most swifts, its tail is not forked, but square-tipped.

The **black-eyed bulbul** is found in the eastern parts of South Africa. Its head is black, its back is grey-brown and its underparts are grey. Bulbuls promote pollination by feeding on fruit, nectar and insects. Their call sounds like *Come back, Calcutta!*

The little **Cape sparrow or** mossie is found almost everywhere in South Africa, except the eastern Lowveld and northern KwaZulu-Natal. Their nests are untidy bundles of dry grass, rags and string, lined with feathers, and are usually built in forked trees, under house-eaves or on telegraph poles.

The **Cape wagtail** is a small bird that struts about with its long stiff tail bobbing up and down. Its back is dark grey and its underparts are whitish with a dark grey band on the chest. It darts over pools, snapping up insects from the surface as it flies.

The **Cape robin** is found throughout South Africa. It has a grey-brown back, bright orange 'waistcoat' and a clear white line above the eye. Although it is rather shy it sometimes takes food from your hand. Its early morning song sounds like *Jan Fred-er-ick*.

The **Cape turtle dove** (below) is very common. Its colour varies, from pale to sooty-grey and it has a dark 'collar' across the back of its neck (it is sometimes called the ring-necked dove). Its familiar call sounds like *Where's father, Where's father* or *Ry stadig, ry stadig!*

Clockwise from the top: rock pigeon, Cape robin-chat, wagtail, Cape sparrow, black-eyed bulbul

AN IMPOSTER
The **white-throated robin** builds its nest of leaves and grass between roots or under a sandbank. Sometimes the red-chested cuckoo (or **Piet-my-vrou**), which does not build a nest, adds its egg to the clutch. When the cuckoo hatches, it rolls the robin's eggs or nestlings out of the nest so that the adult robins attend only to the young cuckoo.

A RING FOR A BIRD
Light aluminium **rings** with identification numbers are sometimes attached to birds' legs. If the bird should be found in some other part of the world, the ring will reveal how far it has travelled. It is therefore possible to trace the route migrating birds have taken.

PLACES TO SEE

ℹ️ Using a field guide such as *The Complete Photographic Field Guide: Birds of Southern Africa* by Ian Sinclair and Peter Ryan (Struik Nature), see how many different bird species you can identify in your garden or in parks

Songs On The Air
Birds' **calls** also vary from species to species. The loud call of the red-chested cuckoo or Piet-my-vrou announces that it has arrived from the north and that winter is over in South Africa. The yellow-and-black bokmakierie, a member of the shrike family, cries *bok, makierie*, sometimes followed by *wit wit wit wit!* Burchell's coucal, sometimes called 'the rain bird', has a call that sounds like water being poured from a bottle with a narrow neck, and warns us to expect rain.

The harsh cry of *ha, ha … ha-deda* heard in the southern and eastern parts of the country is the cry of the hadeda ibis. The spotted dikkop has an excited *pi-pi-pi-pi-pi* and sad whistle. You may be woken at sunrise by the *wheety-wheety-wheet* of the olive thrush as it pokes about for insects. The song of the Heuglin's robin is heard mainly in the north-eastern parts of South Africa. It sings at dawn and dusk, and weaves the songs of the other birds that share its forest territory into its own distinctive melody.

Where They Grow

Southern Africa's vegetation varies from Namibia's true desert to Knysna's evergreen forests. Our five major types, or communities, of vegetation depend on the geographical, climatic and soil conditions that exist in the different parts of southern Africa.

Mediterranean Vegetation or Fynbos

The Western Cape has a climate and vegetation similar to those countries bordering the Mediterranean Sea. Winters are cool and wet, and summers are hot and dry. There are a few remnants of natural forest, but most of this area is covered by dense, mainly low-growing evergreen scrub. This is called '**fynbos**'.

It is said that a square metre of some types of fynbos boasts more plant species in it than a square metre of any other vegetation type in the world. Fynbos is famous for its beautiful proteas and ericas. Because they have to stand up to dry summer conditions, most fynbos plants are tough and leathery. The leaves are often small and spiky to reduce the loss of moisture, and most are a dull green. Many fynbos plants, such as buchu, have a strong, spicy scent.

Occasionally, both natural and man-made fires break out among the fynbos. But fynbos is adapted to fire and many species need it at ten to 20-year intervals for their regeneration. The problem today is that man-made fires are too frequent and can be devastating.

The fynbos vegetation of the Western Cape

Temperate Forests

South Africa does not have many natural forests. Trees once grew more densely in the wetter parts of the country, particularly in the southwest, but 350 years ago man began to destroy them. Today, only a few protected natural forests remain.

The largest natural forest area is in the southern Cape, between the Outeniqua Mountains and the sea, a stip about 180 kilometres long and 16 kilometres wide, stretching eastward from George through Knysna to the Humansdorp district. In the past, stinkwood, yellowwood, assegai, white pear and other trees were cut down with no thought of replacing them, even though it took centuries for some to reach maturity. Today, approximately 36 400 hectares of protected forest exist in this area. Low shrubs and lush tree ferns grow on the forest floor, and twining lianas, or monkey ropes, hang from the high branches of the trees.

Further east, small patches of temperate forest are found along the rainy eastern slopes of the Amatole, Winterberg and Drakensberg ranges. There are also areas of natural forest along the eastern edge of the Highveld in Mpumalanga and the Limpopo Province.

The dense, lush greenery of the Knysna forest

The Temperate Interior

The vegetation of the open veld of the eastern interior and the Highveld consists mainly of **grasses**. These are generally short, except between the escarpment and the east coast, where they may reach a height of about a metre. Some of the best grazing grasses have been replaced by less nourishing species. This happens when the veld is burnt to encourage new growth or by destructive cattle and sheep grazing. Partly because of the dry, frosty Highveld winters and partly because of fire, indigenous trees are rare. Those that exist are generally found only against the sheltered slopes of mountains or along river beds.

SAFE AND SOUND
The lovely **marsh rose**, a member of the Protea family, originated in a small area of the Hottentots Holland Mountains overlooking False Bay, and now occurs in the Kogelberg. It is very rare and is cultivated in the nursery at the Kirstenbosch National Botanical Garden near Cape Town.

THE WOOD THAT STINKS
The strong, heavy and durable **stinkwood** is South Africa's most valuable hardwood. Like yellowwood, exploitable stinkwood around the Cape was virtually eradicated by early settlers. George Rex of Knysna built a brig (a type of ship), the *Knysna*, of stinkwood and the wood was also used to build trek-wagons.

Bushveld or Savanna

South Africa's savanna consists of **grasslands** with occasional evergreen and deciduous trees. It stretches northwards from the Highveld to the Limpopo River, and towards the borders of Mozambique in the east and Swaziland in the south. Dense, dry bush is typical of the Lowveld. Trees that grow among the shrubs and long grass of this area include the mopane, marula, baobab and umbrella thorn.

A more open savanna is found in the Kalahari thornveld. In the dry region towards the west, there are sparse desert grasses and low thorny shrubs. Tall, tufted grasses and thorny camel-thorn trees are characteristic of the wetter, northern parts.

Semi-deserts and Deserts

Most of South Africa's western interior is covered by the semi-desert vegetation of the Karoo. On the dry and dusty ground, low, woody shrubs grow far apart. Between them, and often close to the soil, grow a variety of **succulents**, most of which are found nowhere else in the world. Because they have spreading roots and they store moisture in their fleshy leaves and roots, these fascinating plants can survive in a harsh, arid climate.

Millions of seeds of flowering plants may lie dormant in the dusty soil for years. As soon as good rains fall, they germinate and grow rapidly, covering the land with a carpet of brilliant flowers. They then die and scatter their seed to wait for the next rains.

The only true **desert vegetation** in South Africa is located in a narrow coastal strip in the northern section of Namaqualand and extending a little way along the Orange River valley. Rainfall here is extremely low; in some years there is no rain at all. The vegetation is sparse and consists of dwarf shrubs, succulents and an occasional quiver tree or 'kokerboom'. Like the Karoo, this area bursts into colour when it rains and flowers bloom.

Aloe ferox

THE CAMEL THORN

The camel thorn acacia (kameeldoring) is quite common in Namibia, Botswana, the Northern Cape, North West Province and Limpopo Province. It also grows in the western Free State and Zimbabwe. It grows in dry woodlands and thornveld in arid areas, often over deep Kalahari sands. A well-developed and extremely deep root system enables it to flourish in desert conditions along dry river beds where it taps underground water.

A CARPET OF FLOWERS

The glossy petals of the **Namaqualand daisies** range in colour from yellow and orange to white with purple lower parts. They occur in the seemingly barren Namaqualand, where they bloom for only a few weeks, transforming the dull countryside into a field of colour.

The spectacular wild flowers that bloom in Spring in Namaqualand

THE WONDERFUL WELWITSCHIA

Welwitschia mirabilis has adapted itself to desert life. Virtually no rain falls in the desert where it is found, and there is no surface water. Yet this dwarf 'tree' can live for up to 2000 years, obtaining its moisture from the sea fog that drifts inland and condenses on its leaves as dew. A torn and tattered pair of these long, leathery leaves sprawls over the desert sands, one on either side of a single taproot. Only their tips die off – burned by contact with the hot sand – as the same two leaves continue to grow.

PLACES TO SEE →

ℹ Visit any of the nine national botanical gardens to explore our regional flora

153

Flowers and Trees

A LONELY PLANT

The **powder-puff tree** grows in the warm and humid coastal areas of KwaZulu-Natal. It is the only member of the Lecythidaceae family that occurs naturally in South Africa. The powdered bark has been used as a poison and the fruit is said to be a cure for malaria.

Baobab flower

Trees are the world's largest plants. They provide homes and food for animals and shelter for man. When their leaves fall and decay, they turn into humus and help maintain the soil. Apart from its many different trees, South Africa has a rich variety of flowers. The Western Cape alone is home to over 8 600 species and about 10 000 more are found in the rest of the country.

Different Parts, Different Functions

Roots anchor trees. Fine hairs draw up water that contains minerals. The **crown** of the tree consists of the top branches, twigs and leaves. The **trunk** supports the crown. Each growing season, a new layer of living tissue is added between the bark and the wood. If a tree is cut down, the layers may be seen as separate rings. By counting them, you can sometimes tell the age of the tree.

Crown

Branches

Trunk

Roots

Our Common Trees

The curious **baobab** tree has a very thick trunk and branches that taper before spreading out. Baobabs have large waxy white flowers. Their scent is only pleasant initially; the egg-shaped fruit is edible.

Camel thorn trees grow in the country's dry northern parts, and provide shade for stock feeding on their velvety pods. Their sharp thorns can inflict wounds on animals caught in them.

Cycads dominated the planet between 200 million and 65 million years ago, but only 160 species are now left. They have crowns of hard, spiky palm-like leaves. Instead of flowers, they have male and female cones that are borne on separate plants. Some have large oblong seeds with a bright reddish-orange covering.

Five species of the deciduous **coral tree** grow in southern Africa in Mpumalanga, Limpopo Province, KwaZulu-Natal, Swaziland, Eastern Cape, Botswana and Namibia. The bark is grey, furrowed and covered with prickles. The pods contain 'lucky beans' which are used as beads and ornaments. The leaves and bark are crushed and used in traditional medicine.

Coral tree flower   *Coral tree*

Witmelkhout, or white milkwood trees, grow on dunes and coastal woodland along the south and east coast of the country. They have glossy, leathery leaves, small dark berries and twisted branches that spread out from ground level.

The leafy, evergreen **stinkwood** flourishes in most of South Africa's high forest, but particularly in the Knysna forests where it reaches between 20 and 30 metres high. Leaves have tiny blisters between the veins on their upper surfaces. Often used to make furniture, it has an unpleasant smell when cut.

Baobab

White milkwood

Top: Arum lily; above: Disa

> **PHOTOSYNTHESIS**
> In daylight, leaves take in carbon dioxide and convert it into organic compounds that make up the tissue. As a by-product, oxygen is released into the atmosphere. This is called photosynthesis and makes food for the plant. It can only take place if chlorophyll (the green colouring of leaves) is present.

Wild figs belong to the important ficus group. Some species grow 23 metres high and are crowned with thick, shiny foliage. All fig species produce a milky latex when a leaf or fig is picked. The famous Wonderboom fig outside Pretoria is about 1000 years old. Over the centuries, new trees have sprung up wherever its drooping branches have touched the ground. It is said that 22 wagons, each with a span of 20 oxen, once sheltered under the tree.

Our four species of cone-bearing **yellowwood** trees are slow-growing and the 30-metre-high yellowwoods in the Knysna forests are probably hundreds of years old. The wood is yellow and has a fine grain. It is used for making beams, doors, floors and furniture.

All Sorts of Flowers
Aloes are members of the lily family. They are succulents whose fleshy, sword-shaped leaves enable them to survive long dry periods.

The **red hot poker** thrives in moist areas. It has spikes of flame-coloured flowers that bloom throughout the year, depending on the species.

Watsonias, freesias and **ixias** belong to the iris family, with about 1500 species worldwide, more than half of which are indigenous to South Africa. The flowers grow from corms (bulb-like underground stems with a firm centre surrounded by scaly leaves). Many Cape species die down during the summer months and sprout when the rainy season begins in winter.

Harebells and **river lilies** grow in KwaZulu-Natal and north of the Vaal river.

White **arum lilies** are common on river banks and damp areas of the Western Cape during spring. The dark-green leaves grow from an underground rhizome which pigs enjoy eating. This gives the arum its common name of 'pig lily', although it is not really a lily. The lovely 'flower' is really a special leaf (or 'bract') called a 'spathe'. Some species have yellow, pink or magenta spathes.

Disas belong to the orchid family, of which there are about 18000 species worldwide. The lovely *Disa uniflora*, or Pride of Table Mountain (pictured), grows near waterfalls in the Western Cape. The delicate lilac-blue drip disa grows in damp places in the mountains of the Cape Peninsula and Stellenbosch.

Over 600 **erica** or heath species are found in South Africa. More than 100 grow in the Western Cape, where they form an important part of the fynbos. Erica are narrow-leafed heaths, many with small, drooping, bell-like flowers in shades of red, pink, yellow and white. The

Chinese lantern heath of the Swellendam area, with its gold and green flowers, grows to a height of 1.2 metres. The small, sticky rose heath of the Cape Peninsula has bright pink flowers like tiny bells.

Erica

Red hot pokers

Proteas grow in many parts of South Africa, but mainly among the Cape's fynbos. Because there are so many different kinds of protea, the group is named after the Greek sea-god, Proteus, who could change his shape and form. Some, like the seven metre-high waboom (*Protea nitida*), are fairly large trees. Others, like the dainty mountain rose, are very small.

King protea

The giant king protea is one of South Africa's best-known flowers. Other species are the sugarbush (suikerbos), woolly-bearded protea with its black fringe, and whitish-green Highveld protea. The pincushion, silver tree, blushing bride and rare marsh rose are all members of the protea family. Proteas are also found in Australia, New Zealand and South America.

In spring, colourful succulent **vygies** cover the ground, particularly in the Namaqualand region. Plants as different as the squat stone plants and sprawling sour fig (suurvy), are also succulents.

DANGEROUS FIREWOOD!
Whenever you look for firewood in the veld, be sure not to use **tamboti** wood. It contains a milky latex that is very poisonous and can burn the skin. The smoke from burning twigs is also poisonous. The tamboti is small, with a dark trunk and rough bark. It often grows in valleys and along river banks.

TREES GIVE MORE THAN SHADE
Trees provide shade, homes for birds and food for animals. Trees also produce fruit, some are sources of gum, fibre or chemicals, and others are used for furniture. Wood is still an important fuel in many areas. Trees are also a valuable source of paper and synthetic fabrics, such as rubber and cellophane.

PLACES TO SEE
ⓘ See South Africa's rich floral heritage at any of the nine national botanical gardens

INDEX

159

160

161

163

PHOTOGRAPHIC, ILLUSTRATIVE AND MAP CREDITS

AB = Andrew Bannister
ABWM = Anglo-Boer War Museum
AC = Acilo
ADZ = Adrienne Zinn
AE = Alfred Eisensta
AEL = Aubrey Elliott
AER = Apple Express Rail
AF = Albert Froneman
AFP = Agence France-Presse
AFS = AgeFotostock
AG = Aletta Gardner
AI = Andrew Ingram
AJ = Alexander Joe
AJN = Anthony Johnson
AK = Alf Kumalo
AL = Alamy
AM = Angus McBride
AMA = Alphonse-Marie-Adolphe de Neuville
AMJ = Amida Johns
AMO = Africa Media Online
AND = Ayse Nazli Deliormanli
AP = Archive Photos
APT = Alain Proust
AR = Alexander Raths
ARI = Ariene
ASK = Alex Slobodkin
AVZ = Ariadne Van Zandbergen
AW = Andrew Woodburn
AY = Anna Yu
AZ = Ariadne Van Zandbergen / Lonely Planet Images

B = Beeld
BAHA = Baileys African History Archives
BB = Bluebird13
BBG = Bloomberg
BC = Brett Charlton
BD = Business Day
BDK = Billy de Klerk
BG = Bongiwe Gumede
BGB = Barbara Gibbons
BI = Blend Images
BK = benkrut
BP = The Bigger Picture
BPS = BanksPhotos
BR = Brasil2
BS = Brenda Shelley
BSK = Baris Simsek
BX = Courtesy of Baxter Theatre Centre

CAS = College of Agriculture, Stellenbosch
CB = Caren Brinkema
CDB = Charles Davidson Bell
CF = Carl Fourie
CFR = Craig Fraser
CG = Christeen Grant
CK = Chris Kirchoff
CL = Colour Library
CM = Clifford Mueller
CMM = Comrades Marathon Museum
CMR = Colin MacRae
CMS = Chris and Mathilde Stuart
CS = Clint Scholz
CTAR = Cape Town Archives Repository

CTSO = Cape Town Symphony Orchestra
CU = Christian Uhrig

D = Drum Social Histories
DB = De Beers
DB/VM = Driham Bester/ Voortrekker Monument and Nature Reserve
DBG = Dennis Bagnall
DBR = Die Burger
DBY = Don Bailey
DG = Daisy Gilardini
DHL = David H. Lewis
DK = Dennis King
DLM = dianne555
DSB = Daryl and Sharna Balfour
DV = Danie van der Merwe

EBU = EasyBuy4u
EG = Eric Gevaert
EK = Elske Kritzinger
ES = Erna Schoeman
ET = Erhardt Thiel
EWN = Eyewitness News

F24 = Foto24
FF = Fabio Fizli
FM = Filonmar
FVH = Friedrich von Hörsten

GB = George Branch
GC = Garth Calitz
GD = Gerhard Dreyer
GI = Gallo Images
GK = Gamma-Keystone via Getty
GR = Gerenme
GS = Geoff Spiby
GT = Gautrain
GTY = Getty Images
GW = Graeme Williams

HM = hazelmcqueen
HRH = Helmoed-Römer Heitman
HVH = Hein von Hörsten

IA = Ian Anderson
IDP = imagedepotpro
IL = Ian Lusted
IM = Ian Michler
IMV = Ismael Montero Verdu
IOA = Images of Africa
IP = INPRA
IS = iStockphoto.com
ISC = Inti St Clair
IZ = Iziko Museum

JA = Janice Adlam
JB = James Berrangé
JD = Joe McDaniel
JDP = Jéan du Plessis
JG = James A. Guilliam
JH = John Haigh
JK = jseminiuk
JL = Joe Lena
JLY = John Leroy
JM = Johan Marais
JMO = Juan Mora
JR = Jonathan Reid
JS = James R. D. Scott

KB = Karl Beath
KBG = Keith Begg
KP = Kristo Pienaar
KY = Keith Young

LC = Loretta Chegwidden
LDP = Louis du Preez
LH = Leonard Hoffmann
LHX = Lex Hes
LHR = Loretta Hostettler
LJ = Li Jingwang
LMA = luismmolina
LOQ = Library of Queensland
LP = Library of Parliament
LS = Linda Steward
LT = Lisa Trocchi
LVH = Lanz von Hörsten

M24 = Media24
MA = Museum Africa
MAK = Mark Atkins
MAX = Mary Alexander
MC = Mendelssohn Collection
MCL = Melissa Carroll
MCSA = Media Club South Africa
MCTD = Maria Carolina Troconis Dittmar
MD = Miroslaw Dziadkowiec
MH = Michael Hammond
MHY = Martin Harvey
MLP = Mlenny Photography
MP = Maropeng
MPE = Mark Peters
MPS = MapStudio
MS = Mark Skinner
MT = Matthew Turnbull
MU = Michael Utech

NASA = National Aeronautics and Space Administration
ND = Nigel Dennis
NDT = Natalie du Toit
NHMV = Natural History Museum Vienna
NLSA = National Library South Africa
NM = National Museum (Bloemfontein)
NMC = Nicolas McComber
NMCH = National Museum of Cultural History
NN = Nick Norman
NO = Nicolene Olckers
NOV = Neil Overy
NP = Nicci Page
NSRI = National Sea Rescue Institute

OD = Ola Dusegard
ODZ = Ozgur Donmaz
OS = Oxford Scientific

PB = Paul Burns
PBP = Peter and Beverly Pickford
PC = pictafolio
PD = Parker Deen
PF = Popperfoto
PG = Pgiam
PM = Peter Mukherjee
PMT = Philip Mostert

PP = Per-Anders Petterson
PPT = ppart
PPY = Phil Perry
PR = Photo Researchers
PVW = Piet van Wyk

R = Reuters
RA = Rapport
RAY = Ricardo Azoury
RB = Robert Botha
RBF = Ruvan Boshoff
RBH = Rodger Bosch
RBSA = Reserve Bank of South Africa
RDLH = Roger de la Harpe
RH = Rod Haestier
RHS = Random House Struik
RL = Ryan Lindsay
RRB = Rodrigo Blanco
RRH = Richard R. Hansen
RS = Roger Sedres
RSF = Rainer Schimpf
RSG = Rodger Shagham
RT = RTimages
RY = Ryno

SA = Shaen Adey
SAMC = South African Mint Company
SAP = from the book 150 South African Paintings – Past and Present
SARB = Reproduction authorised by the South African Reserve Bank
SC = Shem Compion
SF = small_frog
SJ = Sharief Jaffer
SJL = Suljol
SO = Scott Orr
SPL = Science Photo Library
SS = Sasol
SSPL = Science and Social Picture Library via Getty
SU = source unknown
SW = Shutterworx

TC = Tony Camacho
TD = Thomas Dressler
TF = TopFoto
TL = Time & Life Pictures
TMK = Tania Monckton
TR = Transnet
TS = Tom Stoddart
TSP = Terrence Spencer

UCT = University of Cape Town
UIG = Universal Images Group

VB = Vanessa Burger
VL = Valerie Loiseleux

WC = Wiki Commons
WD = Wendy Dennis
WH = Warren Heath
WHA = World History Archive
WK = Walter Knirr
WM = William Martinson
WPK = WP Koort

Front cover, clockwise from top left: SA/IOA, WK/IOA, Richard Young/Rex Features/IP, LH/IOA, GT, CK/MCSA
Back cover, clockwise from top left: HVH/IOA, RDLH/ IOA, ND/IOA, GS, WK/IOA, GI/RS